D1030834

American Culture in the 1990s

Twentieth-Century American Culture
Series Editor: Martin Halliwell, *Professor of American Studies, University of Leicester*

This series provides accessible but challenging studies of American culture in the twentieth century. Each title covers a specific decade and offers a clear overview of its dominant cultural forms and influential texts, discussing their historical impact and cultural legacy. Collectively the series reframes the notion of 'decade studies' through the prism of cultural production and rethinks the ways in which decades are usually periodised. Broad contextual approaches to the particular decade are combined with focused case studies, dealing with themes of modernity, commerce, freedom, power, resistance, community, race, class, gender, sexuality, internationalism, technology, war and popular culture.

American Culture in the 1910s
Mark Whalan

American Culture in the 1920s
Susan Currell

American Culture in the 1930s
David Eldridge

American Culture in the 1940s
Jacqueline Foertsch

American Culture in the 1950s
Martin Halliwell

American Culture in the 1960s
Sharon Monteith

American Culture in the 1970s
Will Kaufman

American Culture in the 1980s
Graham Thompson

American Culture in the 1990s
Colin Harrison

American Culture in the 1990s

Colin Harrison

Edinburgh University Press

4/12/11
WW
$100 —

© Colin Harrison, 2010

Edinburgh University Press Ltd
22 George Square, Edinburgh
www.euppublishing.com

Typeset in 11/13 pt Stempel Garamond by
Servis Filmsetting Ltd, Stockport, Cheshire, and
printed and bound in Great Britain by
CPI Antony Rowe, Chippenham and Eastbourne

A CIP record for this book is available from the British Library

ISBN 978 0 7486 2221 4 (hardback)
ISBN 978 0 7486 2222 1 (paperback)

The right of Colin Harrison to be identified as author of this
work has been asserted in accordance with the Copyright,
Designs and Patents Act 1988.

Contents

List of Figures   vi
List of Case Studies   vii
Acknowledgements   viii
Chronology of 1990s American Culture   ix

Introduction: The Intellectual Context   1

1. Fiction and Poetry   35

2. Music and Radio   65

3. Film and Television   97

4. Art and Architecture   133

5. Digital Culture   169

Conclusion: Towards a New Millennium   199

Notes   209
Bibliography   227
Index   237

Figures

I.1	Growth of inequality in the USA (1960–97)	8
I.2	Anita Hill testifying to a Senate Committee (1991)	15
I.3	O. J. Simpson in car chase (1994)	24
1.1	Toni Morrison and Oprah Winfrey (1996)	39
2.1	Teenage mourning at the Kurt Cobain memorial (1994)	75
2.2	Tupac Shakur on stage (1992)	89
3.1	Military press conference in Riyadh, Saudi Arabia (1991)	100
3.2	Video footage of Los Angeles police officers beating Rodney King (1991)	105
3.3	Dinosaur meets clone in *Jurassic Park* (1993)	113
3.4	John Travolta and Uma Thurman in *Pulp Fiction* (1994)	115
3.5	The perimeter wall around the set of *Titanic*, Popotla, Mexico (1998)	121
3.6	Jerry Seinfeld and Jason Alexander in *Seinfeld* (1990–8)	123
4.1	Kara Walker, *Slavery! Slavery!* . . . (1997)	143
4.2	Sarah Sze, *Second Means of Egress* (1998)	149
4.3	Philip-Lorca diCorcia, *Head #1* (2001)	153
4.4	Guggenheim Museum, Bilbao (1991–7)	161
4.5	Zhang Huan, *My New York* (2002)	167
C.1	Riot police at a damaged store in Seattle (1999)	204

Case Studies

Introduction
Post-feminism and the Backlash   16
The O. J. Simpson Trial   22
Bowling Alone (2000)   31

1. Fiction and Poetry
Paradise (1997)   40
Two Asian American Poets: Lawson Fusao Inada and
    Li-Young Lee   48
Frisk (1991)   57

2. Music and Radio
Nirvana (1987–94)   73
Tupac Shakur (1971–96; 1991–present)   87
Napster and Music on the Internet   94

3. Film and Television
Watching the Watchmen: the Rodney King video   106
Happiness (Todd Solondz, 1998)   116
The Simpsons (1989–present)   128

4. Art and Architecture
Kara Walker   144
Bill Viola   155
Frank Gehry   161

5. Digital Culture
Howard Rheingold, *The Virtual Community* (1993)   178
Regulating the Net   189
Body Maps: The Human Genome Project and the Visible
    Human Project   194

Acknowledgements

Thanks to everyone who assisted in the process of writing this book. In particular, thanks to my colleagues in what used to be the American Studies department at Liverpool John Moores University – Bella Adams, Ross Dawson, Joe Moran, Joanna Price and Morag Reid – for taking on some of my teaching duties so that I could spend time on research. Jo, Ross and Glenda Norquay also provided valuable advice and feedback on drafts throughout. Pramod Nayar offered comments on several chapters and helped me rethink aspects of the book's overall structure. Most of all, I am indebted to Martin Halliwell for his patience and attention to detail in the role of Series Editor.

I am grateful to artists Philip-Lorca diCorcia, Zhang Huan, Sarah Sze and Kara Walker for their permission to reproduce images of their work. Thanks also to Ben Andrews, Paul Hegarty, Stephen Kenny, Clive Moran, James Nicholls and Rowan Wilson for various kinds of encouragement, discussion and gifts of books.

Finally, my thanks go to my family for all their support, and to Marie-Anne McQuay, who has been an unfailing source of encouragement and ideas and has made many sacrifices on my behalf.

Chronology of
1990s American Culture

Date	Events	Criticism	Literature
1990	Iraq invades Kuwait. Reunification of Germany. McDonald's restaurant opens in Moscow. Foundation of Queer Nation, New York City. Nelson Mandela released from prison.	Robert Bullard, *Dumping in Dixie* Judith Butler, *Gender Trouble* Mike Davis, *City of Quartz* Eve Kosovsky Sedgwick, *Epistemology of the Closet* Cornel West, 'The New Cultural Politics of Difference'	Robert Bly, *Iron John* Thomas Pynchon, *Vineland* Li-Young Lee, *The City In Which I Love You* John Edgar Wideman, *Philadelphia Fire* Tim O'Brien, *The Things They Carried*
1991	Operation Desert Storm launched to remove Saddam Hussein from Kuwait. Dissolution of Soviet Union. Slovenia and Croatia declare independence from Yugoslavia, beginning three years of national and ethnic conflicts in the region. Birth of World Wide Web. Anita Hill accuses Clarence Thomas of sexual harassment in Supreme Court hearings.	Susan Faludi, *Backlash* Donna Haraway, *Simians, Cyborgs and Women* Fredric Jameson, *Postmodernism, or, The Cultural Logic of Late Capitalism* David Roediger, *The Wages of Whiteness* Saskia Sassen, *The Global City*	Bret Easton Ellis, *American Psycho* Tony Kushner, *Angels in America* Adrienne Rich, *An Atlas of the Difficult World* Jane Smiley, *A Thousand Acres* Art Spiegelman, *Maus* Vol. 2

Film	Television	Music	Art
American Dream (Barbara Kopple) *Dances With Wolves* (Kevin Costner) *Goodfellas* (Martin Scorsese) *Total Recall* (Paul Verhoeven) *Wild At Heart* (David Lynch)	*Beverly Hills, 90210* (1990–2000) *In Living Color* (1990–4) *Northern Exposure* (1990–5) *Twin Peaks* (1990–1) Ken Burns's documentary series *The Civil War* broadcast on PBS	Joey Beltram, 'Energy Flash' Public Enemy, *Fear of a Black Planet* 2 Live Crew, *Nasty as They Wanna Be* Ice Cube, *AmeriKKKa's Most Wanted* Sonic Youth, *Goo*	Jimmie Durham, *Catskill Giveaway* Philip-Lorca diCorcia, *Hollywood* series (1990–2) David Wojnarowicz, *Tongues of Flame* retrospective (cur. Barry Blinderman, Illinois State University) Jenny Holzer is first woman to represent USA at Venice Biennale 'New Works for New Spaces', Wexner Art Center, Columbus, OH
Boyz n the Hood (John Singleton) *JFK* (Oliver Stone) *Silence of the Lambs* (Jonathan Demme) *Terminator 2* (James Cameron) *Thelma & Louise* (Ridley Scott)	*The Jerry Springer Show* (1991–present) *The Ren and Stimpy Show* (1991–6) *Sisters* (1991–6) Court TV launched Rodney King video shown on national television	John Adams, *The Death of Klinghoffer* Guns N' Roses, *Use Your Illusion I & II* Metallica, *Metallica* Nirvana, *Nevermind* First Lollapalooza festival features Nine Inch Nails, Ice-T and Siouxsie and the Banshees	'Dislocations' (cur. Robert Storr, Museum of Modern Art) Mike Kelley, *Hanging Stuffed Animals and Deodorizers* Glen Ligon, *Notes on the Margin of The Black Book* (1991–3) John Miller, *Dick/Jane* Lisa Yuskavage, *The Ones That Don't Want To: Bad Baby*

Date	Events	Criticism	Literature
1992	Bush and Yeltsin sign joint understanding beginning process of post-Cold War arms reduction. Bill Clinton elected 42nd president. Acquittal of LAPD officers accused of beating motorist Rodney King sparks riots in Los Angeles. Opening of Mall of America, Minnesota, America's largest shopping mall. FDA imposes restrictions on silicone breast implants for cosmetic purposes.	Francis Fukuyama, *The End of History and the Last Man* Lawrence Grossberg, *We Gotta Get Out of This Place* Toni Morrison, *Playing in the Dark* Toni Morrison (ed.), *Racing Justice, Engendering Power* Arthur Schlesinger, *The Disuniting of America*	Robert Coover, 'The End of Books' William Gibson, *Agrippa (A Book of the Dead)* David Mamet, *Oleanna* Cormac McCarthy, *All the Pretty Horses* Toni Morrison, *Jazz*
1993	Car bomb detonated underneath World Trade Center in New York City. Clinton announces 'don't ask, don't tell' policy on gays in the military. Eighteen US soldiers die in Black Hawk Down incident in Mogadishu, Somalia. Siege of Branch Davidians at Waco, TX ends in fire killing David Koresh and eighty-one followers. First 'spam' message sent by email.	Paul Gilroy, *The Black Atlantic* Robert Hughes, *The Culture of Complaint* Samuel Huntington, 'The Clash of Civilisations?' Amy Kaplan (ed.), *Cultures of United States Imperialism* First issue of *WIRED*, magazine of cyberculture	Donald Antrim, *Elect Mr Robinson For a Better World* E. Annie Proulx, *The Shipping News* Denis Johnson, *Jesus' Son* Toni Morrison awarded Nobel prize for literature Philip Roth, *Operation Shylock*

Film	Television	Music	Art
Basic Instinct (Paul Verhoeven) *Malcolm X* (Spike Lee) *Reservoir Dogs* (Quentin Tarantino) *Unforgiven* (Clint Eastwood) John Singleton is first black director to be nominated for an Academy award	*Def Comedy Jam* (1992–7) *The Larry Sanders Show* (1992–8) *Picket Fences* (1992–6) *The Real World* (1992–present) Jay Leno takes over *The Tonight Show* from Johnny Carson	Babes in Toyland, *Fontanelle* Dr Dre, *The Chronic* R.E.M., *Automatic for the People* X-102, *Rings of Saturn* 'Cop Killer' removed from Body Count's debut album after protests	Coco Fusco and Guillermo Gómez-Peña, *Two Undiscovered Amerindians Visit the West* Felix Gonzalez-Torres, MoMA Projects 34 (public billboard exhibition) Sally Mann, *Immediate Family* Fred Wilson, *Mining the Museum*, Baltimore Historical Society 'Helter Skelter', Los Angeles Museum of Contemporary Art
Falling Down (Joel Schumacher) *Jurassic Park* (Steven Spielberg) *Philadelphia* (Jonathan Demme) *Schindler's List* (Steven Spielberg) Disney buys Miramax Pictures	*Beavis and Butt-Head* (1993–7) *Frasier* (1993–2004) *Homicide: Life on the Street* (1993–9) *NYPD Blue* (1993–2005) *The X-Files* (1993–2002)	Ice Cube, 'It Was a Good Day' Snoop Dogg, *Doggystyle* Smashing Pumpkins, *Siamese Dream* Whitney Houston, 'I Will Always Love You' Steve Reich and Beryl Korot, *The Cave*	Tony Oursler, *Crying Doll* Jason Rhoades, *CHERRY Makita – Honest Engine Work* Nancy Rubins, *Mattresses and Cakes* 'Abject Art', Whitney Museum Whitney Biennial sees white male artists in a minority for the first time

Date	Events	Criticism	Literature
1994	Ethnic conflict erupts in Rwanda. Republicans win back both houses of Congress for first time since 1954. North American Free Trade Agreement creates world's largest free-trade region (US, Canada and Mexico). Richard Herrnstein and Charles Murray's book *The Bell Curve* incites controversy over the relations between race and intelligence. Protests over Smithsonian Institution's proposed exhibition on end of World War II featuring *Enola Gay*.	Harold Bloom, *The Western Canon* Shere Hite, *The Hite Report on the Family* Tricia Rose, *Black Noise* Donald E. Pease (ed.), *Revisionary Interventions into the Americanist Canon* Edward Said, *Culture and Imperialism*	Denise Chávez, *Face of an Angel* E. L. Doctorow, *The Waterworks* Louise Erdrich, *The Bingo Palace* Lorrie Moore, *Who Will Run the Frog Hospital?* Elizabeth Wurtzel, *Prozac Nation*
1995	Founding of World Trade Organization. Bombing of Alfred Murrah Building, Oklahoma City is most fatal act of terrorism on American soil. Trial of O. J. Simpson for murders of Nicole Brown Simpson and Ron Goldman. Million Man March. Netscape Communications goes public, marking beginning of dotcom boom.	Benjamin Barber, *Jihad vs. McWorld* Walter Benn Michaels, *Our America* bell hooks, *Killing Rage: Ending Racism* Robert Putnam, 'Bowling Alone' Sherry Turkle, *Life on Screen*	Sherman Alexie, *Reservation Blues* Richard Ford, *Independence Day* Chang-Rae Lee, *Native Speaker* Charles Wright, *Chickamauga* John Updike, *Rabbit Angstrom: The Four Novels*

Film	Television	Music	Art
Forrest Gump (Robert Zemeckis) *Go Fish* (Rose Troche) *Natural Born Killers* (Oliver Stone) *Pulp Fiction* (Quentin Tarantino) Paramount Pictures bought by Viacom	*Ellen* (1994–8) *ER* (1994–2009) *Friends* (1994–2003) *TV Nation* (1994–5) Lesbian kiss features on episode of *Roseanne*	Jeff Buckley, *Grace* Sheryl Crow, 'All I Wanna Do' Philip Glass, *Symphony No. 2* Nas, *illmatic* Kurt Cobain commits suicide	Janine Antoni, *Lick and Lather* Matthew Barney, *Cremaster 4* (first of *Cremaster* cycle) Robert Gober, *Man Coming Out of Woman* Vitaly Komar and Alex Melamid, *America's Most Wanted* First Gramercy International Art Fair (becomes Armory Show in 1999)
Se7en (David Fincher) *Strange Days* (Kathryn Bigelow) *Toy Story* (John Lasseter) *The Usual Suspects* (Bryan Singer) Dreamworks SKG founded	*Murder One* (1995–7) *Star Trek: Voyager* (1995–2001) *Taxicab Confessions* (1995–present) Launch of networks UPN and The WB BBC/PBS history documentary series *The People's Century*	Guided By Voices, *Alien Lanes* Emmylou Harris, *Wrecking Ball* Alanis Morissette, *Jagged Little Pill* C. Dolores Tucker campaigns against gangsta rap TLC, *CrazySexyCool*	Kerry James Marshall, *The Garden Project* Allan Sekula, *Fish Story* Jessica Stockholder, *Sweet For Three Oranges* 'Video Spaces: Eight Installations' (cur. Barbara London, MoMA) Richard Meier, Museum of Contemporary Art Barcelona

Date	Events	Criticism	Literature
1996	Clinton re-elected president. Google founded by Larry Page and Sergey Brin. Proposition 209 ('California Civil Rights Initiative') passed, marking beginning of legal challenges to affirmative action programmes in state institutions. Unabomber arrested. Telecommunications Act passed.	Arjun Appadurai, *Modernity at Large* Manual Castells, *The Rise of the Network Society* Kimberlé Crenshaw, *Critical Race Theory* Michael Denning, *The Cultural Front* Hal Foster, *The Return of the Real*	Anonymous (Joe Klein), *Primary Colors* David Markson, *Reader's Block* George Saunders, *CivilWarLand in Bad Decline* David Foster Wallace, *Infinite Jest* Launch of Oprah's Book Club
1997	Successful cloning of Dolly the sheep. *Mars Pathfinder* lands on Mars. Foundation of Project for a New American Century. Clinton issues apology to victims of Tuskegee syphilis experiment. Mass suicide of Heaven's Gate cult.	Lauren Berlant, *The Queen of America Goes to Washington City* Angela Davis, *Blues Legacies and Black Feminism* Henry Louis Gates, *Thirteen Ways of Looking at a Black Man* Manuel de Landa, *A Thousand Years of Nonlinear History* Toni Morrison, *Birth of a Nation'hood*	Russell Banks, *The Sweet Hereafter* Don DeLillo, *Underworld* Toni Morrison, *Paradise* Bharati Mukherjee, *The Holder of the World* Philip Roth, *American Pastoral*

Film	Television	Music	Art
Fargo (Joel and Ethan Coen) *Independence Day* (Roland Emmerich) *Lone Star* (John Sayles) *Scream* (Wes Craven) *When We Were Kings* (Leon Gast)	*Buffy the Vampire Slayer* (1996–2003) *The Daily Show* (1996–present) *Judge Judy* (1996–present) *Millennium* (1996–9) *The O'Reilly Factor* (1996–present)	Aaliyah, *One in a Million* Marilyn Manson, *Antichrist Superstar* Mikel Rouse, *Dennis Cleveland* DJ Shadow, . . . *Endtroducing* Tupac Shakur murdered	Gregory Crewdson, *Hover* Nan Goldin, *I'll Be Your Mirror*, Whitney Museum of American Art Felix Gonzalez-Torres dies of AIDS 'Conversations at the Castle' (cur. Mary Jane Jacob, Atlanta) 'Hall of Mirrors: Art and Film Since 1945' (cur. Kerry Brougher, Los Angeles Museum of Contemporary Art)
Amistad (Steven Spielberg) *Boogie Nights* (Paul Thomas Anderson) *Men in Black* (Barry Sonnenfeld) *Starship Troopers* (Paul Verhoeven) *Titanic* (James Cameron)	*Ally McBeal* (1997–2002) *The Chris Rock Show* (1997–2000) *King of the Hill* (1997–2009) *South Park* (1997–present) Lead character of sitcom *Ellen* 'comes out'	Erykah Badu, *Baduizm* Missy Elliot, *Supa Dupa Fly* Lilith Fair women's music festival Notorious B.I.G. (aka Biggie Smalls) murdered Wynton Marsalis's *Blood on the Fields* is first jazz composition to win Pulitzer prize for music	Robert Colescott is first African American artist to represent US at Venice Biennale Bill Viola retrospective, Whitney Museum Kara Walker awarded MacArthur Foundation fellowship Guggenheim Museum opens in Bilbao Getty Center opens in Los Angeles

Date	Events	Criticism	Literature
1998	Al-Qaeda detonates truck bombs outside US embassies in Kenya and Tanzania. Clinton-Lewinsky scandal leads to impeachment of President. FDA approves Viagra for treatment of erectile dysfunction. Microsoft antitrust case begins. Vice-President Al Gore signs Kyoto Protocol on climate change, though it remains unratified by the Senate. DNA tests suggest that Thomas Jefferson fathered a child with slave Sally Hemings.	Rey Chow, *Ethics After Idealism* Jared Diamond, *Guns, Germs and Steel* Julian Dibbell, 'A Rape in Cyberspace' Philip Gourevitch, *We Wish to Inform You That Tomorrow We Will Be Killed With Our Families: Stories from Rwanda* Avital Ronell, *Finitude's Score*	Bret Easton Ellis, *Glamorama* Yusef Komunyakaa, *Thieves of Paradise* Richard Powers, *Gain* Philp Roth, *I Married a Communist* First issue of *Timothy McSweeney's Quarterly Concern*
1999	World population tops six billion. NATO begins air strikes against Serbia to prevent 'ethnic cleansing' in Kosovo. Protests at WTO talks in Seattle. Two pupils at Columbine High School go on shooting spree, killing fifteen. Six-year-old Elian Gonzalez rescued from waters off Florida.	N. Katherine Hayles, *How We Became Posthuman* Martha Nussbaum, *Sex and Social Justice* John Rawls, *The Law of Peoples* Gayatri Spivak, *A Critique of Postcolonial Reason* Margaret Wertheim, *The Pearly Gates of Cyberspace*	Ha Jin, *Waiting* Cormac McCarthy, *Cities of the Plain* (completing the Border Trilogy) Neal Stephenson, *Cryptonomicon* Ralph Ellison's unfinished novel *Juneteenth* published posthumously Jhump Lahiri, *Interpreter of Maladies*

Film	Television	Music	Art
Bulworth (Warren Beatty) *Happiness* (Todd Solondz) *Pleasantville* (Gary Ross) *Saving Private Ryan* (Steven Spielberg) *The Truman Show* (Peter Weir)	*Sex and the City* (1998–2004) *Sports Night* (1998–2000) *Total Request Live* (1998–2008) *Will and Grace* (1998–2006) Final episode of *Seinfeld* (May)	Dixie Chicks, *Wide Open Spaces* Jay-Z, *Hard Knock Life* Lauryn Hill, *The Miseducation of Lauryn Hill* Britney Spears, '. . . Baby One More Time' Tortoise, *TNT*	Vanessa Beecroft, *VB35*, Solomon R. Guggenheim Museum New York Ilya and Emilia Kabakov, *Palace of Projects* Shirin Neshat, *Turbulent* Sarah Sze, *Second Means of Egress,* Berlin Biennial Zhang Huan, *Pilgrimage – Wind and Water* (PS 1, New York)
American Beauty (Sam Mendes) *The Blair Witch Project* (Daniel Myrick, Eduardo Sánchez) *Fight Club* (David Fincher) *The Matrix* (Andy and Larry Wachowski) *Three Kings* (David O. Russell)	*Family Guy* (1999–present) *Futurama* (1999–2003) *Sopranos* (1999–2007) *The West Wing* (1999–2006) *Who Wants to Be a Millionaire?* (US version, 1999–present)	Eminem, *Slim Shady LP* The Flaming Lips, *The Soft Bulletin* Shania Twain, 'Man! I Feel Like a Woman' Smog, *Knock Knock* Napster published on internet	Doug Aitken, *Electric Earth* Mark Dion, *Two Banks* (Tate Thames Dig) 'The American Century', Whitney Museum Controversy accompanies opening of British show 'Sensation', Brooklyn Museum of Art Daniel Liebeskind's Jewish Museum completed in Berlin

The Intellectual Context

The attempt to identify the main characteristics of the 1990s was under way before much of the decade had even happened. By 1993, the press had come up with a multitude of era-defining labels: favourites were The Sober Nineties, The Gay Nineties, and The Practical Decade. For some it was 'the espresso age', the decade of leanness and thrift; for others it would be a time of liberation and abandon. 'Welcome to the '90s and the era of commuter marriage,' announced the *Los Angeles Times*, noting the rise of fragmented personal lives under the pressures of flexible capitalism. The *Seattle Times* observed a trend running in the opposite direction: 'Welcome to the '90s: aging boomers staying home, sipping chamomile and falling asleep.'[1] To some extent these labels offer an insight into Americans' expectations of the decade to come, and we might want to say that the mood of austerity in many of them reflected a need to put the perceived excesses of the 1980s at a distance, while the sense of restlessness in others was a millennial impulse, recalling the *fin de siècle* spirit of the original 'gay decade' a century beforehand. But what is more significant is simply the frequency with which these premature attempts to classify the decade were appearing. It was as if Americans needed urgently to fix the meaning of the present before they could live in it.

The attempt to understand such labels begs a further question: what does it mean to think of history in terms of decades? As a unit of measurement the limitations are obvious: a decade misrepresents processes of change that do not sit within a ten-year span, and tends to homogenise the events of a period rather than place the accent on conflicts and discontinuities.[2] But the idea of the decade has also become embedded in popular consciousness, influencing the way we think about culture as well as history. Social historian Jason Scott Smith has argued that it has its origins in the turmoil of the late nineteenth century, where it functioned as a means of adapting to a world in which traditional conceptions of time were being overturned. On the one hand, the disorienting speed of modernity produced widespread feelings of nostalgia, while on the other a growing awareness of simultaneous and unrelated patterns of development drove a need for unifying narratives of progress. The decade spoke to both of these impulses, since it helped articulate differences between the present and the recent past and encouraged people to see themselves as part of a generation facing a common destiny.[3]

By the end of the twentieth century, the sense of accelerated change was undiminished: global travel and communications overturned existing perceptions of time and space; advances in information technology created a steady flow of innovations for business and personal use; communist states across Europe were disappearing almost overnight, and new waves of immigration continued to transform the nation's ethnic composition. But the new moderns – the 'postmoderns', in the vocabulary of the day – faced the future very differently. As we shall see, a generational identity was difficult to sustain in a nation that seemed to be fragmenting into numerous different communities all with their own distinct histories. Unifying narratives of progress were also harder to come by in the wake of a century that had seen many of the utopian visions of the modern era result in catastrophe. Scientific and technological developments continued, but the assumption that they were necessarily linked to forms of liberation had become highly questionable. Such 'incredulity towards metanarratives,' in Jean-François Lyotard's famous phrase, distinguished the new sense of time from its predecessor.[4]

A further difference was the greater role played by mass media and popular culture in the formation of historical consciousness. For numerous theorists the reproduction of images of the past (primarily in film and television, but also in architecture, music and fashion) threatened to displace more authentic or politically enabling forms of historical knowledge, reducing history to little more than a set of stylistic variations. 'We are condemned to seek History by way of our own pop images and simulacra of that history, which itself remains forever out of reach,' wrote Fredric Jameson in a landmark work of cultural criticism, *Postmodernism* (1991).[5] Andreas Huyssen named it an 'amnesiac' condition, one in which capitalism, mass media and the growth of the electronic archive posed a profound threat to human experience and provoked an obsession with memory. 'Our culture as a whole is haunted by the implosion of temporality in the expanding synchronicity of our media world,' he judged in 1995.[6] In these and many other accounts the 'crisis of historicity' loomed over the last decade of the millennium, a sign of anxieties about the relationship to the past and a declining ability to imagine the world to come.

Memory and nostalgia are therefore integral to the sensibility that gave rise to periodising by decades, but they also took on a special significance in the 1990s, when it was not simply that the past was rapidly disappearing but that the very modes of remembering and representing it had become problematic. Preoccupations with memory were widespread in popular film, from *Total Recall* (1990) to *Memento* (2000), or in debates over the challenges CGI posed to the film record; controversies over national memory surrounded the Quincentennial celebrations of 1992 and the Smithsonian exhibition of Enola Gay in 1995. The struggle for authority over the representation of the past was also central to the politics of minority groups. In many of the key events and spectacles of the period it was the memory of the 1960s that became the site of conflict, as members of the 'sixties generation' came to assume positions of power and fought bitterly over what that decade ought to mean. For Huyssen, the 'memory boom', experienced across Europe and America, was ultimately a positive response to the crisis – an expression of a basic need for temporal location and a point of resistance to the disabling forces of media and technology. Historian Svetlana Boym makes a similar claim about the nostalgic impulse in her study of the phenomenon in post-Soviet Russia, suggesting that it does not have to be seen as a merely sentimental or conservative reaction to changing social conditions but can also be creative, a means of recovering the forgotten possibilities of the past:

> Creative nostalgia reveals the fantasies of the age, and it is in those fantasies and potentialities that the future is born. One is nostalgic not for the past the way it was, but for the past the way it could have been. It is this past perfect that one strives to realise in the future.[7]

Such observations inform the approach that I wish to take in this book. Above all, I will try to resist the temptation to claim that the 1990s have a definitive spirit and focus instead on the remarkable heterogeneity of the 1990s. If 'twilight' is a pervasive theme in current reflections on the decade – taking up from Huyssen's perception of an era in the aftermath of grand narratives of progress, but also referring to the emergence of a number of discourses announcing the end of dominant cultural and intellectual paradigms (postmodernism, post-feminism, post-ethnicity, post-cinema, post-rock) – then it is worth remembering that decline has always been part of decade-thinking, and risks overlooking the new forms of politics and culture that might be emerging. As Boym says, in any account of the past we need to recover the 'past perfect' – its possibilities and potentialities, realised or not.

Four Perspectives: The Clinton Years, The New Economy, The Information Age and The End of History

Despite the lack of agreement on the decade's defining characteristics, a number of different perspectives have arisen in recent years that influence the way that the 1990s are remembered. In the pages that follow I will outline four of the most common narratives before going on to look at other ways of conceptualising the period. In each of these, the 1990s come across as a 'twilight' moment, a period of transition in which anticipation of the future is mixed with a sense of decline.

In the first narrative the 1990s are 'The Clinton Years', a period of lost opportunities and divisive party politics. Bill Clinton had come into office in 1992 amid a wave of optimism for a Democrat government committed to addressing social inequalities, but his brand of 'third way' politics, which prioritised electability over ideology, soon alienated the left just as much as his style of government antagonised the right. In the minds of many progressives, the political and financial bankruptcy of the previous Bush administration had handed the new president a real chance for reform which he squandered in his desire to appeal to as broad a section of voters as possible. Signs of his failure of nerve appeared early on: an early proposal to end discrimination against homosexuals in the armed forces was hastily watered down into a widely ridiculed 'Don't Ask, Don't Tell' policy; in 1993, the nomination of African American law professor Lani Guinier to the post of Assistant Attorney General was withdrawn without protest after a right-wing campaign to smear her as a 'quota queen', showing how determined the government was to dissociate itself from any suggestions of affirmative action. Furthermore, the unhealthy economy that Clinton had inherited led him to place what even his economic advisers considered an undue emphasis on fiscal responsibility throughout his two terms. Budget-balancing measures may have pleased Wall Street and stolen some of the ground from the opposition, but they came at the expense of spending on social programmes.[8]

As Bruce Miroff has observed, Clinton's lack of adherence to ideo-logical positions made him the ideal president for a post-Cold War situation in which the political assumptions of old no longer applied.[9] If he was disappointing on policy, he was adept at fashioning an image that carried with the public despite his high-profile mistakes and an extraordinary level of animosity from his opponents. The remark-able victories for the Republicans in the Congressional elections of 1994 (engineered by House Speaker Newt Gingrich and his 'Contract with America') left the White House with difficulties in passing even the most uncontroversial of legislation, and created a stalemate over the budget that shut down the federal government twice in 1995. Nevertheless, it was Clinton who emerged from the standoff with the public's support, assisting his re-election in 1996. Even his his-toric impeachment over an affair with White House intern Monica Lewinsky in 1998 did little to dent Clinton's popularity: in fact, during much of the scandal he enjoyed high job approval ratings even though few had any sympathy for him personally.[10] Clinton's talent in this respect was his ability to create a powerful affective relationship between the people and the presidential office, cultivating intimacy as an element of his public authority as few presidents had managed to do before him. This was evident on numerous occasions, for instance in his response to the bombing of a federal building in Oklahoma City in 1995, at that point the nation's worst terrorist attack: assuming the role of 'mourner-in-chief' helped him regain individual stature as well as reaffirm the value of government in the eyes of the nation. In the Lewinsky scandal, the initial drama of denial and confession saw him exploit customs deeply embedded in popular culture: his announce-ment 'I have sinned . . .' may have been no more authentic than the live, on-air contrition of the discredited televangelists of the 1980s, but it was no less fundamentally American for the same reason.

For many, the tragedy of the late years of the Clinton administra-tion was that the preoccupation with the President's personal life dis-tracted both him and the nation from more pressing issues such as the plight of racial minorities, the need for environmental reforms and the growing security threat of international terrorism. But the Lewinsky saga was also significant because it showed how profoundly an obses-sion with personality and personal conduct had penetrated the public sphere, to the extent that an individual's sexual behaviour could become a matter of national interest and a measure of fitness for gov-ernment. Lauren Berlant has called this 'the intimate public sphere', a cultural formation emerging from the 1970s in which 'the sphere of discipline and definition for proper citizenship in the US has become progressively more private, more sexual and familial, and more concerned with personal morality'. As the fetishisation of the personal within the political, rather than an insistence that personal lives can create political interventions, such a trend ran directly counter to the ethos of the 1960s.[11]

The second narrative of the decade frames the 1990s as a period of economic expansion – the era of multinationals and mergers, rising productivity and excitement about the advent of a 'New Economy' which some believed would be liberated from patterns of boom and bust by technological advances and global communications. This was a rare time in which a chairman of the Federal Reserve could become a star: Alan Greenspan, ex-jazz musician and friend of Ayn Rand, held the post for four terms during which he presided over one of the longest phases of growth in the country's history and acquired an aura of infallibility for his capacity to sustain low inflation with low unemployment. With a guarded, oracular manner of speaking that hinted at an awareness of the impact his words might have on investors, Greenspan established himself as a maestro of confidence, that unruly aspect of human behaviour lying beyond the realms of economic reason, threatening to tip markets one way or another. Those who approved of his work praised his ability to maintain levels of confidence to spur investment while restraining the 'irrational exuberance' that would lead to a bubble.

For others, however, it was clear that the New Economy was not going to escape the problems of the business cycle. Joseph Stiglitz, economic advisor to President Clinton and later Chief Economist at the World Bank, eventually became a figurehead for the global justice movement and a rival in stature to Greenspan due to his criticisms of the new capitalism. Instead of seeing a new mode of growth, he characterised the 1990s as a prolonged boom that merely delayed the inevitable downturn, during which too much credence was given to the doctrine of free markets and too much free rein was given to finance. Liberalisation took place in key sectors such as banking, telecommunications and energy, but at the end of the decade the promises of greater efficiency and lower prices had not been fulfilled: the Telecommunications Act of 1996 opened up the telephone industry to $65 billion of investment that dropped to a value of $4 billion in five years, while the deregulation of electricity in California in 1998 led to an energy crisis which almost shut down the state, exposing criminal misconduct at energy trading firm Enron in the process.[12] Free-market thinking also dominated global economic policy, where developing countries were given aid and loans on the condition that they open up their economies to foreign investment, often to the detriment of local markets and state public sectors. Its failures became evident in cases such as the crash that befell Argentina in 2002, though it had already sparked a resistance movement that came dramatically to the attention of the world's leading powers in the protests against the World Trade Organization in Seattle in 1999.

Hence in economic terms the 1990s became known as an era of exuberance and uncertainty, a boom time that made wealth all the more visible but which masked growing inequalities at home and abroad. America may have been richer, but its citizens were more divided and more insecure. Rising levels of employment occurred simultaneously with the business practice known as 'downsizing', which saw over sixteen million Americans dismissed from their jobs in the period 1992–98 (roughly amounting to one in every fourteen working adults); many of these were forced to take a lower-wage job in returning to work. And as general levels of income rose across all sectors, so too did wealth disparities: by 1999 half of the nation's income was earned by the top fifth of the population while the bottom fifth took only 4.2 per cent. As the graphs indicate below, levels of inequality increased much more rapidly in the 1990s than during the 1980s, which was perhaps better known for its excesses.

In this respect the 1990s resembled previous moments of unstable prosperity: Stiglitz calls it 'The Roaring Nineties' and David Remnick, editor of the *New Yorker* magazine, 'The New Gilded Age'. The latter term recalls the emergence of corporate capitalism in the 1880s and 1890s, but the 1920s is the main point of reference for both writers. Remnick begins his introduction to the volume with a description of Bill Gates's new house on Lake Washington, where F. Scott Fitzgerald's warnings about the Jazz Age are recalled in the inscription from his novel *The Great Gatsby* around the dome in the library: 'He had come a long way to this blue lawn and his dream must have seemed so close that he could hardly fail to grasp it.'[13]

Bill Gates brings us to a third perspective: the 1990s as the Information Age. The term refers to a range of developments in science and technology which come to redefine media, communications and the human body, from the mass manufacturing of cell phones to the digitisation of text, music and image, the genetic modification of foods to the Human Genome Project. Most of all, though, it is associated with the exponential growth of the internet and the

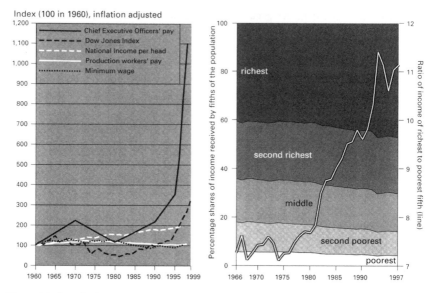

Figure I.1 Growth of inequality in the USA, 1960–97. Source: Bob Sutcliffe, *100 Ways of Seeing an Unequal World* (New York: Zed Books, 2001).

creation of its most popular resource, the World Wide Web. With an unparalleled potential to connect individuals across the globe, the internet promised not only new opportunities for creativity and commerce but also new modes of social interaction and even new forms of subjectivity. Investment in online services and businesses was one of the major sources of growth in the New Economy, and the possibilities of 'virtual communities' seemed limitless. Nevertheless, for many the internet turned out to be more alienating than liberating, while the dotcom industries increasingly failed to meet their inflated expectations. The bubble finally burst in March 2000, and the next two years saw $5 trillion wiped off the share value of technology companies as all sorts of hopeful enterprises proved unable to reach their markets or meet running costs. Some of the most famous 'dot-bombs' (or 'dot-compost': the jokes reflect some of the glee that often accompanies catastrophe) were one-hour delivery service Kosmo.com, pet-accessory store Pets.com and online currency site Flooz.com.

Gates became one of the icons of the Information Age in the 1990s, and not only because his ownership of computer software company Microsoft made him the richest man in the world from the middle of the decade into the new millennium. His commitment to innovation and perpetual change typified the spirit of the 'new capitalism': he was, as Richard Sennett observed, 'someone who has the confidence

to dwell in disorder, someone who flourishes in the midst of dislocation'.[14] In 1995, as his house was being built, Gates was already planning to reorient Microsoft's entire business strategy from PC-focused
software to internet communications: the next two years saw the
launches of Microsoft Network (MSN), web/cable news company
MSNBC and browser Internet Explorer. At a time when political
dreams were in short supply, Gates also stood as an emblem of the
technocratic faith that took their place – a spokesperson for utopias
realised through technological improvement, now that social justice
or economic redistribution seemed unimaginable. His book *The Road
Ahead*, published the same year, offered an upbeat vision of the world
the internet would bring into being: from smart housing to networked
classrooms, telecommuting to interactive entertainment, and trading
systems that would come closer to realising Adam Smith's ideal of
fully transparent markets. At every point Gates stresses the advantages of connectedness over the potential for social fragmentation and
works hard to soften the impact of technological change for those who
are fearful of the coming revolution. Outlining the plans for his Lake
Washington mansion, he is keen to assert that its hi-tech features will
serve human needs and enhance, rather than challenge, social customs
and cultural traditions. Identification pins worn by guests will help
the house's tracking devices understand their preferences, rather
than function as a kind of domestic surveillance; home entertainment
systems and online communication will not discourage occupants
from going out to the movies or interacting with real people; living
with browsable images on screens, rather than paintings, will make
people *more* interested in seeing art in museums, not less.[15] As with
the champions of the New Economy, Gates's ideal is a revolution
without costs: no boom and bust, no environmental damage, no social
alienation and no loss of cultural value.

A fourth narrative that came to characterise the decade, this time
in the fields of political economy and foreign policy, was the 'end of
history'. In the wake of the collapse of Soviet communism, America
suddenly found itself the world's only superpower, facing a new set
of questions about its international role now that the Cold War was
over. At the same time, numerous commentators from universities,
political institutions and the media succumbed to the temptation
to celebrate the 'triumph' of liberal democracy and the system of
capitalism that undergirded it. Francis Fukuyama's book of 1992,
The End of History and the Last Man, resurrected the idea of a
'universal history of mankind' in which western liberal democracy

was on the verge of being revealed as the only truly legitimate political system. 'As mankind approaches the end of the millennium,' he
evangelised,

> the twin crises of authoritarianism and socialist central planning have
> left only one competitor standing in the ring as an ideology of poten-
> tially universal validity: liberal democracy, the doctrine of individual
> freedom and popular sovereignty. Two hundred years after they first
> animated the French and American revolutions, the principles of liberty
> and equality have proven not just durable but resurgent.[16]

Fukuyama's views now sound like a classic expression of American
hubris – an inability to notice political alternatives mixed with a determination to see the conflicts and injustices produced in its own society
as mere imperfections that will be ironed out in due course. But during
the 1990s they helped to propagate a belief in the proven superiority
of American values and provide an intellectual justification for a more
aggressive foreign policy. Fukuyama himself was one of the original
members of the Project for the New American Century, a right-wing
organisation founded in 1997 with the aim of promoting what it called
'American global leadership' – meaning increased military spending,
the safeguarding of American economic interests and the pursuit of
'regime change' across the world in the name of democracy. These
would become central tenets of the neoconservative agenda of George
W. Bush in the next millennium: indeed, many of the signatories to
PNAC's Statement of Principles, such as Jeb Bush, Dick Cheney,
William Kristol, Donald Rumsfeld and Paul Wolfowitz, would go on
to perform key roles in or for his administration.[17]

   Thus in a relative lull between the fall of communism and the rise
of a new adversary in anti-American terrorism – between the end of
history and its resumption, we might say – America's relationship to
world history became the site of fiercely contested ideological battles.
In some respects this has always been the case: America's association
with 'progress' or other ideals of historical development has been
central to its mythology ever since the first conceptions of the conti-
nent as a 'new world', and Fukuyama can be placed in a tradition of
thought emphasising the inevitability of American social forms in the
grand sweep of history that would accommodate figures from John
Winthrop to Alexis de Tocqueville and Frederick Jackson Turner.[18]
But in a more specific sense, Fukuyama and his sympathisers sought to
claim historical change as a predominantly American concern. When

Life magazine's editor Henry Luce first announced 'The American Century' in 1941, it was an appeal to the United States to abandon its isolationism and assume a more active role in international affairs. Clinton drew on this spirit throughout his term of office, developing a policy rhetoric of global cooperation and humanitarian intervention – though he played down the sense of ownership in the phrase ('from the mountaintop of this American century, [let us] look ahead to the next one' is the carefully worded conclusion to his 1999 State of the Union address). The neoconservatives, however, eagerly appropriated the term and certainly meant to imply that the coming century would, or should, belong to America. This was the messianic political fantasy of the *Pax Americana*, a doctrine of 'perpetual war for perpetual peace' that would become a central element of the foreign policy of the next Republican administration.[19]

If the decade is too fragmentary, or still too recent, to have acquired a consensus over the way it should be remembered, the four perspectives I have outlined above are nevertheless central to most attempts to periodise the 1990s. Conveniently, each comes with its own set of bookends: the Clinton Years of 1992–2000 falling between the presidencies of George Bush Sr and Jr; the Roaring Nineties between the recessions of 1991 and 2001; the first phase of the Internet Revolution occurring between the creation of the World Wide Web in 1991 and the announcement of 'Web 2.0' in 2003; and the End of History framed by the fall of two architectural landmarks – the Berlin Wall in 1989 and the Twin Towers of the World Trade Center in 2001. This is not to say that these are the sole or most significant ways to understand the 1990s, and it is certainly not meant to confirm the impression that a decade is a discrete, homogeneous block of time with clearly defined boundaries: such boundaries are always somewhat arbitrary, and any number of momentous beginnings and ends might be selected to give a different nuance to the meaning of the decade. However, they do offer us a set of related contexts for understanding the nation's cultural practices: the various ways in which Americans comprehended, responded to or, indeed, refused to acknowledge the changes taking place around them.

The Sixties in the Nineties

When rumours of Bill Clinton's college experiences with marijuana surfaced during his presidential campaign of 1992, he countered them with an admission that he had once tried a joint but nevertheless 'did not inhale'. This was the first of a number of denials that became characteristic of his presidency, reiterated most famously in the scandal over his sexual liaisons six years later ('I did not have sexual intercourse with that woman, Miss Lewinsky'). Some even saw it as a positive character trait: George Stephanopolous, Clinton's campaign advisor (and author of the famous slogan 'it's the economy, stupid'), once claimed that 'his capacity for denial is tied to the optimism that is his greatest strength'.[20] If it is unfair to suggest that a mixture of denial and optimism characterises American culture more generally, the idea that denial could be a virtue is certainly consonant with a period like the 1990s, in which increased wealth is matched with increased inequality.

Of course, 'I did not inhale' is only half a denial, and it is the equivocation that makes the remark symptomatic of the era. First of all, it is designed to speak to different audiences at once: those who know it to be a lie, and at least partially admire Clinton for telling it because they consider such a misdemeanour irrelevant to politics; and those for whom moral restraint is an important factor in public life, who are nevertheless given a chance to will themselves to believe him. In its dual character the phrase is emblematic of a new, determinedly non-ideological political centrism that seeks to accommodate a range of positions on individual freedom without really appealing to any in particular. But 'not inhaling' also became a memorable line because it represented the decade's ambivalent relationship to the 1960s. Clinton, after all, was the nation's first 'boomer' president, and to his opponents he became a symbol of the threat that the counterculture posed to the nation's core traditions, where it was conceived as unpatriotic and full of the narcissism of youth. Pot-smoking was an obvious signifier of the era, carrying connotations of personal indulgence and political radicalism. By dissociating himself from its effects, therefore, Clinton was indirectly negotiating a relationship to the era and its legacy – acknowledging what the sixties had been, but refusing to credit them with a lasting significance.

In political terms, the 1960s were associated not only with youthful radicalism but also with the implementation of a series of progressive policies designed to improve the lives of disadvantaged groups. Lyndon Johnson's vision of the Great Society emphasised the need to make equality a social and economic reality, in order to fulfil the rights that had been given formal recognition in the civil rights movement. But such policies were tremendously costly, and as Howard Winant has observed, real equality for all Americans would have required nothing less than a total social revolution, something that was distinctly unattractive to the majority of people who enjoyed some form of privilege.[21] Hence the subsequent decades saw a shift away from progressive reform on both sides of the political divide. By the 1980s, conservatives were arguing that the social programmes of the Great Society had not only proved expensive and inefficient but had also exacerbated the problems they were intended to address: thus busing children to schools actually reinforced segregation, bilingual education disenfranchised Hispanics and welfare created habits of dependency.[22] Liberals in turn moved away from defending such programmes as the belief took hold that policies designed to benefit specific sectors of the population were liable to alienate the electorate – in particular, the floating voters known as 'Reagan Democrats' that Clinton had courted in 1992. Thus the 1960s lingered in the 1990s as a kind of spectre: its legacy was worked over, denied and decried in popular culture, in battles over the meaning of multiculturalism, in the politics of race and gender, and in party politics. The attempt to exorcise the ghost produced a number of new discourses proclaiming the end of an era and seeking to establish a new reality: post-feminism, colour-blindness, and the attack on 'the cult of the victim' were all manifestations of this work of remembrance and forgetting.

For women, the story of the 1990s was one of relative progress: a general improvement of living standards and liberties, but always within limits, and falling well short of the feminist movement's ultimate aim of dismantling the system of patriarchy. The mood was captured in the National Organisation of Women's Declaration of Sentiments of 1998, drawn up at a conference celebrating 150 years since the birth of the women's movement at Seneca Falls. Looking back on women's hard-won achievements in securing rights to property, education and suffrage, the manifesto renewed demands for equality and empowerment in all spheres of life – in government, media and the professions; in law and religions, culture and sports, and within the family. But it also sounded a note of exhaustion, recognising that women continued to 'fight the same reactionary forces' as their predecessors.[23]

Statistics on gender differences in labour and political representation give some indication of the nature of these advances and limitations. While men's employment had fluctuated around 75 per cent since the recovery from the recession of the 1970s, women's participation in the workforce had risen steadily each decade, reaching 60 per cent by the end of the millennium.[24] The gender wage gap diminished over the same period, and most significantly for black women workers, whose average earnings as a percentage of those of white men increased from

40 per cent in 1965 to 60 per cent in 1995.[25] Despite such improvements, however, women still had to negotiate barriers such as the
lack of support for working mothers: America was one of the few
countries in the West not to legislate for paid parental leave, and only
introduced the right to unpaid leave in 1993. In politics, too, women
exercised power more then ever before, but inequalities still dominated. Women played a central role in electing Bill Clinton to both of
his terms, making him one of only three presidents to receive a greater
proportion of women's votes than men's (Johnson and Eisenhower
were the others). Participation in government increased across all
sectors, though in larger proportions at state level than in Congress.
In 1990, one in five city mayors and three out of fifty state governors
were women; female senators rose from two to seven in 1993 and representatives from twenty-eight to forty-seven.[26] Both the hopes and
the fears related to women in government were invested in the figure
of Hillary Clinton, who brought an entirely new interpretation to the
role of First Lady, in stark contrast to her predecessor Barbara Bush.
Instead of providing an image of supportive homemaker – one that
Bush had been proud to present as anti-feminist[27] – Clinton took a
more active part in public affairs: her fronting of the administration's
Health Care proposals in 1993, for instance, indicated a desire to
associate the office more explicitly with policy-making and ultimately
transform the image of women's citizenship emitting from the White
House. The subsequent failure of the health plan in Congress grati-
fied many of her critics who considered that she had over-reached the
duties proper to her position.

    For many feminists, one of the decade's landmark moments was the
testimony of law professor Anita Hill to a Senate committee in 1991
regarding her sexual harassment by Supreme Court nominee Clarence
Thomas. The significance of the hearings was compounded by the fact
that both parties were African American, and the case quickly turned
into a national media spectacle. Carol Gilligan referred to Hill as 'the
Rosa Parks of 1990s feminism' for speaking out on a matter that was
still widely neglected and demanding that the nation pay attention to
abuses going on in the American workplace; Lauren Berlant called it
an act of 'diva citizenship', reaffirming the feminist truth that personal
experience had a radical political potential.[28] Hill's testimony did not
prevent Thomas's appointment, but the belligerence of his supporters
and the anachronism of their refusal to concede the significance of
sexual violence was itself felt to be transformative. As well as mobilising a vote against Bush Sr in the forthcoming presidential elections,

Figure I.2 Anita Hill testifying to a Senate Committee on the nomination of Clarence Thomas to the Supreme Court, 11 October 1991 (© Brad Markel/Getty Images News).

it also spurred a rise in the reporting of sexual harassment incidents, which doubled in the next four years.[29]

Less promising, on the other hand, was the way the case exposed a rift between the politics of gender and race. In polls of African Americans as well as in the public statements of their representative organisations, the widespread desire for black representation in the Court appeared to triumph over the wish to acknowledge the injuries suffered by a black woman. Echoing the problems of the Black Power and feminist movements of the 1960s and 1970s, it once again seemed that women were invisible in race politics and race was invisible in gender politics. 'This competition among harmed collectivities remains one of the major spectator sports of the American public sphere,' Berlant observed ruefully.[30]

What was clear was that a range of broad social changes – such things as the decline of manufacturing, the rise of service industries, the proliferation of different forms of family, the relative decline in male-headed households and the emergence of male-oriented consumerism – were having profound effects on gender roles, and while they often opened up new opportunities for men and women they also created anxieties that surfaced in nostalgic reaffirmations of traditional norms of masculinity and femininity. Popular cinema reflected and amplified such anxieties, as with the spate of thrillers of the early part of the decade that dwelt on the threat and fascination of the predatory woman (*Basic Instinct, The Hand that Rocks the Cradle, The Last Seduction*), or movies that made the reconstitution of masculinity their main subject (*Dances With Wolves, Falling Down, Fight Club, American Beauty*). On daytime radio, 'shock jocks' like Howard Stern and Rush Limbaugh delighted in offending progressive liberal sensibilities and attacked so-called 'feminazis' with a virulence that betrayed a deeper disquiet about their own source of authority. In publishing, fashions in pseudo-science and self-help books made the desire to return to a pre-feminist age of gender certainties even more explicit. John Gray's relationship counselling book *Men are from Mars, Women are from Venus*, which reiterated homely truths about behavioural differences between the sexes, remained in the top two of non-fiction bestsellers for three years from 1994 to 1996; Ellen Fein and Sherrie Schneider's unashamedly traditionalist tract *The Rules: Time-Tested Secrets for Capturing the Heart of Mr Right* (1995) almost taunted those who had once dreamed of liberation from gender stereotypes. With section headings such as Don't Stare at Men and Don't Talk Too Much; Don't Meet Him Halfway and Don't Go Dutch on a Date; Don't Call Him and Rarely Return His Calls, the aim to offer advice to young women was patently secondary to the desire to proclaim feminism defeated.

Post-feminism and the Backlash

Susan Faludi was one of a number of cultural critics to notice that a reaction against feminism had been gathering pace since the mid-1980s, but it was her book *Backlash: The Undeclared War Against Women* (1991) that played a leading role in bringing it to the attention of a wider public. Looking back over the previous decade, Faludi observed a range of phenomena occurring in film, television, fashion, advertising and national politics in which negative representations of women's achievements were combined with a rediscovery of traditional gender roles, as if they had been suddenly proven to be the proper way of organising society after all. Thus newspapers reported 'burnout' amongst professional women, rising tides of depressed spinsters and impoverished divorcees, fertility crises amongst thirty-somethings and scare stories about child abuse in day-care centres. Behind such myths was a pervasive desire for the family values of old with their more restricted definitions of femininity: young married mothers back in the home.

Resistance to the idea of women gaining and exercising rights is not new in itself, of course, and Faludi observed that it usually peaks at moments when women are on the verge of making genuine advances toward independence. Since the two main factors securing greater freedom for women have always been the right to determine the value of their labour and the right to control their fertility, we should not be surprised that some of the key manifestations of the backlash in the nineties were the discrediting of working women (such as the vilification of Anita Hill as an unmarried 'career woman') and the rise of a 'foetal rights' movement opposing abortion. What was new, however, was the way that the backlash placed the blame for women's dissatisfactions and suffering on the changes brought about by feminism itself. 'Women are unhappy precisely *because* they are free,' the logic went: 'Women are enslaved by their own liberation.'[32] In this manner the real structural inequalities that women continued to face were entirely neglected, and women were denied a language through which to articulate collective political grievances.

This new phase of reaction against women's rights was also captured in the widespread use of the phrase 'post-feminism', a term implying that the women's movement had either failed or already achieved all of its goals. While it indicated the success of the backlash in devaluing feminist politics, it also spoke to a growing sense of alienation from feminism itself amongst a younger generation of women. The common diagnosis was that the movement had fragmented during the 1980s with, on the one hand, the emergence of multiple versions of feminism making competing claims, and on the other, the growth of academic interest in the idea of sexual difference, which had developed a rich vocabulary for exploring women's 'otherness' at the expense of attending to the continuing struggle for equality.[33] Liberal feminists such as Christina Hoff Sommers deplored this apparent abandonment of the public sphere, while others tried to recover a new discourse of women's agency, moving away from critiques of patriarchy that they believed consigned women to the position of victims. Katie Roiphe earned some notoriety for her suggestion in *The Morning After* (1993) that women bore some of the responsibility in incidents reported as 'date rape', while Naomi Wolf's *Fire With Fire* (1993) looked forward to a new era of 'power feminism' that she saw beginning to emerge out of the backlash – though her evidence was unfortunately limited to a few cultural trends such as the rise in women's gun ownership and the publication of female-oriented pornography.

However important it may have been to critique the forms of feminism that a new generation had inherited from their predecessors, it was disappointing that much of this work remained centred on the experiences and individual opportunities of white middle-class American women. In a climate of social conservatism and economic liberalism, the distinctions between feminist, post-feminist and anti-feminist positions often blurred.

Perhaps Faludi's key insight was that the backlash against women was more usefully seen as a crisis amongst men, who – contrary to the myths propagated in the media – were coming off worse in the statistics on mental health, infertility and quality of life after divorce.[34] Men in lower-income groups who were most at risk from downsizing and most sensitive to the entry of larger numbers of women into the job market – men who, ultimately, were unable to reproduce the prospects and stability of their own fathers' lives – became the main constituency for backlash rhetoric. In the late 1980s and early 1990s this sense of crisis was reflected in the advent of a 'men's movement', a loose collection of support groups, family values advocates, male feminists and New Age spiritualists seeking to establish new or more workable models of masculinity. Poet Robert Bly's *Iron John* (1990) became the handbook for thousands of (largely white) men seeking to 'steal the key' from their mothers to unlock their Wild Man within; conservative Christian organisation Promise Keepers filled stadiums with men willing to commit to reclaiming authority in their marriages and families; and African American men assembled in unprecedented numbers on 16 October 1995 for the Million Man March, convened by Minister Louis Farrakhan of the Nation of Islam. Taken as a whole, the movement was poised somewhat awkwardly on a tension between a feminist-informed awareness of the need to critique male identities and a desire to retreat into the certainties of patriarchy. Despite these contradictions, however, it evidently spoke to a need for revived forms of male sociality and for new ways to understand what men wanted.

The backlash was not just an isolated phenomenon in gender politics in the 1980s and 1990s; it was also a general cultural tendency and a key feature of many of the debates known as the 'culture wars' which raged over matters such as minority rights, multiculturalism and national identity. As the new social movements gathered momentum and the voices of minorities shifted from the margins to the centre, resistance came from numerous quarters on the left and the right. Often speaking in the name of core values and national traditions, such critics questioned the validity of minority claims or suggested they had gone too far and threatened democratic principles. Arthur Schlesinger, advocate of the 'vital centre' in the 1950s, argued in *The Disuniting of America* (1992) that the radical cultural politics of the 1960s had spawned a 'cult of ethnicity' that celebrated cultural difference for its own sake and was hostile to the idea of a common national culture. 'The multiethnic dogma abandons historic purposes, replacing assimilation by fragmentation, integration by separatism. It belittles *unum* and glorifies *pluribus*.'[31] His views echoed those of Dinesh D'Souza, who had asserted the year before in *Illiberal Education* that affirmative action in the universities such as preferential hiring and admissions quotas had not resolved inequalities but only eroded intellectual enquiry and exacerbated tensions between identity groups on campus.

Central to backlash discourse was the belief that identity politics had hijacked the public arena and obstructed reasoned discussion with irrefutable demands made on the basis of past oppression. For art critic Robert Hughes, it was a 'culture of complaint', an elevation of victim over citizen that made for not only bad politics but also bad art. Robert Mapplethorpe, the photographer whose images of gay subcultures took on a special resonance after his death in 1989, was Hughes's example of the damaging effects of identity politics on aesthetic judgment: in his eyes, Mapplethorpe was a minor artist given inflated status because his work affirmed the values of a particular group.[35] Harvard law professor Alan Dershowitz also joined in the condemnation of the cult of the victim in *The Abuse Excuse* (1994), where he suggested that juries were showing a worrying tendency to acquit criminal defendants when they offered evidence of childhood trauma in their defence. One of the most notorious uses of such a defence was in the trial of Erik and Lyle Menendez in 1993, brothers from a Cuban-American family in Beverly Hills who pleaded that they had murdered their parents to escape from an abusive father; the plea was eventually rejected, but only after a retrial in 1996.

While it is true that the public sphere needs to be protected from overly partisan claims on its resources, and it is right to worry about the sentimentalisation of justice when it pays too much attention to the emotions of the victims of crime, it is also the case that criticism of 'playing the victim' was unusually strong in the early part of the 1990s and clearly reflected ideological investments in the culture wars. Ostensibly an argument about the excessive amount of capital to be made out of reference to personal suffering, anti-victim discourse was ultimately an attempt to correct the progressive focus on environmental factors in social problems: it disabled political protest by representing it as individual complaint.[36] The same logic applies to the way that political correctness was caricatured and trivialised in this period (and this is a misrepresentation that has lasted well beyond the decade): in both cases, an attention to the ways that inequalities are structurally maintained – through laws, institutions or language – is dismissed as unnecessary, divisive and slightly lunatic.

There could be no better example of this new conservative attitude and its contradictions than Clarence Thomas – standing for the symbolic position of America's first black Supreme Court judge and denouncing sixties liberalism and identity politics even though he had himself been a beneficiary of affirmative action as a law student. He also gave a notable illustration of anti-victim discourse when he gave this statement to the press during the nomination hearings:

> I don't believe in quotas. America was founded on a philosophy of individual rights, not group rights. The civil rights movement was at its greatest when it proclaimed the highest principles on which this country was founded – principles such as the Declaration of Independence, which were betrayed in the case of blacks and minorities . . . I believe in compensation for actual victims, not for people whose only claim to victimization is that they are members of a historically oppressed group.[37]

Thomas's scandalous rereading of the civil rights movement as a campaign for justice for individuals, rather than historically oppressed groups, shows how deeply the backlash had penetrated into racial politics as well as gender issues and the culture wars.

Colour-blindness and Post-ethnicity

In 1965, President Johnson had placed race at the forefront of the vision of the Great Society when he declared at Howard University that the legal freedoms won by the civil rights movement were not sufficient on their own, but needed to be supplemented by compensatory social programmes. As he famously announced to the audience of black graduates: 'You do not take a person who, for years, has been hobbled by chains and liberate him, bring him up to the starting line of a race and then say, "you are free to compete with all the others," and still justly believe that you have been completely fair . . .'[38] This conviction became the guiding principle behind race-specific policies such as school integration, voter registration, targeted recruitment, quotas and other forms of affirmative action.

By the 1990s, however, the tide was headed in the other direction. The Supreme Court's lack of interest in a substantive interpretation of equality was underlined in its 1989 ruling against the city council of Richmond, Virginia when it attempted to address a drastic imbalance in municipal contracting by setting aside 30 per cent for minority-owned businesses. In California, affirmative action came under further attack in 1996 under Proposition 209, which sought a ban on any consideration of race, sex or ethnicity in public institutions and thereby threatened attempts to increase minority representation everywhere from universities to police forces.[39] Race was being erased from political debate, too, as a result of the defeatist reasoning that Americans were too racist to vote for parties with race on their agendas. The reigning philosophy of the Clinton administration in its early years had been to smuggle in policies assisting racial communities as a 'hidden agenda' beneath an overt rhetoric of benefits for all; from here, the step towards not targeting racial communities at all was only a short one.

A key component of the neoliberal disavowal of race politics in this period was the discourse of colour-blindness. A colour-blind approach stated that neither blacks nor whites should be given special treatment, and that entry to schools, jobs or public positions should be awarded without paying any attention to racial background. Colour-blindness also materialised in the context of the law, where it stood for a principled neutrality and refusal to acknowledge the significance of race in the administration of justice. While the desire to transcend race may be seen as a genuine commitment to the ideals of equality enshrined in the Constitution, or at least as an expression of fatigue with a nation in which racial conflicts seemed so ingrained and unrelenting, critics of colour-blindness saw it as a form of misplaced idealism, if not wilful denial. Colour-blindness held up a vision of a society in which race ceased to matter, labelling any attempt to address inequality through positive discrimination for minorities a form of discrimination against whites. In doing so, it tacitly accepted the hegemony of whiteness, since disregarding race meant denying that whites were already the beneficiaries of historical and institutional privilege.

Thus the decade saw a strange, contradictory turn in the history of race relations in America: largely excluded from official political discourse, race dominated the public arena as never before. The continuing disenfranchisement of non-white citizens, African Americans in particular, was impossible to ignore: the crack epidemic of the 1980s–1990s disproportionately afflicted black communities in the inner cities, and the stringent response to the wave of crime that accompanied the drug only helped to racialise the problem even more. As Manning Marable notes, discrimination operated at every stage of the process: by 1999, even after the panic over crack use had eased, blacks made up 14 per cent of all drug users but 35 per cent of arrests on drug offences, over half the total number of convictions and three-quarters of prison admissions.[40] Throughout the decade, outrageously high levels of incarceration amongst young black men and recurrent reports of police violence – of which the beating of Rodney King in 1991 was only the most famous – further attested to the dire situation for African Americans.

Inevitably, race became an object of fascination in a series of media spectacles that brought the discourse of colour-blindness into direct collision with evidence of social crisis. Following on from the confrontation between Anita Hill and Clarence Thomas, the nation was consumed by the scandal of the Rodney King video and the riots that followed the acquittal of the police officers responsible for the beating. This was succeeded in turn by the highly publicised trial of former football star O. J. Simpson, accused of murdering his former wife Nicole Brown Simpson and her friend Ron Goodman in 1994; over the ensuing months the trial turned into a bloated media operation, dominating news agendas and single-handedly establishing the success of CNN as a cable news channel.[41] Then in 1996 and 1997 the murders of Tupac Shakur and Biggie Smalls, two of rap music's most prominent artists, created yet another moment of trauma that put race under the national spotlight. All of these events provided occasion for reflection and debate on issues such as police brutality, the root causes of poverty and violence in the inner cities, the legacy of black political struggle since the 1960s and the possibilities of integration. However, with the repression of public discourse on structural racism such phenomena often appeared incoherent and mysterious; under such circumstances the violence within black communities could only be explained in terms of pathology or habit rather than attributed to more complex social factors.

The O. J. Simpson Trial

Football star, sports commentator, actor and lucrative advertising quantity, O. J. Simpson was the perfect symbol of a colour-blind America. He laid claim more convincingly than Clarence Thomas to a rags-to-riches story in which the transition from housing project to elite society was based on merit alone; in addition, his marriage (until 1992) to a white woman and well-publicised residence in a white suburb of Los Angeles appealed to a world in which race could be transcended through effort and prosperity. On the field and on screen, he had cultivated a persona that signified inclusiveness: genial, unwilling to be drawn on racial issues and associated with everyday products common to all Americans such as razors, car rental, clothing and orange juice. At the beginning of the trial, as the shock of Simpson's arrest for double murder began to take shape, a comment in the *Los Angeles Times* expressed the racial subtext of this persona with complete candour: 'White people liked O.J. They liked liking him, too. Liking him proved they were not racists. O.J. redeemed them.'[45]

The fall of O.J. the Redeemer amounted therefore to a crisis for the ideology of colour-blindness itself, and its contradictions would become exposed in the course of the trial. Icons of race neutrality such as Simpson commonly functioned as alibis for the continuing existence of inequalities amongst minorities – the (non-)argument being that if a few could succeed, the system was not at fault. When these icons lost credibility, the same inequalities appeared more insistent and harder to explain away. The intensity of the media attacks on the accused and the desire to forgo reasonable doubt to reach a guilty verdict reflected the degree of popular investment in colour-blindness and the anger at being betrayed, as if it, or Simpson, had defaulted on the promise to liberate Americans from their consciences. Correspondingly, the racial difference that had been repressed in dreams of opportunity and neutrality returned in the media in grotesque forms: in popular references to the case as an Othello and Desdemona story; in the morbid fascination with pictures of the white female victim Nicole Brown Simpson, to the virtual exclusion of Ron Goodman; and most notoriously of all, in *Time* magazine's scandalous cover photo of 27 June 1994, a manipulated police mugshot in which Simpson appears darker-skinned. The racialisation of the trial was also evident in the downplaying of polls indicating white support for Simpson's acquittal – 25 per cent of all whites, more than the total African American population – which created the false impression that the verdict split the nation solely along racial lines.

Difference returned in the court process too, with the defence's recourse to an argument that racism within the Los Angeles Police Department discredited the evidence incriminating Simpson. For those who considered that the personal prejudices of police officers had nothing to do with the facts of the matter, this amounted to 'playing the race card', making illegitimate appeals to race in situations that call for objectivity. But it was the unfairness of objectivity that was at issue here – or at least the way that objectivity had traditionally been constructed on grounds that favoured a white majority. When detective Mark Fuhrman denied making racist remarks, the exposure of his perjury also revealed the matter-of-factness of the police practice known as 'testilying', where officers would commonly lie under oath to secure a conviction that correct procedure would have made impossible. As Kimberlé Crenshaw observes, the tolerance given to such police malpractice reflects a privileged position that is already informed by race:

In light of the limited ideological and material scope of race reform, the concrete fear of crime continues to reflect a racial dimension. The problem of testilying, by contrast, raises few concerns among the elite and other populations who are largely exempt from police procedures or who have so rarely been subjected to them that they have little personal concern about the threat that such practices represent.[46]

The jurors were therefore being asked to disregard racism in order to maintain the belief that the police and legal systems were fair 'under the circumstances' – even when those circumstances were highly racialised.

Simpson was acquitted on 3 October 1995, though the verdict did not quell speculation about the case. Instead, it became a kind of mirror reflecting wider public opinion about the state of race and justice in the United States. For some, the trial was a travesty – either an illustration that the rich could buy their innocence whether black or white, or an example of the perversion of the law in the hands of the mob: many attacks were levelled at the jury for failing to understand the scientific evidence or for picking 'a dreadful time to seek an empty retribution for Rodney King', as prosecuting attorney Christopher Darden complained.[47] For others, it was a salutary instance of the law functioning perfectly properly and acquitting where there was reasonable doubt – a commodity all too scarce in many cases involving black suspects.

The sequel to the trial occurred in 1997, when the families of Nicole Brown Simpson and Ron Goodman were awarded damages of $38 million after a civil trial in which Simpson was held responsible for their wrongful deaths. Simpson moved to Florida in order to evade payment, and so far has paid only a fraction of the settlement to the families. In 2006 he attempted to publish his own account of the murders, gruesomely titled *If I Did It*; the book was withdrawn and pulped before the date of release but has now been republished following award of copyright to the Goodman family.

Figure I.3 O. J. Simpson in slow-speed car chase, 13 June 1994 (© Out Look/Corbis Sygma).

If multiculturalism as an educational principle and intellectual paradigm had met with sustained resistance since the 1980s, there was nevertheless no question that the ethnic composition of the United States was undergoing a sea-change. The National Census of 2000 confirmed the remarkable trends in population growth: the decade had seen the largest population rise since the 1950s, with the most significant increases amongst groups of Hispanic and Asian origin. Hispanics now constituted over thirty million, roughly the same size as the African American population, having doubled in size since the 1970s. Over the century the proportion of non-whites had risen from one in eight Americans to one in four.[42]

While these demographic shifts generated a real sense of optimism in some quarters that America could become a model of a multicultural society never seen before – 'tropicalising the national vision of the city on a hill', as Mike Davis expressed it[43] – another consequence was the emergence of whiteness as an identity, brought into relief against the increasing ethnic and racial diversity of American society despite the fact that the majority status of whites was hardly challenged (the proportion of whites declined from 80 per cent to 77 per cent over the course of the decade). Whiteness often appeared as a symptom of crisis, reflecting the anxieties of those who felt disadvantaged by the preferential treatment awarded to ethnic minority groups: the most vivid image is the forlorn figure of Michael Douglas in *Falling Down* (1993), the angry white office worker lost in a Los Angeles wilderness that he progressively discovers to be someone else's territory.[44]

Whiteness was also taken up in academic circles as a new object of analysis – a category that once passed for the universal subject but now needed to be understood as a historical and ideological construct. Scholars in different fields undertook the project of 'denormalising' whiteness: David Roediger in *The Wages of Whiteness* (1991) and Noel Ignatiev in *How the Irish Became White* (1995) showed how claiming whiteness has been central to the political strategies of various groups in American history, often interrupting other alliances that might be made around labour and class, while Ruth Frankenberg examined the dense intersections of race and gender in *White Women, Race Matters* (1993). Richard Dyer traced the presence and power of white imagery in Hollywood film and popular culture in *White* (1997), while Toni Morrison addressed the racial subtext of American literary history in *Playing in the Dark* (1992), where she asked what it meant for a black writer to work in a tradition in which writers and readers are assumed to be white from the start. The contemporary rearticulation of whiteness was treated by Lauren Berlant in her important essay 'The Face of America and the State of Emergency' in which she showed how idealised images of racial diversity in popular culture worked to erase racial politics from history and suppress the realities of immigrant lives. At the heart of her analysis was *Time* magazine's special issue of 1993, 'The New Face of America', whose cover featured a computer-generated composite image of 'Eve', a young woman purporting to be the future outcome of generations of interracial mixing. The image played out a set of fantasies: interracial sex, the Frankensteinian dream of human reproduction through technology, and the submission to surveillance; but above all else it promoted the delusion that racial conflicts would eventually be resolved through private social and sexual relationships rather than any form of political struggle.[48]

A similar fantasy of resolving race through interracial sexual reproduction was presented by David Hollinger, who coined the term 'post-ethnicity' in 1995 to designate his vision of an America freed from the constraints of multiculturalism. For him, the problem with identity politics as it had transpired over the decades was the conflation of race and culture, such that individuals were obliged to identify with an ethnic or racial community even if they felt no particular cultural affiliation to it. Thus he stressed 'voluntary affiliation' – that an individual might choose whatever identity he or she wished – and celebrated the momentous changes of the 2000 Census which for the first time allowed multiple box-ticking across the spectrum of racial and ethnic categories. Hollinger's optimistic liberalism emphasised individual self-development and the progressive potential of hybrid, mixed-race, transnational affiliations, but it relied at least in part on a substitution of politics with biology, and his belief in the power of choice risked neglecting the obvious instances where individuals are racially identified in circumstances they do not control.[49]

Globalisation and National Culture

So far, this introduction has concentrated on the ways in which nineties American culture developed in relation to social conditions and political conflicts specific to the United States – the legacy of the 1960s, the persistence of racial problems, the increasing visibility of ethnic minorities and so forth. But there is a further context that needs to be taken into consideration, one that shifts the weight of the inquiry from the second term to the first: it means asking not only what *culture* is, and how it reflects or mediates historical change, but what *American* means, and how the concept of nationhood is affected by the profound structural transformations that have come to be known as globalisation. While the processes that globalisation refers to have a long history and do not, of course, occur all of a sudden in the 1990s, the scale and intensity of globalising forces in this period made it a widely used concept in cultural and social theory, in many respects superseding postmodernism as a dominant intellectual paradigm. Globalisation's key themes are mobility and deterritorialisation: capital, information and human beings flow at an accelerated pace and often irrespective of national boundaries, with the result that traditional notions of state sovereignty are called into question. While the interpenetration of global markets leaves nation-states less able to control their economies, communities and social institutions are similarly transformed – increasingly subject to global forces, and detached from their former ties with geographical location.

As with other phases of modernisation, globalisation produces both optimism and anxiety: a dream of a united world is matched by a concern for the destruction of local identities and resources or the unfair distribution of economic benefits. The North American Free Trade Agreement of 1994 is a case in point: bringing together Canada, Mexico and the United States into the largest ever common market, it was heralded by its signatories as a model of cooperation and helped to relieve Mexico of a financial crisis, but it also made visible some of the costs and inequalities of liberalisation. *Maquiladoras* – factories that assembled goods from imported components and exported them elsewhere, taking advantage of the cheaper Mexican labour and looser regulation of work conditions – sprung up near the American border, symbols of the new capitalism; in the Southwest of the country, NAFTA's eradication of subsidies for small farmers and removal of rights for indigenous peoples prompted the Zapatista rebellion, which would soon prove a major inspiration for the growing global justice movement. At home, outsourcing hastened the loss of the country's manufacturing base and generated anti-globalist demands for protecting American jobs. Even those who were more optimistic about national opportunities in global markets worried about the potential damage to society: Labour Secretary Robert Reich envisaged a new class of 'symbolic analysts' more inclined to associate with their contemporaries across the world than with their fellow Americans.[50] More radical responses to globalisation were mobilised in numerous local campaigns across the world but they began to take shape as a mass movement in the demonstrations at the World Trade Organization conference in Seattle in 1999 (see Conclusion). Characterised by loose coalition rather than centralised organisation, planned by means of the internet and documented by participant 'citizen journalists', the protests became a powerful, if occasionally idealised, image of new possibilities for political action.

What, then, are the effects of globalisation on the idea of a national culture? More precisely, what can 'American culture' mean, if we acknowledge that culture is increasingly produced from global materials in sites across the world, often under the ownership of transnational corporations, and distributed amongst global audiences in situations that are ever more mobile and delocalised? One common response is to note that American culture is, of all world cultures, especially global, having occupied a dominant position in the media and entertainment industries since World War II. This has led in the past to arguments over the existence of 'cultural imperialism' – whether globalisation equates with Americanisation, implying a tendency towards homogenisation amongst cultural products across the globe ('McWorld', as Benjamin Barber put it in 1995), or whether to a greater extent other cultures are able to borrow, appropriate and translate American materials for their own ends.[51] Thus, to take one area of cultural activity, developments such as industry conglomeration and the creation of MTV helped make American popular music ubiquitous by the end of the century, but if its ideological force is exerted primarily through its forms and modes of consumption – rock functioning as an expression of individual rebellion, hip-hop as a sign of resistance for disempowered groups – its internal logic of innovation and mutation nevertheless provides ample scope for customisation in local contexts.

More recently, debates about cultural imperialism have been displaced by transnational perspectives interested in the mobility of cultural practices and sites of interference between national cultures rather than the essential attributes of national cultures themselves. Paul Giles, for instance, has argued that contemporary global conditions have problematised the idea of national culture to the extent that it makes more sense to think of American culture as 'virtual' than 'real' – that is, as part of a global imaginary, whether a 'residual narrative' within the country itself or an image in the minds of others across the world. Hence a student of American culture should not be looking for 'the real America' in a set of defining characteristics or exceptional circumstances, or even looking at the ways such myths are critiqued from within, but concentrating instead on the ways that America circulates as a signifier in an international arena.[52] Though Giles restricts his enquiry to literary crossings between America and Britain, another way to see the value of his approach would be to think of the films of Ang Lee, who rose to prominence in the 1990s as a new kind of 'global director' – not simply a Hollywood director with a global audience but a film-maker straddling different national industries, whose work is specifically situated on the intersections between different cultures and audiences. Born Taiwanese and trained in New York, Lee moved from early work that thematised generational and cultural difference (*The Wedding Banquet*, *Eat Drink Man Woman*) to films featuring iconic national moments or settings against which Lee himself is positioned as an outsider: Victorian Britain in *Sense and Sensibility* (1995), Nixonian America in *The Ice Storm* (1997) and the Civil War in *Ride With the Devil* (1999). Subsequent works *Crouching Tiger, Hidden Dragon* (2000), *Hulk* (2003) and *Brokeback Mountain* (2005) are truly examples of global cinema (as opposed to 'world cinema', exotically packaged like world music for western markets) in the respect that they are designed for maximum cross-cultural audience appeal while retaining an outer appearance of cultural specificity. Westerns, comic books and martial arts movies have long circulated as global commodities, and related films can therefore tap into a shared global cultural memory even as they are called upon to deliver a sense of being located within national traditions. What is more, these genres also have the virtue of being structured around non-dialogue elements (action sequences, landscape shots, inarticulate monsters) making them more resistant to harm from dubbing or subtitling. In all three of the above films Lee makes a special feature of such elements to create moments of dramatic or emotional intensity that function independently of language – allowing an immediacy to all spectators that uncannily recollects the way early cinema united immigrant audiences before the introduction of sound. Thus Lee's film-making consistently plays with the tension between inside and outside, commonality and difference, inclusion within cultural formations or their representation as foreign and other. And correspondingly, we should address an analysis of a particular film not so much towards what it reveals about American culture (or, indeed, Chinese or British), but which aspects connote a virtual 'America' to global audiences, which aspects resonate with global issues, which aspects remain semantically open for local meanings to be generated and how the film mediates the tension between these different imperatives.

Exploring the virtual dimensions of American culture in the 1990s is unfortunately beyond the scope of this book. I will, however, try to analyse its internal formations with respect to a global context, highlighting those transnational factors that produce a range of effects and reactions within America itself – factors such as the consolidation of multinational corporations, the emergence of online communities, the impact of global media technologies and markets, and the growing significance of diasporic identities. Perhaps the most important consequence of globalisation, one that has been observed by numerous cultural critics and political scientists, is that the weakening of national sovereignty in economic and social domains has led not in fact to the disappearance of nationalism but to its resurgence: reaffirmations of cultural distinctiveness occur in reaction to the perception that it is being lost. Thus in the United States conservatives found success in recasting progressive social policies as a threat to core American values; concern over illegal immigration gathered momentum, reflected in increased penalties and the tightening of border controls; national myths of landscape, frontier spirit and homeland were reasserted throughout popular culture and political discourse. In addition to these defensive impulses, the 1990s also saw attempts to align national identity with global conditions in what Frederick Buell terms 'postnational nationalism'. He explains:

> the term 'global' became less the nightmare that haunted Americans than a word to conjure with – a key term for restructuring the political discourse of national crisis and internal division into a new kind of recovery narrative, one that seemed to blend conservative nationalist and radical post-national positions together into a new kind of nationalism for a global era.[53]

Thus global diversity is conceived in the image of American multiculturalism; environmentalism is recast as an opportunity for American companies to lead in the development of 'green technologies', and the boundless regions of cyberspace are inevitably reterritorialised as an American frontier.

Just as nationalism is reaffirmed in the face of threats to national sovereignty, so too have globalisation's deterritorialising effects produced a series of defensive reflexes at the local level. One of the most notable trends in political thought over the course of the decade was the growth of debate around the concept of community: the extent to which it played an important part in democratic society and, if so, whether it was in worrying decline in the United States. Communitarians such as Amitai Etzioni sought a third way between the laissez-faire economics of the right and the tendency toward centralised state power in the policies of the left: critical of liberalism's idealisation of the individual, they emphasised the merits of small communities, local interactions and social obligations. Although he was careful not to associate himself with communitarianism as an intellectual movement, Robert Putnam's call for civic renewal in *Bowling Alone*, discussed below, was a significant highlight in such debates, if only because his ideas were taken up enthusiastically by governments at home and abroad. In this book he warned of the disappearance of traditional forms of community, and appealed for the revival of democracy in America through the restoration of its old customs of informal voluntary association. Indeed, we might see this discourse of community and democracy functioning very much in the way of Buell's recovery narrative, a means of rearticulating American national identity in a global context. There is a crisis in democratic society across the world, but the remedy is to be found in fundamentally American habits and principles.

Bowling Alone (2000)

For a long time Americans have worried that the national tradition of individualism runs counter to the norms and ideals of community life. Alexis de Tocqueville, one of the country's first cultural critics, suggested in 1840 that democracy inevitably draws citizens apart in the pursuit of their own interests, giving them a dangerous illusion of independence from one another. However, he also observed that such a tendency was kept in check in the United States by the devolution of politics to a local level and the popular practice of joining clubs and organisations. 'Americans of all ages, all conditions, and all dispositions constantly form associations,' he remarked. 'They have not only commercial and manufacturing companies, in which all take part, but associations of a thousand other kinds, religious, moral, serious, futile, general or restricted, enormous or diminutive.'[54] For de Tocqueville this network of informal institutions, known as civil society, was the crucial mediating force between individuals and the state – a means of creating new social values and a bulwark against the tyranny of bureaucratic regulation.

Political scientists gave renewed attention to civil society in the 1990s, looking for clues as to what made a successful democracy at a time when formerly communist European states were restructuring and occasionally facing, as in Russia, the spectre of total social collapse. Robert Putnam had argued in *Making Democracy Work* (1993) that strong democracies relied upon ample resources of 'social capital', opportunities for civic engagement that strengthened bonds between people and increased levels of trust, thereby minimising the costs of security and maximising economic efficiency. This made it all the more alarming when he presented the thesis in 1995 that levels of social capital in America were in dramatic decline. Over the next five years he amassed data on a wide range of different forms of social engagement, from party campaigning to church and union membership, charitable donation to volunteering, involvement in sports to home entertaining, all of which led to the conclusion that the spirit of association so important to de Tocqueville was disappearing. 'For the first two-thirds of the twentieth century a powerful tide bore Americans into ever deeper engagement in the life of their communities, but a few decades ago – silently, without warning – that tide reversed and we were overtaken by a treacherous rip current. Without at first noticing, we have been pulled apart from one another and from our communities over the last third of the century.'[55] Americans were now 'bowling alone', he claimed – increasingly isolated and atomised even in their forms of recreation.

Putnam's idea struck a chord with the nation, turning him briefly into a talk-show attraction and prompting an invitation from President Clinton to consult on the implications for social policy. To many, the findings seemed intuitively to confirm anxieties about the direction of society: interest and involvement in politics was on the wane; grassroots activity in social movements was being replaced by subscription membership in national organisations; more and more people disagreed with the statement 'most people can be trusted'; road rage, speeding and failure to stop at stop signs were all on the up. As for the root causes, Putnam identified increasing career demands, urban sprawl and television as key factors but attributed most of the decline to generational change. In contrast to the 'long civic generation' of the 1910s to 1940s – those whose sense of social commitment was fostered in the collective experience of depression and war – the postwar baby boomers had grown up to think of themselves as 'free agents', suspicious of mainstream politics and social institutions. If this tended to make them more tolerant and reluctant to moralise, it nevertheless made them less committed to a common culture. 'On any given issue, the tolerant, cynical, "laid-back" boomers may have a point, but as a syndrome their attitudes have a high social cost,' Putnam ruminated.[56]

Thus *Bowling Alone* reiterates the conservative indictment of the sixties, if not as a period of moral indulgence then the moment when the seeds were sown for subsequent decades of disengagement. This may have been what was appealing to a president seeking to recast his own background and move away from the boomer stereotype of the 'me generation'; in any case, Putnam's views were ideally suited to the politics of the third way, which trod a fine line between acknowledging social inequalities and paying minimal attention to economic causes. Emphasising civil society as a remedy for social problems was ultimately cheaper, and less politically risky, than government regulation or a redistribution of tax revenues.

Putnam does mention factors such as deunionisation and the withdrawal of businesses from local communities as a result of globalisation, but these play only a small part in the overall picture, which prioritises the recovery of neighbourly ties above democratic participation or specific political issues. The lack of a structural analysis is exposed in his final manifesto for 'social capitalists', which ranges from the commonsensical to the whimsical: more family-friendly workplaces, more pedestrian public space in cities, media proprietors to become more socially responsible and software engineers to develop internet applications that strengthen neighbourly ties.

The real issue that *Bowling Alone* raises, however, is to do with the notion of community and the usefulness of social capital as a means of understanding it. Critics have warned that social capital is not an unequivocal good: anti-democratic organisations may enjoy high levels of social bonding, after all, and strong communities may have little to do with a commitment to justice and equality. Trust can be valuable but hard to establish across group boundaries without the support and intervention of government, and rights for minorities may never be achieved without some form of legal enforcement. (In other words, social capital may mirror, rather than combat, the unequal distribution of other forms of capital.)[57] Seen in this light, Putnam's emphasis on community betrays a degree of nostalgia for a world in which small, local networks of face-to-face relationships – what the German sociologist Ferdinand Tönnies termed *Gemeinschaft* – are more easily sustainable. If these forms of community are disappearing in more complex, highly mediated modern societies, then it is nonetheless possible that new forms of association are emerging that have an equally important part to play in democracy. Online communities involved in blogging, consumer activism, reviewing and troubleshooting would be obvious examples.

Interest in communitarian solutions was thus a central feature of social criticism in the 1990s, when images of social breakdown were popular and politicians looked for a new language to comprehend the transformations of globalisation and multiculturalism. The current neoliberal rhetoric of stakeholding, civic responsibility and faith-based communities owes much to this phase, and Putnam's own work has had a wide reach on both sides of the Atlantic.[58] But as there are other ways of thinking about community, there are also other narratives of democracy: not the crisis of civil society but the expansion of social bonds and the continuing resistance to forms of inequality.

One of the things that this survey of the intellectual context reveals is the extent to which economic neoliberalism cuts deep into the culture of the 1990s. Neoliberalism's idealisation of the market and preference for minimal government allowed the economy to be more flexible to changing conditions but it also brought new kinds of insecurity to many citizens, and their anxieties found expression in various ways throughout the decade. In addition, neoliberalism impacted on cultural production itself, bringing market principles to bear on creative activity and raising fears that culture was becoming nothing more than another kind of business. In a climate of expanding media conglomerates and dwindling public funding for the arts, it was inevitable that the loss of independence and the need for alternative viewpoints would become common preoccupations. Hence the search for spaces of opposition and critique constitute a major theme in the chapters that follow, through literature, music, film and television and art. Chapter 1 looks at the reorientation of the literary field in a culture dominated by electronic media, while Chapter 2 considers shifts in the consumption of music and the role it plays (or ceases to play) in identity formation. The third deals with the restructuring of film and television industries and the emergence of more diversified, hybrid forms of entertainment, and the fourth analyses art's transition from national to international arenas.

Just as significant in shaping the culture of the 1990s is the growth of digital technology: a development that perhaps more than any other deserves to be called revolutionary in that it was relatively unforeseen and proceeded to transform all aspects of human life. Hence the final chapter treats the impact of digital technology as a 'culture' in its own right – looking at the ways it fostered dreams of new social relationships or flight from the limits of the human condition as it became integrated into the fabric of the everyday. A decade on, we are not yet in a position to assess how profound the changes of the 1990s are, nor how significant it is as a decade of transformation. But as the Conclusion makes clear, the search for new forms of creative expression and the sense of possibility contained even in cultural forms that appear highly incorporated should not be forgotten.

Chapter 1

Fiction and Poetry

Fears of the erosion of national culture by mass communication and popular forms of entertainment have been a part of modernity since the nineteenth century, but the sense that literature itself was under threat seemed particularly acute in the 1990s. On the basis of a survey conducted by the Census Bureau in 2002 the National Endowment for the Arts noted that for the first time in America's recent history, reading literature for pleasure was a minority pursuit: less than half the adult population could claim to have read a work of fiction, poetry, or a play in the previous year. More worryingly, it concluded from a comparison with surveys in 1992 and 1982 that the rate of decline was accelerating dramatically, particularly among young adults. Dana Gioia, NEA chairman and a poet himself, warned of a 'culture at risk', speculating that 'at the current rate of loss, literary reading as a leisure activity will virtually disappear in half a century'.[1]

We should be careful not to place too much emphasis on apocalyptic forecasts like this, since the survey was only a record of a moment in time and did not explore the factors underlying the reading trends it identified. These may have been as singular as the fact that the survey year took in the aftermath of the terrorist attacks of 11 September 2001, a time when news and current affairs clearly took precedence over fiction, and even writers questioned the role of the novel.[2] Equally, if the fall in literary reading was to be attributed to the rise of internet use during the 1990s, as the survey suggested, it marked the impact of a revolution that is unlikely to be repeated in the future. Nevertheless, such results showed how dramatically the literary field had changed over the previous twenty years, and they raised questions about the significance of literature in what has increasingly been called a 'post-literate' culture – one in which the centrality of the printed word is displaced by images on the one hand and oral forms of communication on the other.

Reading in a Post-literate Culture

Why should it matter that literary reading is in decline? Gioia's view is a familiar one: he worries about the limited attention span and 'accelerated gratification' that electronic media encourages, and asserts that print uniquely helps develop faculties of thought and expression. But he also makes a case for the social function of reading literature. From the survey's findings that levels of reading correlate with levels of voluntary work he concludes that 'readers play a more active and involved role in their communities. The decline in reading, therefore, parallels a larger retreat from participation in civic and cultural life.'[3] In this way the concern for reading is revealed to be part of a wider set of anxieties about democracy and nationhood, and Gioia's affirmation of the value of literature is incorporated into a broader 'recovery narrative' (to return to Frederick Buell's term): in the face of profound transformations across social and cultural spheres, reading becomes a way of restoring an endangered national unity.[4]

While the assumption that reading literature really is a positive social good needs to be fully debated (though it is outside the limits of this chapter[5]), we should at least observe that support for such a view comes from a number of different sources, and not only from a state institution like the NEA. The case is also made, perhaps paradoxically, in the realm of daytime television – by Oprah's Book Club, a monthly segment of *The Oprah Winfrey Show* begun in 1996 under the stated mission of 'getting the country reading'. Still running to this day, the Book Club is significant not merely for the fact that it offers a rare moment of visibility for books in popular culture, but because Winfrey's own immense power as a brand has made it the primary focus of the book industry and a key forum for discussion on the meaning and function of literature. For publishers, selection for the Book Club is far more important than any literary prize: an Oprah badge on the cover almost guarantees a million sales in an industry of ever tighter profit margins. For authors, it offers the chance to reach a wider audience in a single appearance than might be achieved in an entire career. What it means for readers and the literary field in general has been the focus of a growing amount of critical discussion.

Reading groups proliferated at a remarkable rate throughout the 1990s, and the phenomenon can be understood in various ways: as a response to the atomisation of working life that Robert Putnam laments in *Bowling Alone* (see Introduction), as a reaction to the virtual sociability of internet discussion groups and as part of a resurgence of oral culture, manifest in other literary contexts such as audiobooks and slam poetry events. Oprah's Book Club combines the reading group's emphasis on communal reading with the traditional talk-show format of live interview: the usual format is a dialogue between Winfrey and the featured author, interspersed with reactions from an informed audience and prefaced with clips from an earlier dinner-party discussion. In this way it presents an image of a (generally female) community in which the meaning of the book is rooted, with Winfrey playing a dual role as enquiring reader and endorsing authority figure.

Because of this divided function Winfrey has been both applauded for democratising literature and berated for the influence she exercises as a celebrity. For some, her achievement has been not just to promote reading in general but also to dissolve the distinction between mass-market and 'serious' fiction, as shown in her selection of demanding novels alongside more accessible ones and perhaps most of all in her ability to turn Toni Morrison from a critically acclaimed writer into a popular one. Cecilia Farr has even argued that the Book Club is an instance of 'cultural democracy' in action, breaking down cultural hierarchies and offering a public forum for previously excluded opinions.[6] Winfrey's detractors, however, have argued that the Book Club fails to develop independent reading habits on the evidence from publishers that selections rarely stimulate interest in the rest of an author's catalogue, indicating that viewers only buy what Winfrey recommends. They also question the influence she has over literary markets, citing reports that publishers have been put under growing pressure to commission new work from writers specifically to suit the show's tastes.[7] A further point of contention is the show's therapeutic format, which as Jeremy Green has argued threatens to present the case for reading primarily in terms of its value as a form of self-help.[8]

Green also points out inherent incompatibilities between literature and television. He cites a moment from the January 1998 show featuring Toni Morrison's *Paradise*, where Morrison's attempt to stress the complex and unresolved nature of the text – 'it's not just black or white, living, dead, up, down, in, out. It's being open to all these paths and connections' – is rendered by Winfrey, somewhat awkwardly, as a soundbite: 'That's great. Paradise is being open to all the places in between.'[9] *Paradise* (1997) was the most difficult of all the novels in Winfrey's selection, and probably the least suited to the restricted discussion format of the Book Club; something that the show clearly tried to address by filming the segment in Morrison's professional environment at Princeton, positioning her this time as the specialist teacher of her text rather than friend and confidante. But if it is true that television's drive towards closure does a disservice to the richness of literary texts, the relationship between Winfrey and Morrison also illustrates the advantages it offers in the way of access to public debate. *Oprah* may be benefiting from Morrison's cultural capital to distinguish itself from rival programmes, but the novels also allow Winfrey to extend and deepen a discourse on black history and social issues that has always been a key element of the show. Morrison in the meantime draws on *Oprah*'s mass audience to cast herself as a public writer, speaking to readers across lines of class and race.

In an interesting article on the 'material codes' determining the way her work is understood, from her association with Winfrey to the design of her book jackets, John Young argues that Morrison has set out to construct a 'self-consciously commodified textual authority' in response to the fact that black women writers have been doubly disenfranchised from commercial and canonical success and have no choice but to appear as 'embodied' figures in the public domain.[10] Where white male writers can afford to stand apart from their works – the extreme cases being J. D. Salinger and Thomas Pynchon, whose anonymity functions as a sign of their authenticity – Morrison has strategically cultivated the visibility that has been forced on her. Appearances on *Oprah* are therefore not just a form of promotion but a means of reclaiming authorship by presenting the writer as a 'speaking subject', a presence in the text and a member of a broad community of readers. This positioning is also evident in Morrison's decision to narrate for the audiobook versions of her works (a job usually given to actors and broadcasters): the medium allows her to evoke a renewed intimacy with the reader through the voice, and also draw attention to oral traditions which are fundamental to African American literary history. If the audiobook is conventionally thought of as a degraded form of literature (because it abridges the text and weakens the intensive physical relationship between reader and book), for Morrison it opens up the tension between the written and spoken word, recalling the sense in which a story is a performance, rooted in time and place, as much as a discrete textual object. The image of the talking book which frames Morrison's 1992 novel *Jazz*, or the recursive narrative structure of *Paradise* that gives an impression of the history of an Oklahoma town existing through the collective memory of its inhabitants, are therefore not compromised but made especially vivid by the novels' oral rendition.

Figure 1.1 Toni Morrison (left) discusses her 1977 novel *Song of Solomon* with Oprah Winfrey, 12 November 1996 (© Reuters/Corbis).

Ultimately, what is at issue here is a tension between authorship and the integrity of the literary text. If Green is disappointed by the treatment of the novel on the show (or the treatment of novels by television generally), it is because he is working with literary principles inherited from modernism which privilege a private relationship between reader and text. For Young, Morrison sacrifices this kind of textual integrity to foreground communication between author and reader, and recover the identity of both as participants in an ongoing cultural debate. In this respect she resembles German theorist Walter Benjamin's well-known description of the storyteller, whose stories offer a form of counsel to a community, either as news brought from afar or as local history and folklore. Writing in 1936, Benjamin saw the storyteller as an archaic figure threatened with extinction by the forces of modernity, and his most powerful image in that essay expresses a sense of the destruction of the places in which stories once flourished:

> A generation that had gone to school on a horse-drawn streetcar now stood under the open sky in a countryside in which nothing remained unchanged but the clouds, and beneath these clouds, in a field of force of destructive torrents and explosions, was the tiny, fragile human body.[11]

It would be wrong, of course, to say that Morrison reanimates this same persona. What makes her authorial identity post- rather than pre-modern is that she has no concept of home or place to appeal to, even as something that has been lost. Confronted by a past that could never be imagined in Benjamin's terms, a history cut across with the realities of African American exile and migration and the denials of white Americans, her task is to reinvent an imaginative community through storytelling, to find a place from which to speak in the relationship she forms with readers, viewers and listeners.

Paradise (1997)

Paradise completes the trilogy of novels that began with *Beloved* in 1987 and whose second part, *Jazz*, appeared in 1992. Taken together, they comprise an enquiry into the traumas and repressions of modern American history, tracing an African American presence back into authoritative representations of the past and examining the legacies of racial conflict in the present. Where *Beloved* focuses on the era of slavery and Emancipation and *Jazz* on the Harlem Renaissance, *Paradise* is concerned with the postwar period known to historians as the Second Reconstruction, in which the civil rights movement laid another claim to justice and equality for black Americans that was once again to unravel in the social and political turmoil of subsequent decades. The book focuses principally on the fortunes of the exclusively black town of Ruby, Oklahoma, successor to an earlier community of black homesteaders who left Louisiana and Mississippi in the 1880s seeking a new life in the recently opened western territories. In the story she tells of the genesis of the novel, Morrison was struck by a phrase she encountered in her research into these post-Civil War pioneers, a warning to other migrating families that they would be turned away if they arrived at the new towns without resources to last a year: 'Come Prepared or Not at All.'[12] Morrison took this as a symbol of the divisions that Reconstruction imposed not only between blacks and whites but also amongst black Southerners, and proceeded to write a story from the perspective of those who had migrated only to find themselves rejected and forced to found their own settlement. The fierce isolationism that Ruby inherits as a result of this 'Disallowing', and which ultimately threatens to destroy the town, operates as a muted allegory of race relations in contemporary America – an investigation into the desires and costs of racial identification as much as the prospects for racial coexistence.

The novel's 'present' is condensed into a single event of July 1976 – the massacre of a group of women inhabiting a former convent on the outskirts of Ruby. Morrison comments: 'I wanted to open with somebody's finger on the trigger, to close when it was pulled, and to have the whole novel exist in that moment of the decision to kill or not.'[13] With the plot suspended at the moment of execution, the rest of the narrative heads backwards into the lives of the women and townsfolk in search of the origins of the violence. Here Morrison uses a narrative structure reminiscent of William Faulkner in which the history of the region is revealed fragment by fragment, through the limited perspectives and resolute or faltering memories of the main characters. This places unusual demands on the reader, who can feel quite browbeaten by the repeated obscurities in the text and the labour of reconstructing the chronology of events, but the method has several purposes. In part, the disruptions and silences of the novel pay testimony to the impact of trauma in the lives of the women who take refuge in the convent, where they learn to tell their own stories as a means of overcoming the abuses they have suffered. At the same time, it reflects the historical trauma that gives birth to the town itself, whose inhabitants are compelled to repeat their forefathers' victimisation in becoming persecutors themselves.

The following passage gives an illustration of the extent that the weight of Ruby's past bears down on the present. In one of the key events prior to the massacre, K.D. strikes his pregnant girlfriend in public, causing the families to confront each other over the open secret of Arnette's pregnancy. K.D. reflects on his uncles' reactions:

> However disgusted both were, K.D. knew they would not negotiate a solution that would endanger him or the future of Morgan money. His grandfather had named his twins Deacon and Steward for a reason. And their family had not built two towns, fought white law, Coloured Creek, bandits and bad weather, to see ranches and houses and a bank with mortgages on a feed store, a drugstore and a furniture store end up in Arnold Fleetwood's pocket. K.D., their hope and their despair, was the last male in a line that included a lieutenant governor, a state auditor and two mayors. His behaviour, as always, required scrutiny and serious correction. Or would the uncles see it another way? Maybe Arnette's baby would be a boy, a Morgan grandnephew. Would her father, Arnold, have any rights then that the Morgans had to respect?[14]

The slap K.D. gives Arnette might seem an isolated instance of male force but here it is shown to be fully embedded in a patriarchal system which is perpetuated through historiography as well as name and property. The story of the town has been reiterated to the point that it can be evoked through a few words signifying lost privilege and a mythical journey from wilderness to civilisation (bandits to furniture); even as K.D. fears his uncles, he acknowledges the story and claims his own place within it, as father of the next generation of Morgans. But there is a further detail that should not go unnoticed. The exclusion of the Fleetwoods from the Morgan fortune is described here in words that echo the Dred Scott judgment of 1857, in which the Supreme Court famously ruled that slaves had 'no rights which the white man was bound to respect'. That this phrase – one that enshrined racism at the heart of the nation's Constitution, the outrage of which helped precipitate the Civil War – should be called upon in a

squabble between black families is a sign of how deeply Ruby has internal-
ised the values and language of the world it sought to exclude. Also evident
in the fetishisation of the original settlers' bloodline and skin colour, it is
a sign that Ruby may be free from the presence of whites but it is no less
dependent on racial ideology.

Ultimately, the origin of the atrocity and the main object of Morrison's
critique in *Paradise* is the desire for utopia – specifically the desire to establish a society free from race. The preservation of the founders' dream of
self-determination generates a fear of outsiders, a need to police sexuality
and a righteous rage – all of which ends in the scapegoating of the women
in the convent. 'Unbridled by Scripture, deafened by the roar of its own
history, Ruby . . . was an unnecessary failure,' concludes one of the town's
new generation. 'How exquisitely human was the wish for permanent happiness, and how thin human imagination became trying to achieve it.'[15] We
should note, though, that that false promise of transcending race is not
just the domain of the black nationalism of the 1960s and 70s, but also of
the discourse of colour-blindness prevalent at the beginning of the 1990s.
Morrison had seen the way that a genuine discussion on race had degen-
erated into denial in the Clarence Thomas hearings and the O. J. Simpson
trial; she had also observed in *Playing in the Dark* (1992) that denial informs
American literary history, where fundamentally racialised concepts of
freedom and individualism have passed for universal themes.[16] Hence
Paradise can be seen as an attempt to resist the allure of race-neutrality,
rewriting a black American presence back into the nation's history and
myths while at the same time questioning the grounds on which racial difference is asserted.

Several critics have pointed out that this deconstruction of race is undertaken at the expense of a similar enquiry into gender. While the convent is
no more a utopia than Ruby, Morrison is clearly attracted to the idea of a
therapeutic women's space, and the celebratory passages toward the end
of the novel featuring 'holy women dancing in hot sweet rain' or the closing
images of maternal reconciliation can be hard to stomach.[17] Equally, the
novel's orientation towards a devastating outburst of male violence tends
to overshadow subtleties in the representation of gender elsewhere.[18] But
again, this should be seen in the context of the spectacles of race that consumed the nation at the beginning of the decade. What was revealed in the
confrontation between Clarence Thomas and Anita Hill was the peculiar
precedence that racial politics took over gender in the 1990s, epitomised
by Thomas's successful use of the metaphor of lynching which simultaneously accused his white interrogators and obscured the claims of a black
woman as the victim of sexual harassment.[19] In response, Morrison's decision to stage *Paradise* around a lynching of women, rather than men, is not
so much a dramatisation of absolute differences between the sexes as an
attempt to write against the lynching motif, to challenge the suppression
of women's victimisation that dominant discourses of blackness seem to
require.

Authorship and Voice

Few writers were able to emulate Toni Morrison's success at adapting to the transformations taking place in the literary field. For many, the decline of print culture and the pressures of electronic media signalled a crisis of authorship and authority: the novelist spoke to smaller audiences and was less commonly called upon to offer analytical insights into the culture. In an article written for *Harper's Magazine* in 1996, a gloomy Jonathan Franzen outlined the defeat of his aspirations to write a 'social novel' at a moment when a writer's views no longer had the power to mobilise debate, and when consumerism threatened to annihilate the significance of individual dramas along with the specificities of place. Finding literature no longer equal to its task of social critique, Franzen found comfort in thinking of it instead as a realm of privacy and intimacy: 'to write sentences of such authenticity that refuge can be taken in them: isn't this enough? Isn't it a lot?'[20]

This is a long way from Morrison's politicised storytelling community: an essentially conservative vision of the novel as a form of consolation rather than a potential intervention in public life. But it is an expression of the literary pessimism that was pervasive in the period, which novelists themselves addressed in narratives of marginalised, blocked and usurped writers: the writer taken hostage in Don DeLillo's *Mao II* (1991), sensing that the power to speak to the masses has now passed to the terrorist; the writer given the limited options of acting as terrorist or state informer in Paul Auster's *Leviathan* (1992); the protagonist of Richard Powers's *Galatea 2.2* (1995), stuck on his next novel while employed to input literature into a computer to synthesise intelligence; the 'Reader' of David Markson's *Reader's Block* (1996), whose attempts at autobiography are interrupted (but also informed) by fragments of literary quotation, allusion and anecdote from a life of reading. The related theme of the literary impostor is given comic treatment in two later novels: John Colapinto's *About the Author* (2001) features a desperate writer who discovers the manuscript of his own life in the belongings of his dead flatmate, and proceeds to pass it off as his own autobiography; Percival Everett's protagonist in *Erasure* (2001) becomes the victim of the success of his sub-literate 'ghetto' novel, written in anger after his agent accuses him of not being black enough. In various ways, then, the trope of the writer in crisis is used to explore anxieties about the market's intrusion on creative expression, the erosion of a public sphere and the relationship between writing and identity.[21]

Of course, we should not ignore the fact that with one exception, all of these writers are white men. The crisis of authorship is clearly most likely to concern those who have traditionally occupied positions of power; those from minority positions, on the other hand, are likely to view readerships, public spheres and the market very differently. This is why an alternative perspective on the period would observe not a decline in confidence about the novel's potential but an explosion in literary activity amongst writers of colour – black, Native American, Latino and Asian American – seeking to bring their own experiences to the attention of new and national audiences. The loss of the cultural centrality that literature once occupied – one that Franzen describes in a revealing metaphor as a depressed inner city evacuated by whites – becomes an occasion and an opportunity to articulate cultural difference and contest dominant images of the nation.[22]

In the universities the development was marked by the publication of *The Heath Anthology of American Literature* in 1989: a large two-volume collection that jettisoned the old 'great writers' approach in order to open up the field of study to overlooked writers (women writers of the nineteenth century, for instance), alternative histories (the 'New Negro Renaissance' of the 1920s as a counterpoint to high modernism) and texts previously thought of as 'non-literary', such as folk tales, speeches and songs. The fierce debates it provoked showed what was at stake: not only did it question prevailing standards of literary merit (and by implication, those professors whose practice was still largely based on the New Criticism of the 1950s), it also challenged the idea of a single, unifying, national heritage. As editor Paul Lauter reflects, 'the *Heath Anthology* came to signify – indeed, to promote – a diffusion of cultural authority, both for those who abhor the decline of academic cultural power, and for those who welcome what they see not as a decline but as a socially healthy redistribution of cultural capital'.[23] The anthology's inclusion of non-white voices – from Native American creation myths through slave songs and Mexican American *corridos* to the immigrant memoirs of the modern period and the poetry of today's ethnic communities – contributed to the political efforts of multiculturalism by transforming the meaning of 'being American' from sharing a set of general characteristics to participating in a highly contested space of plural and ever-changing identities.

It is difficult to do justice here to the variety and particularities of what is reductively called 'ethnic literature', but we can make some brief observations about the directions it takes and the issues facing writers in the 1990s. Ethnic writers negotiated a complex set of relationships to literary traditions, the community they identified with and the nation as a whole. Though the circumstances were different in each case, they saw themselves engaged in similar projects of combating racist stereotypes, preserving or re-examining cultural memory and traditions, and asserting the material realities of their lives to a wider readership. At the same time, many resisted or problematised what was known as 'the burden of representation' – the obligation to speak for or within an ethnic group – and sought ways of differentiating themselves through their writing. Bharati Mukherjee, for instance, has expressed her discomfort with being classified as an Asian American writer, while the novelist and critic Gerald Vizenor, proponent of 'post-Indian' identity, questions the mythologising of Native Americans as inheritors of an oral culture to which individual expression is entirely alien: 'this idea that so many interpreters of Indian life story and autobiography have . . . that they couldn't write autobiography because it is antithetical to their being of essential communal experience. Now what rubbish!'[24] Under such conditions, 'voice' becomes a matter of balancing the claims of individual style and artistic vision with the responsibilities of ethnic identification, while being aware that neither exists independently of the other nor provides coherent grounds for subjectivity on its own.

While they share political objectives, each tradition of ethnic writing naturally has its own distinguishing features that derive from a group's specific history in the United States, its places of habitation and its symbolic role in racial ideologies. African Americans continued to write against their social and figurative ghettoisation, whether by asserting the legacies of slavery on the present like Morrison, detailing the effects of social and economic exclusion on urban populations – for instance, in John Edgar Wideman's *Philadelphia Fire* (1990) – or rewriting popular genres to challenge racial assumptions, as in the black noir crime fiction of Walter Mosely. Native Americans addressed the history of nineteenth-century removal as well as the myths of savagery that legitimised it, appropriating the reservation as the site of modern Indian identity; from the magical realism of Louise Erdrich to the black comedy of Sherman Alexie, the reservation is at once a place of trauma and neglect and a source of solidarity. For Latinos, a similar tension between identity and displacement is sustained in the barrio, and the more abstract space of the borderlands – a term elaborated by writers like Gloria Anzaldúa and Helena Viramontes to capture the sense in which the lives of Chicana women take place across and between cultures, economies and languages. This liminal existence provides the basis for a model of cultural interaction even as the geographical borders between nations become more hazardous and rigorously enforced than ever.

As A. Robert Lee has noted, Asian Americans have had to contend with two separate traditions of misrepresentation: one, a phobic racism that extends from the Chinese Exclusion Act of 1882 to the Japanese internment camps of World War II and the anti-Korean violence of the Los Angeles riots; two, an orientalism that takes root in popular culture peddling images of Asians as exotic and inscrutable, with recent variations in the genius school-kid and the model minority.[25] Writers of the 1990s have contested these representations in various fictional modes, returning to the traumas of previous generations and the traditions they had been encouraged to repress in order to articulate a new experience of living as a 'hyphenated' American. In this sense their writing revises an earlier immigrant literature oriented towards assimilation, but it also departs from the more radical assertion of ethnic difference that followed the example of black politics in the 1960s. Assimilationist and 'culturalist' paradigms give way, therefore, to a third position in hybridity, in which multiple forms of identification coexist.[26] Gish Jen's short story 'In the American Society' (1991) offers a subtle treatment of hybridity in the generational differences within a family of Chinese Americans, capturing the irony of a father whose insufficient assimilation leaves him comically unfamiliar with American customs, yet well placed to resist the casual racism of the middle-class community they interact with.[27] In her subsequent novel, *Typical American* (1991), the process of hybridisation is described in the crumbling of boundaries between cultures and spaces, extending across language, custom, consumption and poetic idiom:

> The language of *outside the house* had seeped well inside – Cadillac, Pyrex, subway, Coney Island . . . Theresa and Helen and Ralph slipped from tongue to tongue like turtles taking to land, taking to sea; though one remained their more natural element, both had become essential.[28]

Asian American writers also sought to recover and rewrite the spaces of identity, those places that accommodate or frustrate desires for rootedness: the homeland of previous generations, the camps, the numerous ethnic enclaves in cities like New York, Los Angeles and San Francisco. Chinatown is of course the dominant location in the orientalist imaginary, signifying mystery and libidinal excess, the unruly other against which an image of civic order is constructed (nowhere is this better captured than in Roman Polanski's grim 1974 film *Chinatown*, where it figures as a scandalously abandoned and unredeemable heart of darkness). Writers such as Carol Roh-Spaulding, Fae Myenne Ng and Chang-rae Lee challenged this stereotype in different ways, not least by revealing the everydayness and diversity of ethnic urban neighbourhoods, but also showing them to be places of multiple histories and social practices. For Lisa Lowe, Ng's representation of San Francisco's Chinatown in her novel *Bone* (1993) captures the significance of Foucault's description of 'heterotopia' – places like the museum, prison or colony that are designed to contain forms of deviance and antagonism but merely serve to destabilise the organisation of space everywhere else. Chinatown's defeat of the divisions separating public and private, work and leisure, or forgotten and monumentalised spaces not only makes it resistant to the totalising gaze of the visitor (be they tourist or immigration officer), but also creates the conditions for new alliances, social practices and identities.[29] In Roh-Spaulding's 'Waiting for Mr Kim', the postwar Chinatown of Oakland, California is similarly a highly condensed, textured space, bearing the traces of rivalries between Korean and Japanese Americans, the transition from bachelor to family society (the laundry built over the opium den) and a broader colonial history (house spirits competing with the Holy Spirit to lay the soul of a suicide to rest). This provides the setting for the story of a young girl's self-realisation through, on the one hand, the rejection of Korean marriage customs, and on the other, a refusal to follow her sisters' examples of rebellion against the family. With echoes of Kate Chopin's classic novella *The Awakening* (1899) – its carefully paced, languid prose suffused with the rhythms of breathing (opium, tobacco, the final exhalations of the bachelor who cuts his throat) – Roh-Spaulding describes an awakening into a self that cannot yet be put into language:

> Gracie breathed in deeply, as her sister had done with the hope of her new life – as, perhaps, Mr Han had done, with the hope of his release. Somewhere near, Little Gene laughed out loud in the street. Her mother banged dinner into the oven. Her father waited below, his Bible open on his knees, to greet the missionary ladies, to say goodbye to Mr Kim. Below, a white, slow figure stepped from a door and headed into the street. Again, she breathed in. And what she took in was her own. Not everything had a name.[30]

Here identity is no longer a realisation of one's heritage or a definition of what is proper to a community, but something particular and
provisional, born out of an awareness of the contingencies of history
and place.

Two Asian American Poets: Lawson Fusao Inada and Li-Young Lee

Lawson Fusao Inada is considered to be one of the laureates of Asian
American poetry, inasmuch as his writing is part of a larger social and
pedagogical practice. Along with co-editors Frank Chin, Shawn Wong and
Jeffrey Paul Chan he has been responsible for the publication of landmark
anthologies *Aiiieeeee!* (1974) and *The Big Aiiieeeee!* (1991), which set out
to present the range and variety of Asian American literature and, controversially, to contest what they saw as exoticism in the work of celebrated
women novelists like Maxine Hong Kingston and Amy Tan.[31] Inada's work
dwells centrally on the legacy of internment for Sansei (third-generation)
Japanese Americans, but at the same time it captures the racial diversity
of West Coast culture in a poetics of bricolage, combining jazz forms
and school-yard chants, Native American and black heroes, and the
performance-based styles of beat poetry.

Legends from Camp (1992) begins with a series of poems that work over
the trauma of internment, to preserve its memory but also to test its validity
as a founding narrative of Japanese American identity. 'Instructions to All
Persons' rereads the original military order of 3 May 1942 in an effort to
appropriate its language as the speech of the internees themselves: thus
the words designating the areas to be evacuated become the markers of
another space, as if the plot of a frontier settlement:

Thence westerly. (*Westerly*)
Thence northerly. (*Northerly*)
To the point. (*Point*)
Of beginning. (*Beginning*) (*Ancestry*)[32]

Through this reiteration the evacuation is recast as 'meeting' and 'gathering', and gradually the outlines of a new community emerge. Customs,
institutions and property are imagined, turning the state's order into the
group's social order. The next poem, 'Legends from Camp', takes this
abstract social space and fills it with stories and memories of internment:
the outrage of being instructed to 'dispose of your pets', the longing for
shoyu sauce, a child's dreams of being rescued by superheroes, a boy
lost amid the rows of huts and found again only for it to expose the deeper
sense in which he is lost. Thus Inada attempts to commemorate the lived
experience of internment and recover it from the previous generation's
denial. But at the same time, he is aware of the danger of establishing it as
an insurmountable trauma or the sole defining moment in Asian American

identity. In 'Instructions', he introduces a note of ambivalence where the final words 'Let there be / Order; Let us be / Wise' receive no italicised responses: this might perhaps signify unanimity but also indicate a touch of suspicion towards the voice of authority the poem has achieved, as if it risks mimicking the original power of the state. In 'Legends', the poem ends with a query about the kind of freedom granted to those who are released from the camps: 'What's over the horizon? / What's left to abandon?' If there are echoes of the expectation of America's early pioneers here, the sense of hope and the exhilaration of flight are tempered by the further recognition that the world out there is already occupied and managed: 'What's left to administer?' Hence the poem looks outward to the challenges facing the new community, questioning the solidarity established in the camps.

Li-Young Lee explores similar themes of ethnicity and memory, but where Inada's poems emphasise orality Lee's are more literary, more readerly; where Inada draws on blues and jazz forms, Lee situates himself in dialogue with the predominantly white canon of modern American poetry. His unusual biography is well known: a mother descended from China's first prime minister, and a father who was Chairman Mao's physician, then a political prisoner under Sukarno in Indonesia and eventually a Presbyterian minister in Pennsylvania after many years of travelling in exile. As a consequence of these multiple forms of dislocation, Lee's central concern is not the recovery of a lost cultural heritage so much as the global condition of migration and cultural exchange. Ethnocentric readings that focus on the fusion of Chinese and American elements in his poetry will therefore fail to understand the breadth of cultural reference and the depth of its resonance with poetic traditions.

'The Cleaving', from *The City in Which I Love You* (1990), opens out from an ordinary scene of buying meat in a Chinese grocery into a meditation on immigration through a series of tropes of the body. For Judith Kitchen, it enacts a process of becoming American which is signified in its celebration of eating food ('a hunger at last satisfied, because it is a hunger that *can* be satisfied'[33]) and in its diction – the raw, angular phrasing of its descriptive passages, 'ducks / dangling single file, / each pierced by black / hooks through breast, bill, / and steaming through a hole / stitched shut at the ass.'[34] Certainly, the poem seeks an identification between the poet's persona and the butcher, 'this immigrant / this man with my own face', and it does so through an explicit reference to an American tradition, the butcher's cleaving recalling the forging of nations in Walt Whitman's 'Song of the Broad-Axe' (1860) and the carving of a new poetry in Ezra Pound's 'A Pact' (1913). But it also treats its precursors, and the idea of assimilation, with an ample degree of irony. Lee celebrates the butcher's violence as much as his craft and, in a remarkable series of moves, takes the transcendentalist vision to outlandish extremes – first emulating Whitman's montage techniques in lines that blend the rhythms of sex, chopping meat and ships crossing the ocean, 'hauling / immigrants and the junk / of the poor'; then creating an image of an ethnic mass in all its variety ('dark or light according / to the birth, straight / or humped, whole, manqué, quasi, each pleases, verging / on utter grotesquery'), before turning on transcendentalism's suppression of differences, and the Anglocentrism it preserves, in a passage where Lee imagines eating Ralph Waldo Emerson's head:

I would devour this race to sing it,
this race that according to Emerson
managed to preserve to a hair
for three or four thousand years
the ugliest features in the world.

. . .

And I would eat Emerson, his transparent soul, his
soporific transcendence.
I would eat his head,
glazed in pepper-speckled sauce,
the cooked eyes opaque in their sockets.

Here Lee parodies Whitman's expansiveness and idealisation of the body while creating an analogy between immigrant assimilation and poetic appropriation. But it is clear that what he objects to in Emerson (apart from the obvious affront) is the notion of separate and unchanging racial histories. Lee is ultimately looking for a model of ethnicity that does not fetishise origins in the same way, and this is why he is drawn to the image of the butcher: 'No seed, no egg has he / whose business calls for an axe.' The butcher's cleaving – both death and nourishment, both splitting apart and binding together – offers a more fluid image of race and ethnicity, placing an emphasis on interaction and change rather than distinct roots.

Following postmodernist concerns with the dissolution of the subject, avant-garde poetics of the 1990s are noted by their repudiation of the persona, the 'I' of the poem that designates an individual consciousness situated in space and time.[35] Not surprisingly, therefore, Lee has been taken to task by some critics for his return to lyrical modes in poems that foreground intimacy and emotional authenticity. To some extent this can be defended as a means of moving away from the limited subject matter and appeal of poetry that concerns itself solely with ethnicity since, as Helen Vendler points out, the lyric is a more abstract form of expression, representing 'the self when it is alone with itself, when its socially constructed characteristics (race, class, color, gender, sexuality) are felt to be in abeyance'.[36] But the simplicity of Lee's work is deceptive, and his lyricism is often problematised by the self's situated actuality. 'This Room and Everything in It', for instance, presents a scene in which the poet seeks to capture the significance of a moment with his lover, committing it to memory through an art of mnemonic association taught to him by his father, in which ideas are assigned to objects around him. The exercise breaks down when the poet becomes distracted by the presence of the room and his lover's body: 'my idea / has evaporated. . . your hair is time, your thighs are song . . .' As in William Carlos Williams's 1920 poem 'Portrait of a Lady' (which this resembles), the collapse of connotation is a technique for revealing the image in all its immediacy: the anxiety to preserve a moment in the past gives way to the sensual plenitude of the present. But the reference to the poet's father carries with it the trace of other contexts of remembrance, and indicates how Vendler may be wrong in thinking that the self can ever be 'alone' and replete in itself. At the same time, we should note that the poem is not about the loss of specific-memories but about the failure of a mnemonic device, and is therefore less concerned with the preservation of certain traditions across generations than the more radical questions about the forms through which history is mediated.

Voice, as a mode of individual expression or a fragment of a wider cultural ambience, was a key terrain on which literary disputes of the 1990s were played out. While writers from marginalised groups prioritised voice as a point of access into the relation between personal experience and group membership, such an approach seemed to imply a model of subjectivity that ran counter to prevalent post-structuralist theories. The common wisdom that the self was an autonomous being in possession of interiority and consciousness had long been challenged in western thought, which posited other models of the subject as an unstable amalgam of psychic drives, a construct of dominant ideologies or a mere effect of discourse – no longer the author of its own utterances but, in Lacan's phrase, 'spoken by language'.[37] Correspondingly, avant-garde poets had been exploring the relation between language and subjectivity since the 1970s, and treated the flourishing of identity-based writing, which seemed to need to speak of and through a more coherent self, with some reservations. Poet Charles Bernstein, for example, raised concerns about not only the lyric 'I' but what he called the 'neolyric "we"', suggesting that speaking in a representative voice created the impression of communities that were known, bounded and closed, denying their capacity to change. He went on to criticise the new multicultural anthologies such as *Heath* and *Norton* for capitulating to middlebrow audiences and selecting those ethnic writers who fit within conventional verse forms: not only did this repress aesthetic innovations taking place across numerous communities, it also threatened to resurrect a logic of assimilation where it implied that all cultural experience already existed within known forms of representation. Against this tendency Bernstein championed poetry as a formally inventive practice which conceives of the self and experience in more provisional terms.[38]

Another factor in the bifurcation of poetry and the problem of voice was the transformation of spaces of production and distribution.

Poetry 'happened' in an increasing number of places, and in increasingly diverse ways: from the new creative writing departments springing up on the edges of the university to the alternative poetry scenes of cities like Boston, Buffalo, New York City and San Francisco, supported by local venues, small presses and, by the end of the 1990s, the internet. As Richard Silberg observes, the peripheral position of creative writing departments meant that the poets they supported were as much attuned to the market as to theoretical concerns, and as much given to open discursive styles as to homogenisation in the form of 'schools'.[39] At the same time, the rapid growth in popularity for poetry readings and performances across the country further emphasised the speaking voice. At the far end of this spectrum is the phenomenon of poetry slams, emerging in the mid-1990s, in which poets competed in head-to-head contests with the audience/crowd as arbiters. The limitations of the slam are plain – the competitive format, subordination of reflective listening to immediate response, and severe time constraints – but it has nevertheless been central to the development of new audiences for poetry, and the space it gives to individual testimony is surely one of the reasons it has developed a strong association with hip-hop culture.

Universities were still important centres for poetry, not least because it was there that access to the internet was well established before it became available to individuals in the latter part of the decade. Electronic magazines such as *We*, *Grist* and *Rif/t* were active from 1993, and university sites such as the Electronic Poetry Center at Buffalo and the online journal *Postmodern Culture* at Virginia provided vital forums for debates and experiment in poetics; the internet itself, meanwhile, developed from a medium of distribution and communication into a new form of textuality.[40] Such contexts gave a renewed impetus to language-based poetry which sought to disrupt or extend the semantic capabilities of words through attention to their material properties – exploring spatial and typographic arrangements, mixing text and image, and foregrounding tonal dimensions – often with the aim of deconstructing modes of authority inherent in conventions of speech and writing.

Thus a feminist poetics is advanced in the work of Susan Howe, Johanna Drucker and Lynn Heijinian, who seek in different ways to subvert patriarchy inscribed in historical documents, literary tradition and popular culture. Drucker's book *Narratology* (1994), for instance, combines text and images that mimic the clichés of genre fiction and female comportment manuals, but through subtle revisions it captures a sense of lived experience as a negotiation of writing and representation, rather than a reality apart. Chicano poet Alfred Arteaga moves far beyond a poetry of ethnicity where he interrogates a postcolonial condition in a poem like 'The Small Sea of Europe' (1991), which explores linguistic as well as historical relationships between colonies, capital, slaves and seas. The play between c/s (itself at the heart of Chicanismo, where the *cs* of anglicised Mexico is softened into the Hispanic *ch*) runs through numerous languages throughout the poem, evoking a world of endless exchange and translation ('trafficking') which escapes and opposes forms of authority in speech, writing and poetry itself (derided at the end as 'some big *Dichtung*').[41] Michael Palmer's poetics of difference in *At Passages* (1994), on the other hand, is a matter of finding an exit from the quasi-totalitarian orchestration of consent – achieved with 'an extraordinarily skilful contempt for anything that might say no to it' – that prevailed during the Gulf War. The poems that make up the collection recover opposition by setting the minimal authority of the poet's voice against the languages of philosophy, history and the state.[42]

Another indicator that voice and authorship were the defining problems of the 1990s was the burgeoning of memoir and autobiography, which grew to dominate non-fiction sales in the course of the decade. These ranged from the writer's memoir, the celebrity autobiography or the tales of the temporarily newsworthy (five jurors in the O. J. Simpson trial produced their own version of events) to illness narratives such as Elizabeth Wurtzel's bestseller *Prozac Nation* (1994), which presented the author's depression as an index of a culture afflicted by anxieties over the loss of traditional forms of security and life expectations. The popularity of memoir was such that it raised numerous qualms about a pervasive narcissism that encouraged all-comers to expose their personal lives for general approval: novelist William Gass, for instance, scornfully called it the genre of 'Look, Ma, I'm breathing'.[43] Gass's essay is little more than a complaint about the rise of the masses and the blurring of boundaries between history and fiction (what he calls a 'vulgar copulation'), but more sophisticated critiques placed memoir in a wider context of changing conceptions of privacy and publicity.

In *How Our Lives Become Stories* Paul John Eakin claims that the 1990s saw a turn away from autobiography in the conventional sense and towards a writing of 'relational selves', in which identity is presented as a feature of dependence on and collaboration with others. Among his examples are Art Spiegelman's *Maus* (1986 and 1991),

Philip Roth's *Patrimony* (1991), Henry Louis Gates's *Colored People* (1994), Barbara J. Scot's *Prairie Reunion* (1995) and Mary Gordon's *The Shadow Man* (1996), all of which represent the author through their relationship with parents or a wider community. Eakin reads this as evidence of a declining interest in the idea of the autonomous self, or the declining function of autobiography to assert the individual as sole possessor of her life and author of her own story. In fact, he confides that it has become increasingly difficult to define the boundaries of the self at all: 'I prefer to think of "self" less as an entity and more as a kind of awareness in process'.[44]

Boundaries are blurred even further in the related publishing trends of 'bloodsport biography', where the biographer battles with an uncooperative subject for authority over the life; or in the collaboration that produces an 'authorised' biography at the expense of both life and writing – the book here being little more than an extension of the brand.[45] Problematising the question of authorship further is the practice of 'ghost writing' in celebrity autobiographies, where the writer has to suppress all traces of style in order to act as a 'medium' for multiple clients. In many respects this is just another outcome of a post-literate culture, in which those who live the most valued lives no longer have the ability to put them into words. But if it appears to return us to the archaic relationship between kings and chroniclers, it certainly deals another blow to the modern idea that identity is linked to the telling of one's own story.

In all of these arenas, then – literary celebrity, audiobooks, ethnic writing, avant-garde experiment, poetry performance and memoir – the relationship between authorship and voice was continually being revised and contested. In different ways, the tensions reflect a set of anxieties about the role of writing in a culture of electronic media, the possibility of authentic subjective experience and the compulsion to assert the validity of personal experience in the public sphere. Perhaps it is no coincidence that an explosion of memoir and identity writing occurs at a moment when individuality seems harder to grasp: such texts both reaffirm the idea of the self and reveal a continued commitment to an ideology of possessive individualism which is deeply ingrained in American culture.

The Ends of Postmodernism

What happened to postmodernist fiction? By the 1990s, the concept was already twenty years old and the weaknesses of the term were becoming apparent. From Ihab Hassan's *The Dismemberment of Orpheus: Towards a Postmodern Literature* (1971) to Fredric Jameson's *Postmodernism: The Cultural Logic of Late Capitalism* (1991), the attempt to describe a general cultural shift had tended to generate a restricted canon of texts exemplifying key characteristics, while the interventions of post-structuralism and deconstruction, originally intended to cast suspicion on the authority of given discourses and concepts, became all too readily accommodated as the lingua franca of the university. In literature, postmodernism's initial playful scepticism towards form evolved into a more melancholy epistemological uncertainty as the millennium approached. Paul Auster's solemn Borgesian mysteries captured the mood well: in works like *The New York Trilogy* (1987) and *The Music of Chance* (1990) central preoccupations are the unintelligibility of signs and the loss of identity in the play of doubling and difference. Writers become entwined in plots not of their own making, and fiction itself seems less a means of liberation than a trap, a solipsistic exercise in creating worlds that achieve a correspondence with reality only by indirect means.

The 'blank fiction' writers of the late 1980s and early 1990s repudiated metafictional pyrotechnics and opted instead for a minimal voice barely distinct from the superficial, deracinated consumer landscape they took for their subject matter. They captured the sensibility of a largely young, white, affluent class seemingly adrift in a culture without historical reference points, and examined the penetration of the commodity into all spheres of life. Canadian writer Douglas Coupland's *Generation X* (1991) was taken up as the handbook of this loosely defined movement, though its nostalgic tone, angst-ridden characters and hankering for the desert as a place of healing and renewal make it perhaps more modernist than postmodernist. It is Bret Easton Ellis's *American Psycho* (1991) that more powerfully deploys the blank, affectless mode of writing as a form of critique.

American Psycho tells the story of Wall Street yuppie-cum-serial killer Patrick Bateman, a figure whose murderous sprees combine with an obsession with conspicuous consumption to offer an indictment of the excesses of the 1980s. What is distinctive about the novel is that it not only depicts violence but enacts it on the reader, through relentless pornographic scenes that are designed to provoke repulsion and stimulation at the same time. Trapped inside Bateman's first-person narration, the reader is denied the comfort of distance from a spectacle that is usually contained within narrative conventions or a basic distribution of justice – an approach that is made explicit in the novel's final words, 'THIS IS NOT AN EXIT'.[46] Perhaps because of this suppression of a redeeming moral framework (if not for its scenes of generally misogynistic brutality), the book was dropped by original publishers Simon & Schuster and provoked outrage from several quarters on its eventual release. Even Norman Mailer recognised the stakes involved: 'One does not want to be caught defending *American Psycho*,' he remarked.[47] Ellis's critique of the serial nature of consumer society is explicit in the satirical parallel he sets up between Bateman's descriptions of his murders and his repetitious dissections of fashion, dining and popular culture, both of which amount to an onslaught on taste and the reader's patience. But the novel is more interesting as an exploration of the particular imaginative and affective properties of literature at a time when the representation of interior consciousness lacks credibility as a method. The corrosion of boundaries between fictional and textual space that occurs in *American Psycho* (the slippage from violence *in* the novel to the violence *of* the novel) is a major feature of Ellis's later work: in *Glamorama* (1998) a fashion model is recruited to an organisation of terrorists who appear to be both filming themselves and being filmed by others; in *Lunar Park* (2005), a quasi-autobiographical story, Ellis is caught up in a series of murders committed by what may be Bateman, a copycat killer or the author himself.

Looking for ways to take postmodernist fiction in a different direction was David Foster Wallace, whose essay 'E Unibus Pluram: Television and U. S. Fiction' (1993) was received as a kind of manifesto for a new generation of writers in the mid-1990s. Here he argued that literature still had to contend with a culture of images, but it could no longer rely on the strategies developed by earlier postmodernist writers since 'it is now television that takes elements of the postmodern – the involution, the absurdity, the sardonic fatigue, the iconoclasm and rebellion – and bends them to the ends of spectacle and consumption'.[48] For Wallace, television had so thoroughly outmanoeuvred fiction that its techniques had become stripped of their critical powers: where irony had been a means of 'exploding hypocrisy' for the writers of the 1960s, it was now in danger of becoming little more than a stylistic pose. Hence he condemned the blank fiction of authors like Bret Easton Ellis, with its deadpan tone and flat, undifferentiated depictions of mass culture, for being inadequate to the task of representing real human experience.[49] But rather than reject irony altogether, as if it were possible to forget the insights of postmodernism and return to a state of uncorrupted sincerity, Wallace tries to push it to extremes, creating highly playful and reflexive texts that go so far as to reflect on the reasons for becoming reflexive (some critics have called this 'meta-ironic'), while at the same time foregrounding the emotional intensities of contemporary life.[50]

Frisk (1991)

Published in the same year as *American Psycho*, Dennis Cooper's novel *Frisk* also elaborates on the motif of serial murder, though to a different end. Where Ellis's novel asks to be read as a diagnosis of a general national and historical condition (a specifically eighties American pathology), Cooper's is less explicitly allegorical and more focused on the intimacies of desire. Although there is a similar emphasis on taboo-breaking and visceral effects, with scenes that go just as far to test the reader's tolerance, it is somehow still possible to say that this is a touching book, and strangely redemptive, in that it seeks to recapture the particular sensibilities and affects that are so horrifically absent in Ellis's characterisation of a postmodern condition.

Frisk is the first of a five-novel cycle spanning the decade and ending with *Period* (2000), portraying the lives of young white men in a minimally described suburban California. Through a relatively limited set of themes and narrative episodes – gay sado-masochistic relationships, paedophilia and necrophilia, pornography and drugs – Cooper deals with the relationship between sex, death and knowledge; in this respect he can be thought of as transplanting the French tradition of transgressive writing (that of Jean Genet, Georges Bataille and back to the Marquis de Sade) into a contemporary setting, exploring the limits of the sacred and profane in a world dominated by the mediated image. In *Frisk* itself, the narrator is the Sadeian libertine, one who seeks to achieve a kind of godhead/freedom through the disregard of moral laws and a kind of knowledge of others through opening up their bodies. Of course, these goals are only ever possible in their imaginary, unrealised form, since the desire for self-creation through murder is met only with the banality of death and 'knowing otherness' in this way means destroying it entirely. The terrible narcissistic circularity of this impulse is dramatically played out in an image like this: 'I shoved one hand down his throat, one hand up his ass, and shook hands with myself in the middle of his body, which sounds funny, but it wasn't.'[51]

What makes the novel fascinating rather than merely repulsive are the literary techniques that Cooper employs to engage and disconcert the reader. Like Ellis, he violates the conventions of fiction and textuality, first by naming the protagonist Dennis to undermine authorial distance, then by giving him a narrative perspective that disregards identity boundaries, inhabiting the minds of other characters as much as his own ('My eyes looked kind of drugged. Amphetamine, maybe. Julian didn't know how else to place the tinniness of my expression').[52] Additionally, Cooper folds another layer of fiction into the text by making Dennis a writer whose acts of carnage are revealed to be no more than pornographic fantasies, but not before we have been invited to share in them. 'I just realised that if you're still reading you must be the person I want you to be,' states Dennis/ Cooper at one point, establishing a punctum in the text that fuses reader and potential accomplice in the same position.[53] The point is to confront us as readers with our complicity in the reality of these scenes – not as acts but as fantasies construed through a culture dominated by the image and the object. It is, after all, a series of snuff photographs that is offered as the motivating factor behind Dennis's obsessions, and even his desire for authenticity, to get beneath the surface of things, is continually haunted by the mediations of popular culture. Fantasies of tearing victims apart quickly revert to tawdry scenes from splatter movies or cartoons in which pirates run their hands through gold coins.

Later books extend the corrosion of boundaries between real, mediated and fictional spaces – in *Guide* (1997), for instance, a character reputedly drugs and seduces Alex James from the British band Blur (poorly disguised as 'Smear'); in *Period* characters continue narrating even after their death. Blurring, indeed, is a thematic and stylistic feature throughout: in part, it is an attempt to evoke the characters' drugged, languid and disoriented states of consciousness; in part it is a carelessness that amounts to a deliberate renunciation of narrative authority – sentences tailing off into 'whatever', 'etc' or a grudging 'oh, so what?'[54] Thirdly, it is a means of remaining faithful to the outlook and idiom of the teenagers that inhabit the novels, as Cooper has indicated in an interview: 'making the charac- ters inarticulate . . . it's a kind of respect for them – that their uncertainty is what's important.'[55] If only for an indication of how beautifully honed this rendering of inarticulacy is, here is a sentence from *Guide*:

> Then his eyes become two thrift-store painting-like takes on my emotions re Luke that are so much cheesier than the thing they depict that they're sort of like souvenirs you'd pick up at Niagara Falls or whatever.[56]

Using no more than the worn, limited materials of teenage speech, Cooper generates a highly concentrated image – and, moreover, one that high- lights the crucial difference between feelings that lie beyond comprehen- sion and the mass-produced derivatives that threaten to overcome them. A further example describes a teenager's expression: 'The kid's face was just permanently sly, like a rock is permanently a random pattern wrapped around a roughly spherical form.'[57] The impact of this line is not just in the brutal way it treats a child's undeveloped expressive capacities, but the way it rewrites even the slow process of geological formation in terms of contemporary design practices, indicating that everything in Cooper's universe is subject to the regime of simulation.

This precision within imprecision, or play between high- and low- definition, is Cooper's stylistic signature. In *Frisk*, it is introduced as a formal device in the opening passages on the snuff photographs, which home in on a mysterious blurred spot at the heart of an obscenely explicit close- up, to be recapitulated at the end where Dennis recreates the pictures that have obsessed him. By now the fakery is clearly evident in the wound: 'It's a bit out of focus. Still, you can see the fingerprints . . .'[58] The rest of the novel occurs between these two sections, and therefore between the two aesthetic responses they signify: on the one hand, the desire to submit to representation in the name of a Real that lies beyond, which is death, and on the other, the will to dominate representation by attending to the elements of the real, which is artifice. Cooper's writing continually oscillates between these two points, figuring a transcendent realm beyond experience but also reasserting the value of the literary act, and thereby re-establishing the boundaries between fiction and reality. This has an ethical dimension too: as Dennis admits, he writes because he is unable to kill.

Julian Murphet writes that Cooper's 'latter-day romanticism achieves, miraculously, the banal sublimity of the true particular, the unassimiliable, in an age of purified equivalence.'[59] Romanticism is perhaps a strange sensibility to come across in the context of writing about a postmodern condition, but its emphasis on style and artifice is a means of reconstructing a critical and cognitive difference. This is no less than the recovery of specific emotions from the speech of teenagers apparently crippled by failures of language; the recovery of love in an age of sex; and the recovery of a space of mourning for the victims of AIDS from the trivialisation of death.

Infinite Jest, Wallace's magnum opus of 1996, is a comic novel running to over a thousand pages, a hundred of which are 'Notes and Errata' that simultaneously signify the scale of its fictional universe and the author's interest in playing with literary conventions. A reader soon realises that the notes are not only there to offer clarifying information but may also involve entirely irrelevant digressions or, occasionally, essential elements of the plot. The technique overturns the hierarchy between text and margins and means that the usual linear process of reading is continually interrupted, making for an experience that is both entertaining and laborious. The labour of reading is clearly part of Wallace's point, since the central narrative concerns the quest for a notorious film – the 'Infinite Jest' of the title – which is so watchable that it leaves a viewer perfectly sated and therefore fatally incapacitated.

The implied critique of a culture dependent on consumption and media images is reinforced by the novel's setting in a future America where even time is sponsored (most of the action takes place during the Year of the Depend Adult Undergarment) and by intertwined stories of addiction and denial. Key characters are tennis prodigy Hal Incandenza, son of the film's creator, battling with his partially marijuana-induced self-consciousness to come to terms with the death of his father, and recovering addict Don Gately, whose experiences with Alcoholics Anonymous offer a certain promise of redemption. If Wallace holds out the possibility of deliverance from the cycles of dependency that make this a nightmarish vision of contemporary America, it is not through a principled withdrawal or abstention from the pleasures of modern culture but through an insistence on culture as communication and the power of the imagination to exceed habits of thinking. Although the film symbolises entertainment as a kind of dangerous drug, Wallace has its maker return as a ghost to defend its intended function as something to liberate the imagination from his son's tendencies towards solipsism: 'a magically entertaining toy to dangle at the infant still somewhere alive in the boy, to make its eyes light and toothless mouth open unconsciously, to laugh. To bring him "out of himself", as they say.'[60] Here we can imagine the author making a similar claim about the novel – that it should also be seen not as a perfect and self-enclosed work of art but as the basis for ongoing dialogue and inspiration.[61]

Wallace's work has inevitably been called 'post-postmodernist', but Paul Giles's more illuminating phrase is 'sentimental posthuman-ism', denoting Wallace's attempt to reconcile the writer's task of representing what it means to be human with a world that is progres-sively being understood in terms of biological systems and patterns of information, modes of thinking that no longer privilege traditional humanist conceptions of the self.[62] In Wallace's universe, conscious-ness is colonised by all manner of intrusive forces (from drugs to television images), the body is no longer governed solely by con-sciousness (as Hal's tennis training demonstrates) and yet individuals are never fully reducible to their biological and mechanical existence. Wallace reiterates this outlook throughout his work, but the point is succinctly made in an essay on Swiss tennis player Roger Federer from 2006, one of the last pieces to be published before the writer's death. In a sport played at speeds that exceed the capacity for con-scious thought, with racket technology that overwhelms individual styles of play and threatens to take the game to a point beyond which it can no longer evolve, Federer is distinguished most of all by his intellectual abilities:

> his intelligence, his occult anticipation, his court sense, his ability to read and manipulate opponents, to mix spins and speeds, to misdirect and disguise, to use tactical foresight and peripheral vision and kinaes-thetic range instead of just rote pace – all this has exposed the limits, and possibilities, of men's tennis as it's now played.[63]

The line could just as easily be read as Wallace's statement on the repertoire of skills a writer must have to think beyond the innovations of postmodern fiction and open up new potential in the literary field.

National and Global Histories

Another way of conceiving the developments that occurred in fiction subsequent to postmodernism is as an expansion of horizons in accord with a growing awareness of globalisation. For many key writers of the period, the task was how to tell stories that captured the significance of a moment of expanding social relations, borderless economic forces and increasingly complex patterns of cultural exchange. Writers such as Jhumpa Lahiri and Bharati Mukherjee examined the formation of transnational identities in stories that placed the immigrant experience in a broader global context. *The Holder of the World*, Mukherjee's novel of 1997, reinterprets Nathaniel Hawthorne's classic novel *The Scarlet Letter* (1850) to assert a world history that is all too often forgotten in narratives of America's national origins. Don DeLillo's approach in *Underworld* (1997) is to bring together scattered narratives around the central themes of waste management, networks of information and commerce, and fears of nuclear disaster. In *The Corrections* (2001), Jonathan Franzen develops a hybrid of family saga and political thriller which takes in American railroad history, the development of capitalism in post-Soviet Europe and the pharmaceutical industry's colonisation of the personality. The problem that all such works had to face was that the attempt to represent the abstract processes of globalisation put pressure on the novel as a literary form, compromising its necessary emphasis on the lives and actions of individuals. Hence the flattened characters of blank fiction were often compounded by contrived plots, to the disappointment of readers who came to the novels with the expectations of a more realist representation of human experience. Naming the trend 'hysterical realism', critic James Wood complained that too many writers were prepared to sacrifice a serious treatment of the way human beings act and feel in particular situations to the imparting of information about the world.[64] Norman Mailer levelled a similar criticism at Franzen, whom he accused of too great a dependence on internet research: 'it is as if he offers us more human experience than he has literally mastered'.[65]

Many writers of the previous generation – postmodernists such as John Barth and Robert Coover, and realists such as Saul Bellow, John Updike and Mailer himself – continued to publish into the 1990s, but it was Philip Roth's achievement that stood out from all others. For him this was a period of extraordinary creativity: between *Deception* (1990) and *The Dying Animal* (2001) he published seven works of fiction and one memoir, receiving national awards for six of them. Of these, the three novels that make up his 'American Trilogy' constitute a major landmark in the literary history of the decade, and their retrospective appraisal of the nation at the end of the century make them a fitting conclusion to this chapter.

Taken as a whole, the trilogy is an interrogation of moments in America's history that Roth suggests are somehow unfinished, whose unresolved politics continue to cast a shadow over the present. In *American Pastoral* (1997) it is the sense of an unbridgeable chasm opening up between the generations in the cultural turmoil of the 1960s and 1970s, after which traditional myths of national identity begin to seem obsolete. In *I Married a Communist* (1998) it is the Cold War, a period which sees the decline of the class politics of the old left and the disintegration of inner-city communities. The third novel in the series, *The Human Stain* (2000), addresses the impact of identity politics in nineties America and the 'ecstasy of sanctimony' that consumed the nation during the Clinton–Lewinsky scandal. In each case the portrait of an era takes the form of a memoir of a 'representative man' beset by a combination of his own failings and destructive influences around him – a communist radio actor betrayed by his wife during the McCarthy witch hunts, a former football star whose daughter sets off a bomb in protest against the Vietnam War and a professor of classics forced out of his post after an innocent remark is interpreted as a racial slur. The conduit for the memoirs is Nathan Zuckerman, Roth's returning narrator/alter ego, now in his later years and intent on retreating from the world around him. Using Zuckerman allows Roth to introduce a degree of irony into the third-person narrative perspective of historical realism, offering the pleasure of insight into the interior consciousness of individuals caught up in historical forces they cannot control while asserting that such a perspective is always an illusion – 'an astonishing farce of misperception', as Zuckerman puts it at one point.[66]

The recurrent theme across the trilogy is the perilous desire for certainty in life – the violence committed in the name of one's beliefs, the pettiness of the morally righteous, the inevitable clash between the urge for perfection and the essentially unruly nature of individuals. What makes us human, Roth implies, is ultimately our inability to conform to the designs for life that we make up for ourselves: this, ultimately, is the human stain, the element of 'brute humanity' that resists idealisation.[67] Ira Ringold in *I Married a Communist* is not a revolutionary hero so much as a man pulled in different directions by his left-wing ideological convictions, Jewish background and bourgeois lifestyle: as his brother explains to Zuckerman at the end of the novel, 'Eve didn't marry a Communist; she married a man perpetually hungering after his life. That's what enraged him and confused him and that's what ruined him: he could never construct one that fit. The enormous wrongness of this guy's effort.'[68] Coleman Silk, the protagonist of *The Human Stain*, is similarly a man in pursuit of a self-fashioned life, as an African American who has passed for fifty years as a Jew. If his determination to escape his past is admirable – and, as the narrator points out, entirely in line with 'the democratic invitation to throw your origins overboard if to do so contributes to the pursuit of happiness' – it is also monstrous, a desire for autogenesis so absolute that it demands renouncing his own mother. 'Anybody who has the audacity to do that doesn't just want to be white. He wants to be able to do that,' Zuckerman realises with horror.[69] Hence when the seventy-year-old Silk compounds his pariah status by beginning an affair with a young cleaner at the college, it is to be taken as a sign of his letting go – a welcome relief from the exercise of his will.

American Pastoral tells the story of the souring of the American dream: the fall of a blond Jewish sports hero with a life 'most simple and most ordinary and therefore just great, right in the American grain' who marries Miss New Jersey, takes over his father's glove manufacturing business and raises a daughter only to watch her turn into a terrorist.[70] Zuckerman's reimagining of the life of Seymour 'Swede' Levov gives Roth the opportunity to reflect on the legacies of the counterculture and the ruined ideal of assimilation: the promise of acceptance that lay within the grasp of whoever embraced middle-class aspirations, espoused by a generation which their children now accuse of blindness and complicity with injustice. If there are traces of O. J. Simpson in Zuckerman's portrayal of the Swede – for instance, in the way he transcends his ethnicity through sporting excellence ('No striving, no ambivalence, no doubleness – just the style, the natural physical refinement of a star'[71]) only to have it return after the fall – then another source is *King Lear*: the king driven mad by a daughter's ingratitude, whose pain as a father becomes indistinguishable from the collapse of his moral universe.

'And what is wrong with their life? What on earth is less reprehensible than the life of the Levovs?' The question on which the novel ends has been implicit from the start, emblematic of the traumatised and circular thinking which Zuckerman imagines having afflicted the Swede ever since the bombing. To some extent the reader is invited to share in the father's anguished belief in his own innocence, since there can be no explanation for his daughter's actions other than the unpredictability of all human behaviour ('She is obliged to be as she is. We all are.'). At the same time, however, the Swede's brother shouts his disapproval from the sidelines, blaming the permissive father and suggesting, as so many conservatives did in the 1990s, that liberalism lacks moral vitality: 'Sure, it's "liberal" – I know, a liberal father. But what does that mean? What is at the *centre* of it? Always holding things together. And look where the fuck it's got you!'[72] As we might expect, it is not a case of locating the author amongst these different positions, be it the Swede's earnest idealism, his brother's conservative outrage or the manic laughter at a crumbling civilisation that echoes in the final pages. Instead of passing judgment upon an era, Roth is more concerned with representing the impact of historical change on the interior lives of individuals, capturing the tension between an appreciation of beliefs now scorned and the recognition of realities not previously acknowledged. In the face of a decline in reading and the diminishing significance of the novel in American cultural life, Roth's writing in this period is a powerful defence of the work that only literature can do.[73]

Chapter 2

Music and Radio

Steve Albini, record producer and member of a string of hardcore punk bands from Big Black to Shellac, published an angry essay in dissenting magazine *The Baffler* in 1993 that offers us an insight into some of the changes taking place in music during the 1990s. With a bluntness typical of his own recordings he described the prospect facing new bands as a race to swim through a trench of filth for the prize of a contract that will only leave them indebted to a record company for years afterward, even as they bring millions of dollars into the industry. The article goes on to identify other music business sins: employing ex-musicians as A&R men to disguise the rapaciousness of the corporations; sanitising a band's sound in the studio to make it more marketable; introducing digital recording techniques that undermine the craft of sound engineering. Overall, his concerns are the alienation of music from its practitioners in what seems to be an increasingly rationalised industry, and the loss of independence that keeps musical culture alive. 'Some of your friends are probably already this fucked,' he concludes, at which point it seems futile to have any musical ambitions whatsoever.[1]

Albini puts the case in an extreme manner, but his views can be taken as an indication of a general sense of unease about the prospects for music at a time when the industry was undergoing a dramatic restructuring. After a wave of mergers and acquisitions starting in the mid-1980s, the field became dominated by huge media corporations that threatened to absorb and/or obliterate independent labels. Expansion and consolidation would come to affect music across the spectrum, bringing with it a shift from regional sensitivities to global markets, a concentration of wealth and attention on a select group of megastars, and a convergence of music with other media to form a new kind of audiovisual product. As we shall see, a further effect of the corporate control of music production was a growing tension between commercial and creative imperatives. Burdened with the costs of conglomeration, the corporations were inherently conservative, preferring to seek new sources of revenue from existing assets rather than take risks on untested material. Not only did this impact on artists in the ways that Albini outlines, it also had lasting consequences amongst audiences, where increasingly naked commercial imperatives threatened the powerful role popular music has played since World War II in creating new identities and forms of solidarity amongst young people.

This chapter will consider the way the tension between the commercial and the creative is played out in the decade's two dominant musical genres, rock and hip-hop, observing the narratives of decline that afflict them both. Rock's numerous mutations from indie to grunge, lo-fi, post-rock, goth and metal were framed by claims about its demise as a subversive force. Similarly, hip-hop's explosion from a localised music culture into a global phenomenon was accompanied by fears that its commitment to progressive racial politics had given way to cynicism and greed. These views need to be problematised, of course, but it is a measure of the pressures on popular music at a time of incorporation that authenticity became an urgent issue in both cases, a prize over which fans and record companies struggled alike. Unfortunately, it is a further sign of the times that the infatuation with authenticity was fed by death and its representations. The loss of Kurt Cobain and Tupac Shakur and the forms of mourning their deaths engendered played an important part in reasserting the power of popular music as a cultural practice, even as it extended the commercial life of the artists.

The stranglehold of corporations is not the only story to be told of the 1990s, however. As many commentators have pointed out, music always exceeds efforts to convert it into product, simply because it is cheap to make, and because what makes it valuable to people is highly unpredictable. John Lovering, for instance, remarks that 'the pleasures of playing, dancing and listening are too Dionysian, too social, too easily adapted to new technological possibilities, to be entirely codified and commodified by monster entertainment corporations'.[2] Some of the new directions in music take the form of scenes, highly localised spaces where performance and listening are part of a wider set of activities; others relate to the technological possibilities opened up by the shift from analogue to digital, already glimpsed in Albini's essay and gathering pace through the decade. The digitisation of music was to prove perhaps the most significant development of all, revolutionising music-making but also creating new forms of access and new modes of listening.

The National Entertainment State (Mickey's Got a Bottom Line)

The incorporation of music has its roots in the unstable economic climate of the 1980s. The success of the compact disc, which allowed companies to resell the same recordings on the basis of improved sound quality, had revived the fortunes of a flagging industry and attracted the attention of multinational media corporations seeking to insure themselves against fluctuations in other markets. The first of these was German media group Bertelsmann, continuing its expansion in music and publishing with the purchase of RCA in 1986. Next, Dutch company Phillips took full control of PolyGram and started buying up American labels, increasing its stock of creative content in a way that complemented its hi-fi equipment production. Sony, Phillips's competitor in CD manufacturing, was also keen to combine hardware and software after the recent calamitous demise of its Betamax video format, and took over CBS in 1988; the same reasoning led another Japanese giant, Matsushita, to buy MCA in 1990, though it would later sell it on to Canadian drinks producer Seagram in 1995. Thus in the space of less than a decade all the major US record companies were foreign-owned with the exception of Warner, which had merged with publishing house Time Inc in 1989.

A few independent record labels remained as they were, but most were affected by the corporations' control over promotion and distribution. By the end of the millennium around 90 per cent of the national market was controlled by just five companies. Universal Music Group, owned by Seagram until 2001, comprised labels such as Island, A&M, Motown, Geffen and Decca; Warner Music Group controlled Reprise and Rhino along with the original triad of Warner Brothers, Elektra and Atlantic, and held stakes in Maverick, Tommy Boy, SubPop and Giant. After the purchase of CBS, Sony Music Entertainment became owner of Columbia and Epic Records, while Bertelsmann Music Group's takeover of RCA made it the home of hundreds of labels including Arista, Ariola, Jive/Silvertone and Deconstruction. British company EMI owned a number of US labels including Capitol, Priority and Astralwerks. The 'Big Five' would soon become four, with the merger of Sony-BMG in 2004.[3]

The new companies cashed in on their prodigious back catalogues, enjoying the revenue from CD reissues until the mid-1990s, but over the longer term conglomeration did not appear to rescue the industry from crisis. Mining existing assets took precedence over cultivating new talent, and the key developments lay in marketing and packaging. Older stars, thought to be more bankable, were signed to blockbuster contracts that took money away from smaller acts and occasionally fell apart in disputes like those between George Michael and Sony, Prince and Warner, or XTC and EMI.[4] In order to recoup the investment on these performers, companies relied on long tours and increasingly spectacular concerts, not always with positive results. Irish band U2's minor embarrassment with its Popmart tour of 1997 is a case in point: ticket sales were the second highest of all US tours that year but it still failed to turn a profit on the American leg, and the band's faux-ironic celebration of commercialism was generally scornfully received.[5] Additionally, companies exploited alliances with other media such as films and (later) video games: the fact that four of the five top-selling singles of the years 1991–5 were movie tie-ins showed just how much music was becoming part of a branded audiovisual package rather than a product or an activity in its own right (see box below). All of these developments, and the relatively flat sales figures toward the end of the decade, contributed to a growing sense that the industry had lost its way, having disillusioned its audiences and bankrupted music's promise of liberation through fun.[6]

Bestselling US singles, Billboard Hot 100 Charts

1990:   #2: Roxette, 'It Must Have Been Love' (*Pretty Woman*)
1991:   #1: Bryan Adams, '(Everything I Do) I Do It For You' (*Robin Hood*)
        #2: Color Me Badd, 'I Wanna Sex You Up' (*New Jack City*)
1992:   #1: Boyz II Men, 'End of the Road' (*Boomerang*)
1993:   #1: Whitney Houston, 'I Will Always Love You' (*Bodyguard*)
1995:   #1: Coolio, 'Gangsta's Paradise' (*Dangerous Minds*)

Radio was also undergoing profound transformations in this period, and faced similarly difficult prospects for the future. The phenomenon of the 1980s had been talk radio, emerging out of the migration of music broadcasting to FM stations to become the nation's second most popular format by the early 1990s, despite a dwindling share of listeners still tuned to AM. Talk radio spoke to the needs of many Americans who felt removed from the centres of power, patronised by mainstream news media and isolated in the narrowly defined communities of the Reagan era: such people could listen or call in to impassioned debate on issues of the day and enjoy the thrill of unbridled, sometimes taboo-breaking opinion from the hosts. The most prominent of these figures, such as Rush Limbaugh, Don Imus and Howard Stern, were skilful in giving their audiences a sense of select membership in a club that saw through the lies of government, the platitudes of the liberal media and the vanities of celebrities. Limbaugh, for instance, decried television's fascination with O. J. Simpson in the run-up to the trial with the line 'No O. J., none of the time'. With between ten and twenty million weekly listeners in this period, Limbaugh could exert a real political influence by defining issues and galvanising Republican voters: in the Republican primaries of 1992 his endorsement for Pat Buchanan was instrumental in pulling George Bush Sr further to the right, and he even claimed credit for the electoral victories that put Congress in the hands of Republicans in 1994.

Talk radio did more than act as a conduit for conservative political opinion, however. As Susan Douglas has argued, it was also a medium through which specific types of masculinity were fashioned for a largely male audience. Stern's persona wavered erratically between vulnerable child, loutish adolescent and grown cynic, mediating some of the contradictory demands placed on men at a time of changing gender roles while giving relief from the obligations of political correctness. Limbaugh created a wholly new discourse that Douglas calls 'male hysteria': his rants against the emblems of liberal society ('feminazis', 'multiculturalists', 'tree-huggers', 'compassion fascists' and 'the condom crowd') presented an image of emotional manhood that seemed more authentic than the limited stereotypes available on mainstream television broadcasting.[7] The complexity of this position – analytical and irrational, self-deprecating and vitriolic, adopting 'feminine' traits but denying women's political claims – can be seen in the following extract from Limbaugh's morning show, a typical anti-feminist tirade:

Now, I find this interesting [reading]: 'Women Tell the Truth: A Conference on Parity, Power and Sexual Harassment.' Who's the keynote? A liar! Anita Hill. I wish I could go. I would like to dress up as a . . . you think I could pass as a woman? I could pass as a feminist woman. I'll bet you I could . . . Just put on a hat, don't shave my legs for a couple of days – I do that, you know – wobble in there on high heels, and spy on this bunch. Ha ha ha ha ha![8]

Limbaugh and Stern were both celebrated as 'rock and roll' hosts, bringing a spirit of rebelliousness to a medium that had become bland and quaint. But the example above shows how nonconformity and irreverence were enacted within a highly traditional, conservative frame, ultimately concerned with putting women back in their former place. The shock jocks reinvigorated the possibilities and fortunes of AM radio, but what they communicated to their listeners was not a new model of masculinity so much as a strange, manic kind of gender nostalgia.

The Telecommunications Act of 1996 initiated the next revolution for radio. This was a radical overhaul of the regulations governing telecommunications, much of which had remained unchanged since the 1930s, with the aim of promoting competition within and across all sectors – telephone and cell phone networks, cable television, internet provision and radio. Companies were allowed to own a greater portion of local markets and all restrictions on national ownership were lifted, meaning that a single company could operate stations across the country, with up to eight stations in the large cities and as many as six in the smallest markets where there were fourteen or fewer stations in total.[9] The Act received broad support in Congress, indicating that it did not split parties along ideological grounds, but it was controversial amongst media analysts, many of whom correctly predicted a concentration of ownership and a consequent loss of diversity in programming. By the end of the decade almost a third of the nation's ten thousand stations had changed hands, and broadcasting was dominated by only four companies – Capstar/Chancellor Media, CBS, Clear Channel and Jacor – controlling 70 to 90 per cent of market share. And as we have already seen in the case of the music industry, consolidation meant immensely powerful but debt-ridden companies, beholden to their investors rather than the listening public and disinclined to take risks on the music they played. In the words of a music director whose station was bought by ABC/Disney in 1997, 'If you're reporting to Mickey Mouse, Mickey's got a bottom line.'[10]

The number of formats multiplied in the wake of the Telecommunications Act (because it made little sense for a company to compete against itself with the same product), but anyone who has listened to the radio on a long drive across the States in recent years will know that this has not resulted in a wide variety of music to listen to. Formats are geared towards carefully defined niche markets to maximise advertising revenues: thus Modern Rock splits into sub-categories like Active Rock (aimed at the younger male listeners) and Modern Adult Contemporary (older women); playlists, correspondingly, are tightly controlled to prevent a show from losing its audience share. Directors and marketing consultants (rather than DJs) choose the tracks, usually limiting them to a range of twenty to fifty current singles to establish familiarity, and computer software such as Selector determines the order of play, regulating the tempo or the gender of the artists to maintain a level of variety within predictability. Because of the bottom line, stations are overwhelmingly concerned with capturing the fleeting listeners who boost ratings; and because these are likely to be more fickle, impatient with unfamiliar tracks or unprepared to develop sustained listening skills, the chances for introducing real diversity or a larger proportion of new music are dramatically reduced. As the research of campaign group the Future of Music Coalition has discovered, multiple formats mean little when there can be as much as 75 per cent of 'playlist overlap' between them.[11]

As well as restricting the possibilities for diversity in music programming, industry consolidation has made it more difficult for listeners to hear a range of political opinion, and more difficult to maintain locally responsive broadcasting. Public services that local stations have traditionally provided are threatened, critics have argued, when stations are owned by national corporations supplying the same content to all regions. An incident from 2002 shows what is at stake: when a train crash released a cloud of ammonia gas over Minot, North Dakota, police called local radio stations to alert the inhabitants only to find that Clear Channel, who owned six of them, had no one to answer the phones.[12] Equally serious is the problem of anti-democratic tendencies in the new oligopolies: corporate ownership inevitably compromises journalism, and the conglomerates wield a great deal of lobbying power. A stark illustration of this fact was the revelation in 2003 that Clear Channel, now owner of more than 1,200 stations, had covertly organised a number of patriotic rallies to counter protests against the failing war in Iraq. The *New York Times* speculated that the company was either currying favour with the government in the run-up to further deregulation, or it was simply a manifestation of the close personal ties between its vice chairman and the Bush family.[13] Developments such as these have fostered a growing movement of dissent, much of it located on the internet, against Clear Channel in particular and media monopoly in general.

For many the concentration of power in music and broadcasting raised the spectre of a monolithic culture industry whose interests posed a real threat to democracy. Mark Miller traced the networks of media ownership in a map printed in *The Nation* in 1996, warning that the emergence of a 'National Entertainment State' would compromise journalistic freedom.[14] Douglas takes a similar view of what happened to radio, arguing that what is lost with the decline of local independent stations is the role that radio plays in the formation of citizenship, encouraging people to imagine themselves as part of a wider community of listeners. Some of the hopes for alternative media were focused on the new possibilities opened up by the relatively uncontrolled space of the internet, where independent stations began streaming radio in 1994, and the growing free radio movement, which broadcast illegally with low-power transmitters to small communities across America. But both of these were subject in their turn to the pressures of commercialisation and restrictive regulation, and by the end of the century the prospects for any upturn in radio's fortunes looked bleak.[15]

The Death of Rock

The key moment, 'the axis upon which history shifts', as Mark Andersen put it, was the release of Nirvana's *Nevermind* in 1991. This was the album whose enormous success marked the transfiguration of grunge music from a local independent scene into a nationwide phenomenon, breaking through generic boundaries and defining a generation in the process. The convergence of underground and mainstream was evident in the category shift from 'indie' to 'alternative' in retail, radio formats, MTV charts and Grammy awards: 'alternative' suggested a trend towards broader listening habits and a loosening of the purism associated with rock and its derivatives, but it also denoted a real loss of independence to the major labels and corporations. Ultimately, grunge's new-found popularity brought with it both expectation and trepidation – the sense that music could still energise a population and articulate the feelings of those who had little power and authority, but also a fear that commercialism would stifle its radical potential. Andersen's remarks were those of a youth leader (with organisation Positive Force in Washington DC) looking back on the era to observe that the excitement around grunge corresponded with a drop in involvement and activism amongst audiences previously motivated by punk's do-it-yourself ethos: 'What it led to was a dramatic transformation of the punk rock community, in ways that were extremely destructive . . . even as they carried the seed for some profound transformations.'[16] The fraught relationship between music as a commodity and music as a force for change would be an enduring tension throughout the 1990s.

'Grunge' describes all aspects of the scene – place, aesthetics and identity – at once: the dreary weather and post-industrial landscape of Seattle and surrounding towns where the music began in the mid-1980s; the slowed-down, bass-heavy, fuzzed guitar sound recalling the poor acoustics of domestic garages where the first performances and recordings took place; and the cruddy, unkempt look that signified dispossession and aimlessness. Kim Thayil of Soundgarden, one of the bands on the foremost grunge label Sub Pop, called it 'sloppy, smeary, staggering, drunken music', showing how the lines between sonic impact, musicianship and social status were often blurred.[17] But this was by no means the sound of a social movement: if anything, grunge's fascination with the lumpen aligned it with the cult of abjection that was being explored in the art world at this time, rather than the politics of the marginalised that Andersen longed to recover. Mudhoney's anthem 'Touch Me I'm Sick' (1988) is typical – the singer claims 'creep' and 'jerk' as badges of honour, while a lurching guitar riff and a bawled chorus convey drunken disorientation and a sense of disgust with conventional song structure. Outside of Seattle, another good example is Chicago's The Jesus Lizard, who used the focused anger of punk but stretched the music out and distorted it to make a woozy, dirgy sound, with often incoherent vocals recorded through what sounded like a paper cup. What made this music communal rather than alienating was a message of inclusiveness that tempered the self-abasement – 'come as you are', as the Nirvana song put it. Grunge created a collective sense of equality through low expectations that spoke powerfully to young people whether they shared those limited prospects or not.

Nirvana (1987–94)

Nirvana's career was short but the band casts a long shadow over the decade, and not just because of the death of its iconic lead singer. More than any other band, Nirvana embodied the contradictions of rock in a corporate age: their mass popularity was hard to reconcile with the indie ethos that had defined them in their early days, and the anti-rock/anti-pop gestures that they staged as an attempt to work through the conflicts only served, predictably, to make them all the more precious a commodity.

Nevertheless, the passion with which they railed against the system that contained them offered their audience (predominantly young, white and middle class) a kind of comfort, a means of accommodating themselves to a culture that allowed very few truly alternative spaces.

Nevermind was Nirvana's second album, recorded shortly after drummer Dave Grohl joined Kurt Cobain and Chris Novoselic and the band left Sub Pop for David Geffen's label DGC Records. What was groundbreaking about this record was its blend of heavy metal riffs, indie rock stylings and simple pop melodies, all of it finished in a glossy production that cleaned up the usual grunge sound. The iconic cover art, a baby submerged in clear blue water, dollar bill dangling in front of it like bait, emphasised the key affective elements of the music – vulnerability, a sense of imminent suffocation and a kind of hallucinatory transparency that allowed listeners to feel an intense personal relationship to the songs. The album's standout track, and one of the definitive singles of the decade, was 'Smells Like Teen Spirit': a four-chord stomp whose slow-and-quiet/fast-and-loud routine, borrowed from indie rock bands like The Pixies, became the signature of the genre and opened up new possibilities for rock-pop fusions.

Lyrically, the key to 'Teen Spirit' is its promise of a revelation of meaning that is never fulfilled, always yet to come. Cobain's delivery is often slurred or hoarse, and even where it is clear, brought into relief by the ringing guitar notes of the verse, for example, his words are on the verge of incoherence: 'Load up on guns, bring your friends,' he begins, but the sense of mutual purpose quickly breaks down into apparently random phrases with varying degrees of obscurity. Grohl, indeed, cautioned against people reading too much into lyrics that were often composed at the last minute, when 'you need syllables to fill up this space or you need something that rhymes', and phrases like 'Hello, hello, how low' are clearly there for tonal reasons as much as to make a statement. Nevertheless, there is an emotional coherence if not a meaning in the song, which is its attempt to reconcile inexpressible personal angst with the desire for community – just as greeting and despair are combined in the above line.[18] This is reinforced by the music's quiet-loud structure, the lone voice dissolving into a collective frenzy of noise, which culminates in the bitterest parody of a revolutionary demand: 'Here we are now: entertain us!' The words assume the authority of the voice of a generation as they take the will of a crowd of consumers to such an extreme, and such a level of volume, that it becomes a rejection of everything on offer.

Cobain's substantial knowledge of music history, as well as his own scepticism, meant that such sentiments could not be expressed without a note of irony, given that disaffection and the desire for rebellion have been among the main subjects of rock and roll since the 1960s at least. The title, recalling a brand of cheap deodorant, gives it away at the start: nostalgia for the first sensual pleasures of youth is inseparable from the recognition that these are always already commodified – just as rock itself is marketed at kids as the spirit of their teenage years. For critic Greil Marcus, this was the chilling sound of rock music aware of its own defeat, the end of a genre that 'no longer seems to speak in unknown tongues that turn into new and common languages, to say anything that is not instantly translated back into the dominant discourse of our day'.[19] Thus the video gives us the usual rock clichés but in an awkward, off-key manner: a school-concert setting with joyless pupils, cheerleaders with the anarchy sign on their vests but the dance routine of storm troopers, a half-hearted performance from Cobain, the machismo of heavy metal gestures undone by rhymes like mosquito/libido. This self-consciousness about the emptiness of rock grew with Nirvana's mass popularity, and led to numerous attempts to repudiate the authority that came with it, from dressing up in drag at concerts to a refusal to lip-synch on the British television show *Top of the Pops*, and a deliberate attempt to shed listeners with an Albini-engineered back-to-basics approach on the next album *In Utero* (1993), complete with sarcastic track 'Radio-Friendly Unit Shifter'.

The complex and private circumstances of Cobain's suicide at the beginning of April 1994 should not be reduced to single causes like a brutal music industry or the destructive power of celebrity; but the note he left behind, read out in a taped message from his wife Courtney Love to a grieving crowd at a memorial gathering on 10 April, showed that the conflicts he treated ironically in his music had never been properly resolved in his own life. Seduced by the myth of rock authenticity to the end, he wrote with envy and disdain of his inability to become an entertainer like Freddie Mercury, and his guilt at not being able to feel the pleasure of performing in front of fans. The delusion was all too plain to Love, who noted bitterly, 'All the wordings from Punk Rock 101', and paused at the last moment to denounce his affirmation of 'burning out', rather than fading away, as a lie.[20] The title of her own band Hole's next album, *Live Through This*, was to be her own response to this most dangerous of rock clichés. If this was a more salutary message for rock music to be offering in the 1990s, the shift from defiance to endurance is telling.

Figure 2.1 Teenage mourning at the Seattle Center memorial for Kurt Cobain, 10 April 1994 (© John Van Hasselt/Corbis Sygma).

So rock did not die with Kurt Cobain; it was already dead: its gestures of shock and rebellion had become exhausted, and the role it once had as a medium through which young people made sense of their lives or felt inspired to imagine other ways of life had vanished. The question remained as to whether a progressive cultural politics was being articulated in other genres and scenes – in hip-hop or dance music, for instance – or whether the loss of music's power to affect people was endemic in popular music as a whole; but the anxieties about rock music, at least, were starkly exposed in the reactions to Cobain's death. The widespread expressions of mourning and the sanctification of the star in memorial services, pilgrimages, commemorative t-shirts and elegies in the national media suggested that what was at stake was not just the loss of an individual talent but a public desire to believe that rock lived on. Cobain's suicide perfectly suited this desire, since it vividly dramatised the myth that music could matter so much that it was worth sacrificing oneself to. Thus, the tragedy was made to serve an authenticating function, restoring integrity to a failing institution – much in the way that the death of Labour Party leader John Smith a month later helped to restore faith in British politics in the United Kingdom, or the death of Princess Diana revived popular sentiment for the Royal Family in 1997.

One of the key voices in the discourse of 'rock in crisis' was Lawrence Grossberg, whose 1994 paper 'Is Anybody Listening? Does Anybody Care? On "The State of Rock"' argued that rock's decline concerned not only a loss of status relative to other musical genres but the disappearance of a whole mode of experience that had been central to youth culture since its inception. Originating in the 1950s, rock music's significance derived from its power to articulate the sensibilities of young Americans at a time when youth emerged as a new social category, seen as the embodiment of hopes for a new future as well as a threat to social order. This is not to say that it gave them a language with which to express particular views, or even that it was genuinely subversive, but that it provided tools for creating new identities and values within the limits of everyday life. Its emphasis on differences (between generations, between hip and square) generated important points of resistance within the social fabric; its privileging of connoisseurship in popular music consumption established new canons and standards of judgment; and its celebration of the transformative possibilities of fun, sexual or otherwise, set young people against the constricting norms of the adult world they were destined to enter. Grossberg calls this (after French cultural theorists

Gilles Deleuze and Felix Guattari) rock's 'deterritorialising function' – a spirit of restlessness and mobility, a disruption of forms and
boundaries: 'it is as if it imagined that Saturday night was outside the
discipline of territorialisation, and projected a world in which every
moment could be lived as Saturday night'.[21]

By the 1990s, the conditions determining the relation between
youth and popular music were very different. In the intervening
decades teenagers and young adults had been steadily transformed
into consumer groups, markets for an expanding range of media and
lifestyle products such as fashion, computers, video games and youth-
oriented film and television. The entrenchment of conservatism in
economic and cultural spheres had also taken its toll, as it left young
people facing reduced prospects and increasingly repressive controls
on their behaviour. Grossberg sees this as a betrayal on the part of the
baby-boomer generation of the 1960s, who supported policies that
disenfranchised the young while they claimed a kind of proprietor-
ship over the meaning of youth; more recently he has suggested that
America is in the midst of nothing less than a 'war on kids' conducted
by a cynical society reluctant to imagine the social alternatives that
children represent.[22] Under such circumstances popular music culture
is weakened and fragmented, no longer at the centre of young people's
lives and no longer the focus of deterritorialising energies. To put it
in shorthand: society has less invested in youth, and youth has less
invested in music. Grossberg summarises the change as a shift in priorities: 'Rather than dancing to the music you like, you like the music
you dance to' – though his words also betray something of the rock
enthusiast's fear and incomprehension of the newly emerging cultural
formation of dance music.[23]

Nothing captured this transitional phase in popular music culture
better than Mike Judge's animated cartoon *Beavis and Butt-Head*,
which ran on MTV from 1993 to 1997. Beavis and Butt-Head were
two dim-witted pre-pubescent rock fans destined to fail in life but
heroes of their own couch where they spent much of the day watching music videos; the innovative programme format switched from
conventional narrative episodes to sections where they commented
over the top of videos being shown full-screen, in imitation of MTV
viewers themselves. The appeal of these characters lay in their glo-
rification of the moronic, immature, and inarticulate in the midst of
insistent demands to grow up: these were not teenagers in rebellion
against an adult world but children denying it was even there, revel-
ling in their refusal to engage in even the most basic forms of social

interaction (not even punks would have used 'Words Suck' as a t-shirt slogan). Just as important, though, was the image of the music fan they projected in their video commentaries: their unremitting judgments of what ruled and sucked affectionately satirised the MTV generation, forced to undertake the task of taste-formation through the formulaic caricatures and minute stylistic differences offered up by the music industry, while somehow managing to be discerning and witty within their limited range of understanding. Entirely contained within a world to which they would never be fully entitled, and trained to develop a refined set of discriminating faculties that would largely come to serve the purposes of consumption, Beavis and Butt-Head's taste nevertheless exhibited traces of a sovereignty that could, in turn, never be entirely contained within consumer society.

Grossberg's narrative of the decline of rock and the crisis of youth is relatively un-nuanced, however, and we would do well to consider alternative critical perspectives, particularly from the point of view of gender. The rumour that the title of 'Teen Spirit' was inspired by a piece of graffiti written on a wall at Cobain's home by Kathleen Hanna of the band Bikini Kill opens up a different history for rock in the 1990s, one that highlights the presence of women challenging and refashioning rock aesthetics. '*Kurt* smells like Teen Spirit': Cobain's self-erasure in the song title is characteristic, but equally significant is the gentle mockery in the original line, indirectly levelled at rock's macho aspirations.[24] Hanna was one of the progenitors of Riot Grrrl, an influential feminist punk movement formed in 1991 in a collaboration between women in Olympia, Washington State and Washington DC (where meetings took place in Andersen's Positive Force centre). Riot Grrrl's aims were to create networks of communication and activism as well as to mount a critique of sexism within music culture. Short-lived as it was, the movement developed a repertoire of strategies and styles that was empowering for young women in addition to taking rock in new directions.

True to the spirit of indie scenes, the making of music was closely related to the production and distribution of fanzines through which participants developed a sense of solidarity and a rudimentary political awareness: 'BECAUSE viewing our work as being connected to our girlfriends-politics-real lives is essential if we are gonna figure out how what we are doing impacts, reflects, perpetuates or DISRUPTS the status quo', the manifesto declared.[25] This feminist consciousness was reinforced in live concerts where mic-sharing routines brought female fans on stage to take over the vocals or testify to their own experiences of abuse, while moshing, a kind of ritualised shoving from which women were generally physically excluded, was relegated from the front of the venues to the peripheries. Band members often appeared with words like BITCH, SLUT and RAPE written onto their bodies, partly to force issues of sexual abuse into the public arena but also as a way of literalising the male gaze, making it difficult for men to enjoy the sight of women performers as an erotic spectacle.[26] Riot Grrrls also mocked conventions of femininity in their styles of dress, a typical example of which was the harlot/baby-doll look, which disconcertingly collapsed innocence and sexual knowledge onto each other.

Such attempts to transform and politicise relations between performers and audiences were complemented by a critique of sexual politics in the music itself. Riot Grrrl bands such as Bikini Kill, Bratmobile and Heavens to Betsy, and their slightly more mainstream counterparts like Hole, L7 and Babes in Toyland presented very different models of female rockers than had previously been available in punk or indie scenes. Not limited to challenging the assumption that women were only suited to providing lead vocals for a band (a role that confused musical contribution with visual presence), they also attacked and appropriated the gendered codes on which the whole system of rock rested. The traditionally masculine gestures of transgression – speed and volume, a confrontational stage presence, screaming, profanities – became something else when adopted by women: screaming, for example, could signify rage in the usual way but also a kind of ecstasy that was not necessarily addressed at men. For example, when Kat Bjelland from Babes In Toyland screeches 'Yooouuu . . . got this thing that really makes me hot!' on 'Bruise Violet' from *Fontanelle* (1992), it is hard to decide whether to hear it as the threat of a maniac stalker, a parody of a male solicitation or a conventional female come-on ironised to the point of exhaustion.

Readers with a memory of nineties American popular music will either find this history hard to square with the mainstream female rock and pop that emerged in the latter part of the decade or see all too clearly how those progressive styles and principles were watered down, mutated and travestied to suit wider audiences. 'Grrrl riot' was eclipsed by 'girl power', the brand of assertive teenage femininity the Spice Girls brought with them from the United Kingdom in 1997. Where the former movement had sought to mobilise young girls through DIY methods of networking and consciousness-raising, girl power promoted empowerment alongside normative images of sexuality (self-confidence on the condition of remaining attractive to boys), making it a highly conservative if not cynical version of gender politics. The baby-doll look, too, was borrowed and reproduced, though drained of all its defiance, in the new wave of teen pop that followed. Britney Spears's naughty schoolgirl image from the video of her debut single '. . . Baby One More Time' (1998) was clearly more of a marketing strategy than a political one – an attempt to appeal to younger female and older male audiences at the same time. Rather than challenging the male gaze, it became the site of an awkward tension between innocence and sexuality where the demands of those audiences came into conflict – just as the song juxtaposes female assertiveness (a raunchy singing style, team sports in the video) with hints of eroticised violence towards women ('Hit me . . .'). Spears successfully cultivated this kind of provocation early in her career, appearing on the cover of once-purist rock magazine *Rolling Stone* in 1999 when she was seventeen and still famously a virgin, clutching a Teletubby and dressed in her underwear; however, the tension between the different audiences became increasingly difficult to manage in later years, and her inability to live up to the image of a sexy teen idol left her an easy target for vitriolic and misogynistic attacks from the tabloid press.

In addition to teen pop, the late 1990s also saw the emergence of a new generation of female rock and pop stars targeted at older audiences. Tori Amos, Fiona Apple, Meredith Brooks, Sheryl Crow and Canadian Alanis Morissette were among numerous artists who returned to the more intimate modes of the singer-songwriter tradition but incorporated elements of rock attitude into their sound and image and were taken up as icons of a new kind of post-backlash feminism. Like Riot Grrrls, they challenged stereotypes by appropriating male instruments and mannerisms, dealt with women's sexuality in a direct, unapologetic manner and sought new spaces of performance such as the annual women's music festival Lilith Fair (1997–9). What differentiated them was a lack of discomfort with the conventions of beauty and glamour on which much of their popular appeal relied, and a focus on individual rather than collective empowerment. Their politics, such as it was, was one of testimony – giving voice to the complexities of women's lives by describing their own in as open and authentic a manner as possible. Thus Amos and Apple made reference to personal experiences of rape and eating disorders; songs like Brooks's 'I Need' (1997), Crow's 'All I Wanna Do' (1994), Morissette's 'All I Really Want' (1995) and '21 Things I Want in a

Lover' (2002) persistently emphasised the importance of individual desires; and a particular premium was placed on sincerity as a mode of presentation. On the David Letterman show in 1993, Crow felt compelled to claim that the song 'Leaving Las Vegas' was partly auto-biographical, much to the annoyance of its original writer[27]; similarly, on the decade's bestselling album *Jagged Little Pill* (1995) Morissette cultivated a raw confessional voice that masked the fact that all the tracks were written by Glen Ballard. (Indeed, given the marketability of sincerity at this time we should think twice about laughing at the notoriously poor definitions of irony in the hit song 'Ironic'; being seen to be ironic was simply not in the singer's interests.)

The problem with the feminism of the 'Angry Young Women', as they came to be known, was that they left patriarchal structures within and outside the music industry largely untouched. Meredith Brooks might appear to use tactics similar to Riot Grrrl self-branding in a song like 'Bitch' (1997), appropriating sexist terms of abuse and asserting the contradictory, uncategorisable nature of women's identity ('I'm a sinner, I'm a saint / I do not feel ashamed') but her statement of independence is entirely framed within the context of a relationship to a male partner: 'You know you wouldn't want it any other way . . .' Equally, Fiona Apple protests women's right to powerful sexual desires in 'Criminal' (1996), but when it came to the video she was unable to resist being positioned in all too conventional terms as a sex object. Shot in grainy, shadowy spaces, lying on the floor or undress-ing in the kitchen, she appears like an underweight supermodel in one of Nan Goldin's photographs. Where the Riot Grrrls had focused on body image and eating disorders in order to mobilise young girls, Apple's aims were, in the end, merely individualistic and sadly naive about the relationship between artists and the music business. In a *Rolling Stone* interview she explained her strategy: 'Start out being lean and the absolute perfect marketing package, and slowly, as I get more power, becoming more of myself and exhibit the happiness that comes from that . . .'[28] This separation of a language of empowerment from a critique of the consumption of music was a key characteristic of what we must more accurately call the pseudo-feminism of the 1990s.

Hip-Hop Nation

The flip-side to the decline of rock was the tremendous rise in popu-larity for rap music over the course of the decade. *Time* magazine acknowledged the fact by announcing in 1999 that America had become a 'hip-hop nation': rap was now outselling all other genres, and hip-hop penetrated the mainstream in ways that other music cultures never had, influencing pop, Hollywood film, high-street fashion, advertising and even styles of business. Despite this near-total integration with entertainment and leisure industries rap had also taken over rock's deterritorialising function, offering its fans moments of flight and freedom from the limits of the everyday. As Russell Simmons, head of New York label Def Jam, observed, 'Rock is old . . . It's old people's s___. The creative people who are great, who are talking about youth culture in a way that makes sense, happen to be rappers.'[29] All the complexities of rap's appeal to its different audiences were wrapped up in the notion of 'making sense': young people denied the social vision of their parents' generation were drawn to rappers' various messages of hope or displays of nihilistic bravado; whites, now 70 per cent of the market, consumed hip-hop's images of blackness with a mixture of voyeurism and a genuine desire to identify with otherness; African Americans – especially young black men, who as a group faced disgracefully high levels of social exclusion – valued the music for its realism and critical force.

The distance that rap music had travelled can be measured by comparing the *Time* article with *Newsweek*'s dismissive feature from March 1990, written at the height of a panic over the music's effects on young Americans, when it still seemed marginal enough for the magazine to offer to 'decode' it for readers as if it were an alien language.[30] The discourse of rap-as-threat, of which this is a good example, combined a distaste for rap's musical qualities with a fear of black inner-city life that bordered on outright racism, as revealed in the following description of 'the rap attitude': 'Bombastic, self-aggrandizing and yet as scary as sudden footsteps in the dark.'[31] This sense of threat had been fuelled by gangsta rap – a variant emerging on the West Coast at the end of the 1980s which dwelt on racial conflict and emphasised confrontation with institutional power (usually the police), but through criminality rather than politics. Where New York's foremost political rap band Public Enemy framed protest in a language of black nationalism – their 1988 album *It Takes a Nation of Millions to Hold Us Back* succeeded by 1990's *Fear of a Black Planet* – artists like Ice-T, Ice Cube and associates NWA (Niggaz With Attitude) rejected political organisation of all sorts in favour of garish images of crime and violence in the 'ghettoes' of post-industrial urban America.

The prominence of gangsta rap signalled the end of New York City's hegemony as the origin of hip-hop. Regional centres of production had already begun to emerge in cities like Los Angeles, Miami, Atlanta and Philadelphia, initially defining themselves in opposition to New York but soon evolving local styles. The Miami sound, popularised by 2 Live Crew, was a deep, reverberating bass inflected with 1980s electro, while in California the rapid-fire delivery of early gangsta rap gave way to G-funk – a smooth, laid-back sound heavily indebted to George Clinton's Parliament/Funkadelic, in which the gangster figure displayed his authority through aloofness and lack of effort rather than overt toughness. Snoop Doggy Dogg's imposing presence and distinctive melodic drawl made him the most celebrated rapper of the genre after his appearance on Dr Dre's key album *The Chronic* (1992), and his own debut *Doggystyle* (1993) became one of the bestselling rap albums of the decade.

One reason for the disappearance of the dense sample collages of old-school hip-hop, which reached a peak with Public Enemy and white Brooklynites the Beastie Boys circa *Paul's Boutique* (1989), was purely economic: few artists could pay for copyright clearance. After Biz Markie was sued for sampling from a Gilbert O'Sullivan song in 1991, and 2 Live Crew the following year over their use of Roy Orbison's 'Pretty Woman', the message was that hip-hop's aesthetics of appropriation and mixing were legally subordinate to traditional notions of authorship on which the commercialisation of recorded music had long depended.[32] Henceforward, sampling went two ways: the collagist approach explored increasingly obscure source material to evade the notice of copyright holders, while the bigger-budget acts paid to use portions of familiar tunes and gave them a more central role in the final track. But rap's aesthetics were also influenced by local environmental factors. New York's largely pedestrian spaces had produced a specific set of musical practices concentrated on the relation between body and street: outdoor block parties and break-dancing, a 'walking' rhythm (as in Grandmaster Flash and the Furious Five's 1982 hit 'The Message') and a treble-accented sound that catered to the widespread use of personal stereos and walkmans.[33] West Coast rap, on the other hand, was music for an automotive culture, characterised by a resounding bass and cinematic imagery that reflected the pleasures of cruising through the city.

Take the song 'It was a Good Day' from Ice Cube's 1992 album *The Predator*: a lush, down-tempo track depicting a day in the rapper's life. The precise images of everyday spaces, the play between street-level and aerial perspectives and the sense of flow, both lyrical and visual, all contribute to the cinematic effect. But what makes the track

particularly distinctive is the absence of rupture that usually characterises gangsta rap – the sudden breaks, the barrage of samples or the
switching from one rapper to the next – just as the remarkable thing
for the protagonist in the song is the absence of the usual occasions of
violence or police activity in the neighbourhood. 'Saw the police and
they rolled right past me / No flexin', didn't even look in a nigga's
direction / as I ran the intersection': for a moment life is unhindered,
and the freedom of movement – on the streets, the basketball court
and in sex – is what gives the song its powerful self-assured feel.

'Good Day' is by no means free of the machismo and sexism that
upset many of gangsta rap's detractors, but it has a light touch and a
genuine wit that the outraged rarely acknowledged – as when Cube
plays with the gangster stereotype: 'Today I didn't even have to use
my AK / I got to say it was a good day'. The humour has a darker
purpose, of course, which is to suggest that what many people accept
as ordinary life is often a luxury for the inhabitants of deprived inner-
city areas: a perfect day in South Central LA is not drinking sangria
in the park, but simply not getting arrested or killed. And if this
seems like an exaggeration in keeping with the myth of the gangster
life, we should remember the statistics that attest to the extent of the
crisis amongst African Americans at this time: in South Central Los
Angeles, a district with high levels of poverty, 50 per cent unemployment for black men and infant mortality over twice the national
average, aggressive anti-gang police initiatives such as Operation
Hammer had recently placed over fifty thousand youths under arrest;
across the country, almost a quarter of all black men aged 18 to 30
were in prison or on parole, amounting to a larger population than
black men of all ages in higher education.[34] The recent acquittal of the
officers tried for beating Rodney King was further evidence of the
racialisation of criminal justice, and the sense of rage that erupted in
the Los Angeles riots of 1992 is everywhere present in *The Predator*.
Even in 'Good Day', the brief moment of ghetto pastoral is suffused
with a nervous tension which is the knowledge that this is merely
the temporary suspension of force. The video ends with a swarm
of police descending on the rapper's house as he goes inside; on the
album, the song is cut short with Cube's own interjection 'What the
fuck am I thinking about?' and the ominous voice of control: 'Peace,
quiet and good order will be maintained in our city to the best of our
ability.'

This brings us to the heart of the dilemma facing rap in the 1990s:
simultaneously a confrontational music speaking truth to power

at a time of social crisis, and a commercial music whose rhetorical provocations and images of violence were key commodities. Most consumers were entirely comfortable with this tension, as they were able to pick and choose which messages to identify with and which to disregard, but it made rap an easy target for others with a political agenda. In the aftermath of the Los Angeles riots, for instance, the candidates of the 1992 presidential campaign were conspicuously unable to address claims that institutional racism might be a cause of the violence, but both sides made a point of condemning rap to appeal to conservative voters. Bill Clinton misrepresented remarks by rapper and Public Enemy protégée Sister Souljah to accuse her of fomenting racial hatred, while Republican Vice-Presidential candidate Dan Quayle joined the Los Angeles Police Department in attacking Ice-T's song 'Cop Killer', even though it had been available long before the riots without causing controversy (and, besides, was not actually rap but heavy metal). Anti-rap outrage was a way of converting the real political problems of race into moral problems, and thereby distracting the electorate from the root causes of unrest and injustice for which politicians might have taken some responsibility. [35]

Criticisms of rap also came from within the African American community, however, and none carried more weight than those of C. Delores Tucker, former civil rights activist and now president of the National Congress of Black Women. Tucker took the battle to the media corporations themselves, appearing at shareholders meetings to accuse them of profiting from obscenity, and she had a hand in Time Warner's decision to divest itself of its hip-hop interests in 1995. Forthright as her opponents, Tucker denounced gangsta rap as 'genocidal prose' and refused to credit it as anything other than an exploitative form of commercialism much in the tradition of blackface minstrelsy:

> Rap in its purest form was an artform of prose and poetry which expressed life in the same sense that the spirituals did. Gangsta rap is a perverted form which has been encouraged by those who have always used the entertainment industry to exploit and project the negative stereotypical images to demean and depict African Americans as subhuman, which is the antithesis of what we as African American people are.[36]

As Nelson George has pointed out, the trouble with this species of complaint is its commitment to a myth of black innocence: it rehearses a familiar story of the appropriation of black culture by a white industry without admitting that African American hip-hop artists had an unprecedented degree of autonomy to produce offensive material of their own.[37] In George's account, Tucker's naivety on this point led her away from a principled and necessary critique of rap's sexism and into some unholy alliances with figures who should have been her adversaries, such as record label boss Suge Knight and Republican moral crusader William Bennett. But the storm she ignited also revealed a deep generational rift in the cultural politics of African Americans, especially where relations with mainstream media were concerned. By the 1990s, the veterans of the civil rights movement had come to assume a kind of guardianship over the meaning and purpose of black endeavours, and it was their authority that was threatened by the new breed of hip-hop entrepreneurs, many of whom paid little heed to established black institutions like the church or the NCBW and laid claim to a different cultural heritage – one that comprised not only blues, jazz, and spirituals but mainstream white pop, children's comics, kung-fu and, indeed, Italian American gangster movies. On top of this challenge, hip-hop's delight in offence and transgression seemed a direct affront to those who had worked to secure real advances for African Americans largely through an appeal to the nation's moral integrity. Whether wilful or playful, they saw the lawlessness celebrated in gangsta culture as nothing less than a generational betrayal.

The concept of 'hip-hop nation', then, contains an unresolved tension between civic nationalism and black nationalism: sometimes (as in the *Time* article of 1999) it means an idea of America united by common musical tastes and consumption patterns, while at other times it refers to specifically African American, if not Afro-centric, forms of solidarity and identity. But the gangsta figure, who appeared to pose such a threat in the mid-1990s and is still integral to the hip-hop imaginary, is a kind of third term, outside of both – defined by his antagonism to the state and resolutely identifying with posse and hood rather than a more abstract and sentimentalised 'black community'. While the posturing can easily look absurd and may be self-defeating as a form of cultural politics, it is nevertheless possible to understand the gangsta (and the equally troubling designation 'nigga') as a kind of necessary force of negativity within hip-hop, a resistance not only to the policing *of* black communities but the policing that takes place *within* black communities, through figures like Tucker.

Tupac Shakur (1971–1996; 1991–present)

As the dates indicate, Tupac Shakur's death has not terminated his career. Currently the best-selling rap artist of all time, Tupac has almost twice as many posthumous studio albums to his name than the five he released during his lifetime and over four times the sales. He is the subject of numerous books, films, a clothing line and foundation for the performing arts, with new work still forthcoming. This extraordinary legacy is testimony both to the large amount of material Tupac left behind and the determination of parties within and beyond the music industry to capitalise on his memory. But it also provides an opportunity to compare styles of mourning for the great icons of popular music in the 1990s, and examine the different ways that death signifies in the rock and rap 'formations'.

In the myths of Tupac and Kurt Cobain, both artists feature as symbols of lost promise. Cobain's death, as we have seen, was incorporated into a narrative that cast him as the last great rock star and victim of his success, thereby affirming an ideology of authenticity as resistance to the market. Hip-hop, by contrast, has always worked on and within the mechanisms of the market, and conceives of authenticity more in terms of commercial mastery or 'adaptation to the force of commodification'.[38] Indeed, one of the reasons for Tupac's pre-eminence while alive was his skilful manipulation of the codes of rap authenticity: drawing on contemporary gangsta styles and his own background as son of a famous Black Panther mother, his image was a composite of multiple personae ranging from activist and visionary to outlaw and player. Bare-chested, tattooed and perfectly toned, Tupac was both the beautiful warrior of black nationalism and the dysfunctional spectre of 'thug life'; bespectacled and impeccably dressed, he was scholar or businessman, the vanguard of a new black middle class.

A further difference is the way that death itself is commodified in the subgenres of hardcore rap that were dominant in the mid-1990s. Snoop Dogg's trial for accessory to murder in 1993 had already cast a spotlight on the disturbing relationship between rap's imagery and the real lives of its performers, but Tupac and his former friend Biggie Smalls (aka The Notorious B.I.G.) reworked the theme, dwelling obsessively on their own demise. B.I.G.'s 1994 album *Ready To Die* was followed up with *Life After Death* (1997), while Tupac considered martyrdom on *All Eyez on Me* (1996), claiming with wry humour, 'My only fear of death is reincarnation' ('No More Pain'). This fixation on death seemed grotesquely prophetic when, after an escalating personal rivalry that was also a battle for industry supremacy between Los Angeles label Death Row Records and New York's Bad Boy Entertainment, Tupac was shot dead in September 1996 and Biggie six months later.

The murders were variously taken as symptoms of the excesses of the music industry or instances of a pathology of violence amongst young African American men. Others argued that they were a function of cultural as well as social alienation. 'It's bigger than rap,' commented Chuck D of

Public Enemy. 'Until black people control our reality, not only will art imitate life, but life will start to imitate art.' [39] This struggle to determine reality rather than submit to a way of life imposed by others was essential to hip-hop's ethos of 'keeping it real' and has been a key concern throughout black culture. But the irruption of the reality of death into the spectacle of gangsta rap also signified a troubling form of political alienation, since it revealed the degree to which black Americans' lives had been reduced to a condition of 'bare life', so excluded from citizenship that the inhabiting of a space outside the law seemed a preferable mode of existence.[40]

The loss of Biggie and Tupac left the hip-hop community deeply shocked, and effectively brought gangsta rap to an end. Death Row imploded after the indictment of Suge Knight on unrelated charges in 1997, and Bad Boy, under the direction of Sean 'Puffy' Combs, began to lead hip-hop further towards mainstream pop, incorporating more soulful vocal styles and emphasising glamour rather than violence. If this was the beginning of rap's domination of popular music, the signs of its limited creative aspirations were already evident in his tribute to B.I.G., 'I'll be Missing You', which unashamedly plundered The Police's hit 'Every Step You Take'. Tupac's own legacy was commemorated in 'Changes' (1998), which reused much of Bruce Hornsby and the Range's song 'The Way It Is'. Although the song had been completed before his death, its elegiac mood and reflection on the potential for change made it a central text of mourning.

'Changes' contains two apparently contradictory discourses: on the one hand, it presents a litany of social problems that urgently demand change, from racist police and crowded prisons to misguided policies on drugs; on the other, it falls back on the gangsta's radically individualistic outlook, born of a belief that structural change is impossible. The tension between progressive and defeatist positions is present in the refrain itself, a revision of Hornsby's original lines which evokes both changelessness and a sense of rupture with the past: 'That's just the way it is / Things will never be the same . . .' It is easy to see how such words could be reinvested with mourning for someone whose loss seemed inevitable, but if they have another meaning it is the suggestion that the past once contained a possibility for change that now no longer exists. In this respect the song is a meditation on the significance of the previous generation's politics in the present, an assertion that a radical break has occurred between the 1960s and the 1990s that has made collective action for change inconceivable. This is something that Tupac hints at early in the song, with reference to the recent murder of Black Panther Huey Newton – 'It's time to fight back that's what Huey said / Two shots in the dark now Huey's dead' – but he also considered it in an interview in February 1996, reflecting on his relationship with his mother:

> My mom and [the Panthers] envisioned this world for us to live in, and strove to make that world. So I was raised off those ideals, to want those. But in my own life, I saw that that world was impossible to have. It's a world in our head. It's a world we think about at Christmas and Thanksgiving. I had to teach my mother how to live in this world like it is today. She taught me how to live in that world that we have to strive for.[41]

This conflicted discourse, a kind of nostalgic realism, is utterly of the 1990s. Tupac's attempt to preserve a memory of the previous generation's political idealism while denying its relevance to the present acutely articulates the pain of a post-historical condition: what it is like to live in the aftermath of a revolution in which nothing was liberated except the market. Here the difference between the significance of Tupac's death and Kurt Cobain's becomes clear. Mourning Kurt meant believing once again in the values of rock culture – the rebellion and negativity of youth, and its search for alternative spaces of identity construction; mourning Tupac meant looking back on the failed hopes of black Americans and recognising that the struggle for social justice had been superseded by the pursuit of individual goods. On the other hand, what *was* truly revolutionary was the way that the commemoration of Tupac placed this failure at the heart of the national imaginary. The death of the rap star was in this respect not an authenticating event but a legitimating event, a way for rap to lay claim to its own sacrificial heroes and establish its significance as a mode of articulating the memory and sensibilities of the nation as a whole.

Figure 2.2 Tupac Shakur on stage, 1992 (© Raymond Boyd/Michael Ochs Archives/Getty Images).

New Musicking

'Rather than dancing to the music you like, you like the music you dance to . . .' If Grossberg is right about this shift in priorities, then the emergence of dance music from the mid-1980s has transformed popular music more radically than any of the developments in rock or hip-hop. Although it never had the monumental impact on youth culture in America that it did in Europe, dance challenged many of popular music's basic practices and aesthetic principles, from the way music was made and performed to notions of authorship and song structure. It also developed a very different set of relations between music and identity: in place of rock's commitment to identity formation through rebellion or hip-hop's articulation of black identities through commodification, dance music to a large extent put questions of identity to one side to explore and experiment with the affective qualities of sound. Even though the club scenes that fostered dance music were necessarily rooted in particular locations, the music was determinedly outward-looking, embracing new influences and mutating often at breakneck speed. Similarly, clubbers themselves enjoyed a powerful sense of community but one that was defined in the loosest and most inclusive of ways, with little attention to specific social differences. Dance music focused on perception, rather than representation; notions of personal identity were abandoned in the embrace of an ego-less subjectivity and the ecstatic sociality of the dancefloor.

Dance music's two principal forms, house and techno, were nevertheless born out of conflicts in black music and cultural traditions. House emerged in Chicago from the remnants of a disco scene that had become the object of hostility from rock fans on one side and funk fans on the other; its repetitious rhythm, excessive sensuality and synthesised sound were direct extensions of the elements that disco's critics had found inauthentic and offensive (not without touches of racism and homophobia).[42] Techno originated in Detroit, capturing the nervous melancholy of a place in transition from industrial powerhouse to urban blight in a music that was sparse, relentless and conspicuously devoid of 'soul'. Coming from a black middle class that the motor industry had brought into existence before its decline, techno's pioneers turned away from the city's Motown heritage as well as the ghetto-identified modes of contemporary hip-hop and looked to Europe for their influences, creating strange fusions of seventies funk and European electronic pop. 'Just like Detroit, a complete mistake,' as Derrick May famously described it. 'It's like George Clinton and Kraftwerk stuck in an elevator.'[43]

By the 1990s, a burgeoning rave scene and attendant drug culture drove many of the next generation of techno producers into more minimalist and conceptual territory. The four-four drum patterns, limited chord progression, harsh percussion and looped bass lines from equipment like the Roland TB 303 generated a sound that was simultaneously mechanistic and organic, elemental rather than human, and well suited to the favoured science fiction topics of megacities, alien worlds and unstable states of being. Works like Cybersonik's 'Technarchy' (1990), Suburban Knight's 'The Art of Stalking' (1990), X-102's *Rings of Saturn* (1992), Jeff Mills's *Waveform Transmission* (1992–4), Robert Hood's *Internal Empire* (1994) and *Night-Time World* (1995), and Model 500's *Deep Space* (1995) give an idea of techno's posthumanist themes, as well as the common tendency to assume aliases that masked or minimised the presence of the individual creator in the music. 'Underground' displaced 'street' as the key site of authenticity, reflecting the borderline legality of the early club scene but also imparting a feeling that the music was a kind of secret communication between initiates sustaining the idea of revolt during repressive times.

As Simon Reynolds points out, a tension between militarism and mysticism is central to the cultural politics of African American music: at the political ends of jazz, funk, soul and rap the focus for resolution to social injustices or the restoration of community shifts between the here and now, and a mythical past or future.[44] The same dialectic is evident in techno, which moved from the Afro-futurism of a group like Drexciya to the explicitly insurgent stance of label collective Underground Resistance. A mysterious duo who never revealed their identities, Drexciya posed as messengers from a mythical marine species that evolved from pregnant slave women thrown overboard during the Middle Passage ('Is it possible that they could have given birth at sea to babies that never needed air?' suggests the sleeve notes to their 1997 album *The Quest*). Equally covert were the operations of Underground Resistance, founded by Jeff Mills and Mike Banks in 1989, which presented its releases as weapons in an ongoing sonic revolution ('Transmit these tones and wreak havoc on the programmers!' the website declares). A decade on, Banks and Mills look back on UR's politics quite differently, though they correspond in their expression of a desire to resist and transcend current racial representations. Banks:

> [W]e lived and grew up in an environment that was being bombarded
> by audio and visual stereotypes that are essentially a guide for failure
> ... We wanted a label and a sound that depicted brothers in a different
> darkness and a different light.

Mills:

> Underground Resistance wasn't militant, nor was it angry ... the music
> that I make now has nothing to do with colour. It has nothing to do
> with man/woman, East/West, up/down ... The mind has no colour.
> There's this perception that if you're black and you make music, then
> you must be angry. Or you must be 'deep'. Or you must be out to get
> money and women. Or you must be high when you made that record.
> It's one of the four.

This kind of purism has led to Mills being accused of taking techno
into a dead end, cut off from the renovating energies of the dancefloor,
but it is also an attempt to refuse to be categorised as (merely) a 'black
artist' in order to claim a place in a broader avant-garde tradition.[45]
   So what happened to techno? Why was it that its producers became
stars in Europe but failed to cross over in the United States? In part,
it was because many early artists had signed to European labels which
did not have the budgets to promote the records on the other side
of the Atlantic; another reason was that the American market of the
1990s was much more rigidly segmented, and the major corporations
too cumbersome to figure out how to sell dance music of any sort.
The trend for multiple aliases and the lack of a performance element
(whether vocals or playable instruments) made dance hard to fit into
a rock/MTV marketing model, and it was not until 1997 that the
industry made a concerted effort to bring it into the mainstream, with
a rebranding as 'electronica' and a number of high-profile signings
of European artists. One of the major deals was Maverick's contract
with Prodigy, a former rave act from the UK which significantly had
already made efforts to restyle itself to appeal to rock audiences.[46]
   Dance music did not quite break out from the underground, then,
but its radically different approach to the making and experience of
music did have a wider impact. The departure from the song form was
also undertaken by bands at the more progressive end of alternative
rock like Tortoise and Godspeed You Black Emperor, who produced
extended exploratory pieces where the voice is largely used as instru-
mentation and the listener is enveloped in a multi-layered, open-ended

sonic landscape. Reynolds argues that this involves a shift away from rock's ego- and identity-oriented processes toward a more decentred engagement with the music, and the parallels with techno are clear:

> At the heart of rock and roll stands the body of the white teenage boy, middle finger erect and a sneer playing across his lips. At the centre of post-rock floats a phantasmatic un-body, androgynous and racially indeterminate: half ghost, half machine.'[47]

Hip-hop evolved a similar approach in the subgenre known as 'turntablism' – a return to the original skills of the DJ that had become somewhat marginalised in gangsta and pop-oriented rap. While the spectacle of the DJ set continued (notable figures being DJ Premier, Cut Chemist, Peanut Butter Wolf and the virtuoso Californian collective Invisibl Skratch Piklz), studio albums such as DJ Shadow's *Endtroducing . . .* and DJ Spooky's *Songs of a Dead Dreamer* (both from 1996) emphasised mood and texture over performance, bringing an array of recorded sounds into the mix from jazz rarities to antique public announcements in order to create surprising juxtapositions and activate the recesses of memory in the listener's mind. Such artists played with the familiarity and cultural resonance of the sample, moving between its referential quality and its material presence as mere sound freed from its original context. The mixes they produced worked less like songs, communicating specific meanings to their audiences, and more like collages: rearrangements of pre-existing fragments in which the whole of audio history was offered up as potential raw material for reuse and reinterpretation.

The widespread culture of sampling is one of the most salient aspects of the new music formation that grew out of hip-hop and dance music in the 1990s. Structurally, sampling marks the erosion of the boundary between music and environmental (or ambient) sound in a manner linking hip-hop with the *musique concrète* of the European avant-garde; at the same time, it contributes to the dissolution of boundaries separating high and low, classical and popular. The distinction here – made by Robert Fink in a superb article on music's decanonisation in a post-classical age – is between sampling that sustains the difference by foregrounding it, as in Coolio's use of Pachelbel's *Canon in D Major* for 'C U When U Get There' (1997), and sampling that is so dense, obscure or brief that the high culture connotations disappear, as when Beck introduces Schubert's *Unfinished Symphony* into a track from *Odelay* (1995), a sound Fink describes as 'so gloriously out of any possible context that it has a hallucinatory immediacy'.[48]

Sampling also describes the new modes of listening that have emerged in the last couple of decades, especially with the rise of digital technologies in production, distribution and playback. Turntablism itself is a kind of collapsing of the previously distinct acts of listening and music-making into one composite practice, since what we listen to is, apart from other things, the DJ him or herself listening to the world around – record collections, genres, 'classic' tracks, film and television soundtracks, whatever has been captured on tape or vinyl in the past. A further example would be the way that digital formats are now allowing a level of interactivity with the music commodity – where, for instance, a CD contains a number of unlocked tracks for ordinary consumers to remix on their home computer. In such cases (and in the culture of remixes generally) the musical artefact is no longer a fixed object but a text disseminated across studio production, public performance and private consumption.

Napster and Music on the Internet

Alongside the wave of conglomeration in the music industry was another revolution: the World Wide Web, expanding at an exponential rate from its inception in 1991. A clash between the two was inevitable, given that the industry had a great deal invested in copyright and distribution while the web had its roots in a non-commercial ethos dedicated to the free flow of ideas. As soon as music became information – when it became possible to separate ('rip') audio from its physical formats to convert it into digital files (such as mp3) – an entirely new audio culture came into being, which posed a serious threat to the business of music. Earlier innovations such as cassette and video taping had already come with claims they were killing their respective industries, but in those there was a significant measure of degradation that sustained the value of the original product. Digital music, on the other hand, could be copied an infinite number of times and stay identical, while the internet enabled it to be sent to any number of listeners without cost.

Prior to the advent of Napster, music was available on the internet in a number of different forms. The Internet Underground Music Archive (1993–2006) helped bands access a potentially vast global audience by hosting publicity and tracks in return for a monthly subscription; internet radio broadcasting arrived with the release of RealAudio's streaming software in 1995 and ventures such as Emusic, MP3.com and Liquid Audio tried to coax the hesitant corporations into providing material for legitimate download. Some forward-looking artists like David Bowie and the Beastie Boys turned to the internet to develop new ways of reaching their fans, offering access to unreleased material, news of tour dates or the occasional free download, often against the wishes of their own label. Thus, in the absence of a serious commitment from the industry, web-based music quickly developed in more informal ways amongst hobbyists, students and communities of fans. It was this seam that Napster tapped so effectively.

Napster was an early 'peer-to-peer' file-sharing program that enabled users to access each other's personal music collections. It worked by scanning hard drives for mp3 files and posting the filenames – not the files themselves – to a central site, where users would search for the material they wanted and then connect to others' computers to download it. The beauty of this procedure was that it spread the burden of information transfer amongst the file-sharers rather than overloading a main server; the threat to the record companies, of course, lay in the fact that the site was never in possession of the music that it helped to redistribute, and so it could deny liability for the transactions that took place. Napster's simplicity, viral capacities and disregard for conventions made it the ideal internet application (a 'killer app') and its inventor, Shawn Fanning, a kind of cult hero – the embodiment of a rock and roll spirit that had long disappeared from the music itself. When *Time* placed him on its cover in October 2000, just over a year from its initial release, Napster was already the fastest-growing application in net history, on 25 million computers across the world.[49]

Not surprisingly, this caused a storm in the recording industry. Dr Dre and his protégé Eminem were outspoken in condemnation of file-sharing, demanding that their songs be removed from the service; Madonna protested when her single 'Music' appeared on Napster prior to its release date in 2000; heavy metal band Metallica went so far as to produce a printout of over 300,000 names of downloaders it wanted banned.[50] (Among the ironies here was the fact that the band had benefited in its early years from encouraging fans to tape and exchange recordings of their concerts. Such was the grey area that file-sharing occupied, and the reason why it produced such zeal amongst its supporters: it brought deeply rooted and legitimate fan practices into direct collision with the consumer behaviour required by the corporations.) The argument of Napster's opponents was straightforward: file-sharing was a form of theft denying artists their rightful income and undermining the investments of the labels. Napster's defenders pointed out that free downloads did not necessarily mean lost sales, and it was just as likely that they helped to promote artists or revive interest in music languishing in the labels' back catalogues. John Perry Barlow, one-time lyricist for The Grateful Dead, argued that free access to music actually increased its value, just as tape-swapping brought more fans to their concerts and videotaping boosted the film industry. As did Chuck D of Public Enemy: 'To the pirates, I say the more the merrier. Success comes from the fans first – if someone is going to pirate something of mine, I just have to make sure to do nine or ten new things. I mean, you can't download me.'[51]

The truth was, file-sharing increased the value of the artist's persona and creativity ('you can't download me') while it decreased the value of recordings (or rather, reduced the over-inflated values the industry had been placing on them for decades). This difference highlighted the conflicting interests of labels and artists: an artist, after all, could capitalise in other ways on the fame the internet generated – through concerts, merchandise or film appearances – while the corporations only had an inert commodity to sell. Recent attempts to combat this problem have been to license songs for use in films, advertising and mobile phone ringtones, and to market 'landmark recordings' in lavishly packaged CD box sets. In addition, companies have resorted to litigation to force file-sharing to the outer reaches of the web and replace it with commercial download sites. This strategy began with the Recording Industry Association of America's lawsuit against Napster in December 1999, which eventually found Fanning guilty of contributory copyright infringement and led to its closure in July 2001.[52]

Much of the early excitement surrounding the internet has now passed, and record companies have, at least in the short term, managed to secure their own model of distribution against erosion by file-sharing, but the impact of applications like Napster should not be glossed over. In pooling people's personal music libraries, file-sharing opened up the possibility for individual listeners to develop musical interests beyond the increasingly narrow confines of radio, retail outlets and labels' release schedules. But in a more profound sense, it transformed their relationship to the history and temporality of popular music: all of a sudden, the hard drives of millions of users across the world functioned as a kind of collective musical memory in which listeners could rediscover the long-forgotten and long-deleted, or simply browse the once-private affective realms of entire strangers.

Fink's term 'musicking' is useful for understanding the changes taking place at the end of the twentieth century, since it treats music as a set of cultural practices encompassing not just the development of specific genres but modes of listening, spaces of listening and other forms of engagement with the world.[53] From this perspective the most significant aspects of the music of the 1990s come into focus, where what mattered were not particular stylistic developments so much as the way that music was being made and listened to. Since the 1980s, music had increasingly been consumed audiovisually, through video, film soundtrack and the 'personal soundtrack' experience of the walkman. It also became more ubiquitous, appearing more frequently as a background element in contexts from clothing stores to call waiting or greetings cards.[54] Digital formats such as mp3 accelerated these trends in the 1990s, making music not only more portable but also more disposable – far less concerned with hi-fi quality than previous formats like CD or vinyl (as the current tendency for teenagers to play their music on tinny mobile phone speakers on buses will testify). All these developments do not necessarily amount to a devaluing of music; but they do indicate that the relation of music to other cultural activities is changing dramatically.

Chapter 3

Film and Television

As with music, the story of film and television in the 1990s is one of new technologies, shifting markets and anxious corporations struggling to keep ahead of the game. Many important developments were the outcome of changes wrought in the previous decade. Cable television was now firmly established, having captured over 30 per cent of the audience after a period of growth and consolidation: new channels such as Cable News Network (CNN), Court TV, Comedy Central and Cartoon Network helped to define the media landscape as one of niche markets. Anti-monopolistic regulations that had been challenged throughout the 1980s were finally relaxed, allowing networks to produce more of their own programmes and leading to a renaissance in serial drama and situation comedy. The threat that home video had been expected to pose to film and television industries never materialised, but the availability of the new technology had other important consequences. In cinema, the success of the eighties 'high concept' movie resulted in an increasingly formulaic output that began to disappoint audiences and helped create the conditions for a revitalised independent scene. Again, as with music, the crucial questions are to do with the relation between culture and media ownership. To what extent does it matter that film and television production is dominated by no more than a handful of multinational corporations? What space is there for independent creative activity, and how much opportunity for social or ideological diversity?

An additional feature of the visual culture of the 1990s, one that parallels the trend towards 'ubiquitous listening' in music, is the expansion of moving images beyond the traditional bounds of film and television to penetrate all aspects of everyday life. Closed-circuit television cameras proliferated not only in shops, workplaces and city streets but also in the home, initiating a domestication of personal surveillance that would accelerate with the advent of webcams and mobile camera phones. Flat-screen technology allowed advertising to reach new spaces from waiting areas in banks and post offices to taxis and buses. Video screens became integral to sports and music events, relaying the performance to ever-larger crowds while collapsing the separation between the event and its representation. The blurring of the lines between actual event and televised drama was also evident in a number of media spectacles that fascinated American audiences in the decade: for instance, in CNN's broadcasting of live images of military strikes in Iraq during the Gulf War of 1991; in cult leader David Koresh's awareness of the cameras accompanying the FBI during the siege at Mount Carmel Center, Waco in 1993; or in the uncanny made-for-TV car chase between murder suspect O. J. Simpson and the Los Angeles Police Department the following year. Under such circumstances, it is not surprising that the nature of reality and the status of film and television images become central preoccupations of the decade.

The chapter will therefore deal with the major changes that took place in the industrial organisation of film and television, while also examining selected textual examples to see how they illustrate or reflect on wider social issues. First, though, we need to consider the part played by television in the national media spectacles of the 1990s.

Media Spectacles: The Gulf War

On 16 January 1991, with the deadline for compliance with United Nations resolutions expired, President Bush Sr appeared on television to 160 million viewers, the largest audience in American history, to announce the forthcoming attack on Saddam Hussein's Iraqi troops illegally occupying Kuwait. His words indicated the degree of symbolic investment in the war: 'I have told the American people before that this will not be another Vietnam, and I repeat this here tonight. Our troops will have the best possible support in the entire world and they will not be asked to fight with one hand tied behind their back.' Whatever the political objectives, one goal of the war would be the restoration of national pride, erasing the memory of a previous ignominious defeat. Thus it was, in Bruce Cumings's words, 'a war fought in the interest of forgetting', meant to address the problems of America's past as much as those of the present.[1] Tellingly, Bush also hinted that the war would involve a new approach to the media, whose coverage of US actions in Vietnam was thought to have played a part in generating popular opposition back home and hampering the war effort. If media organisations were not to tie the troops' hands this time, they would need to be integrated more effectively with official sources.

In the eyes of CNN reporter Peter Arnett, it was with the previous year's invasion of Panama that war first became a media event: news teams were embedded with troops, live feeds were introduced and audiences at home were treated to continuous coverage of a bizarre siege in which rock music blared through the night in an attempt to force the opera-loving General Noriega to surrender.[2] But it was in the Gulf that the integration of media and military reached such a level that the very reality of the event seemed in doubt. Public relations firm Hill and Knowlton was hired to muster support in the run-up to the war, and gained some notoriety for fabricating a story about Iraqi troops removing babies from incubators during their invasion of Kuwait. During the war itself the government attempted to streamline media representation of events with its own, operating a pool system for the press in Saudi Arabia and controlling access to information. Reporters from the more left-wing magazines such as *Harper's*, *Mother Jones* and *The Nation* were denied visas, and soldiers were prohibited from carrying their own camcorders. In one of the clearest demonstrations of media incorporation the US Air Force gave a ride in their new F-15E fighter plane to awestruck CNN anchorman David French two days into the war; this and many other moments of weapons fetishism such as shots of aircraft carrier landings or tank manoeuvres in the desert helped to ensure a correct emphasis on war as an instrumental process rather than a political activity or an ethical problem.[3]

The most iconic image of American force was not an object, however, but a field of vision. Seven per cent of the ordnance discharged at Iraqi forces and territory were so-called 'smart' weapons, equipped with remote guidance systems and nosecone-mounted cameras that tracked the flight of the missile up to the point of impact. The pictures they captured were broadcast to the public to demonstrate a precision not otherwise to be found in the bombs launched at Iraqi troops and cities (over 70 per cent of which missed their target), and showed just how much American audiences had become an object of military strategy. Eros and Thanatos combined, the images bypassed editorial controls and gave viewers thrilling access to what was literally the front line of conflict. At the same time, of course, what they could not show was the missile's impact. The aftermath of the strike remained mysterious and unreal, delicately veiled behind the grey screen of a break in transmission.

Figure 3.1 General Charles Horner displays videotape footage of a missile strike, at a military press conference in Riyadh, Saudi Arabia, 18 January 1991 (© Jacques Langevin/Sygma/Corbis).

Such weapons epitomised the visual culture of the Gulf War, offering a sense of power to television audiences while distracting them from the real effects of violence. The logic of denial was evident in other aspects of the conflict – in the romanticised naming of the campaigns 'Desert Shield' and 'Desert Storm', in the media blackout imposed during the attack on retreating Iraqis on 26 February 1991 and in euphemisms like 'friendly fire' and 'collateral damage'. For many commentators the central contradiction of the Gulf War was that its unprecedented visibility on television entailed specific kinds of blindness, undermining the traditional function of media in a democratic society as an instrument of the public sphere. As Elaine Scarry reflected the following year, the spectacle 'suspended, rather than incited, the population's capacity for deliberation and debate'.[4]

This is not to say that television stations were entirely in collusion with the Pentagon in the representation of the war, nor that manipulation of viewers' perceptions was total. Examining the spectacle more closely reveals that the media functioned as a separate system whose own economic, political and aesthetic demands occasionally brought it into line with state interests but which could also generate points of friction or resistance. As Daniel Hallin and Todd Gitlin noted, the costs of reporting in the Gulf required many stations to be reliant on military press briefings; commitments to local markets and communities often led to a bias towards patriotic rather than critical features, and the narrative drive of television news helped shape the war as a personal conflict between the two heads of state at the expense of political analysis.[5] But in other instances press coverage was less compromised and differences from the official story could emerge, as with CNN's pioneering decision to post correspondents 'behind enemy lines' in Iraq. Using new satellite phone equipment, Peter Arnett and John Holliman set up in a Baghdad hotel at the outbreak of the war and broadcast live commentaries during the aerial bombardment, later travelling under Iraqi supervision to sites of bomb damage. The reports they filed often provided valuable information to military commanders as well as the wider public, but their interactions with Iraqi authorities also provoked accusations of bias toward the enemy. Arnett notes in his 1994 memoir *Live From the Battlefield* that he was both congratulated for his contribution to the war effort and accused of treachery; he prided himself on his skills in evading Iraqi censors during the live chats with CNN anchors, while he was nevertheless suspected of falling victim to the Stockholm Syndrome, reproducing the views of his captors. After his televised interview with Saddam Hussein on 28 January 1991, both sides claimed a public relations victory: Saddam's prediction that the war would become 'the mother of all battles' was read as honourable defiance in Iraq and an expectation of mass Iraqi casualties in the United States.[6] Thus the application of new technology and the new methods of reporting that came with it generated radical ambiguities in the messages being broadcast.

On conclusion of hostilities the war's symbolic objectives appeared to have been accomplished: confirming the President's assurances, the *Wall Street Journal* duly celebrated on 1 March with the headline 'Victory in Gulf War Exorcises the Demons of the Vietnam Years'. But the spectacular nature of the war seemed to have created only an illusion of closure, and only for a short time. Politically, much was unresolved: Saddam remained in power in Iraq, able to construe himself as an undefeated Arab leader who dared challenge the West; the country's victimised populations of Kurds and Shiites were now more at threat than ever after rising up to find themselves bereft of foreign support; and hopes for greater stability in relations between Israel and Palestine had been obstructed by the entanglement of the two crises. In subsequent years the conflict passed into popular memory not as a turning point in America's military history but as a war that was so overdetermined by its media representations that it never seemed fully real. Jean Baudrillard's famous proposition that the Gulf War 'did not take place'[7] was echoed in novels such as James Chapman's *Glass (Pray the Electrons Back to Sand)* (1995) and films such as *Three Kings* (1999), where soldiers are shown attempting to live out Hollywood fantasies, making deals with television reporters and perplexed by the absence of combat. 'Are we shooting people or what?' asks one in the very first line.

Three Kings is notable for its use of a wide repertoire of visual styles to connote the different orders of representation that mediated the actuality of the war: hand-held camera to signify documentary authenticity, fast and slow motion to undermine claims to realism, still photographs to evoke personal memories or the historical record. The film also makes use of the 'bullet time' special effect, commonly known from *The Matrix* of the same year, in which the action is slowed to follow the progress of a speeding bullet. If this effect recalls the perspective of the missile nosecone camera, then it shows how military modes of vision feed into popular culture, vividly illustrating Paul Virilio's argument that warfare and cinema have shared an intimate relationship ever since the invention of serial photography in the late nineteenth century.[8] But, in what are perhaps the film's signature sequences, the film continues where the missile camera stops, following the bullet as it pierces the human body and lodges in a mass of organs and tissue. At this point, whatever claim the technique may have to penetrate the invisibility of the war in the name of the real, showing the death that never appeared on television screens, is offset by the viewer's assurance that this can only be a simulation after all, a clever piece of cinematic illusion. In this way the troubling memory of the war's scandalous television images is smoothed away and a form of closure is achieved.

Spectacles of Race

If the Gulf War offered Americans the chance of a nationally unifying spectacle (in which even the expression of opposition to the war could be taken as evidence of democratic freedoms), the domestic media spectacles of the 1990s had the opposite effect, opening up deep rifts between Americans along lines of race, class and gender that the immense amount of coverage and discussion they received failed to resolve. In the hearings that followed Anita Hill's accusation of harassment against Supreme Court nominee Clarence Thomas, the riots provoked by the acquittal of Los Angeles police officers tried for beating motorist Rodney King, and the trial of O. J. Simpson for the murders of Nicole Brown Simpson and Ron Goodman, what was exposed on television screens was the nation's continuing failure to address the problems of racial inequality. All three incidents would become sites of struggle over the significance of race and the legacy of the race-sensitive reforms of the 1960s. But what also makes them interesting is the special role television played in structuring the meaning of the events: the rise of surveillance, televised court proceedings and the availability of video technology to private individuals made them 'happen' as spectacles, and highlighted the complex relationship between law, media and the public sphere.

The Hill-Thomas confrontation began when a report produced for Thomas's nomination process was leaked to the press and Hill was called to testify at a televised hearing on 11 October 1991. Ten years previously she had joined Thomas's team as a legal advisor at the Equal Employment Opportunity Commission, where she alleged sexual harassment had taken place. Not long after the conclusion of the Gulf War, news networks welcomed the opportunity to recover some of the ground lost to CNN and covered the hearings in meticulous detail. Thomas was a conservative choice and his nomination provoked a number of liberal groups who worried about his opposition to affirmative action and abortion rights, but what made the event so highly charged was the fact that both participants were African American. This doubled the stakes, since what was at issue was not just the significance of race in the Supreme Court but also the visibility of sexual injury amongst black women.

In an op-ed for the *New York Times* on the eve of the Senate's vote, sociologist Orlando Patterson sided with Thomas and celebrated the dispute as a sign of progress, a 'ritual of inclusion' which normalised conflicts between African Americans and allowed black and white spectators to engage in the issues across racial lines.[9] But for others it was a more lurid affair that paraded stereotypes of black sexuality and exposed irreconcilable conflicts between race and gender politics. Reports of Thomas's use of pornography were met with counter-accusations that Hill was an erotomaniac, and while Thomas attempted to portray himself as an ordinary family man Hill found herself demonised as an unfeeling and unmarriageable career woman. Then, in one of the decisive moves in the dispute, Thomas denounced the investigation as 'a high-tech lynching for uppity blacks who in any way deign to think for themselves'. The remark was a masterstroke in that it intimidated the Senate committee – none of whom wished to bear comparison with a lynch mob – and at the same time undermined Hill's authority, giving her no position from which to claim the right to speak. As many commentators pointed out, associating the hearings with lynching imposed an image of racial victimisation within which the suffering of black women had no place; Hill could only be cast as the *white* false accuser in the story. For Critical Race theorists – part of an intellectual movement that formed in response to the crises of race at the beginning of the decade – what happened to Hill was only one example of the way that black women's experience was repeatedly eclipsed in American culture, where feminist and anti-racist politics tended to rely on dominant identity positions that neglected 'intersectional' experiences of oppression.[10]

When Thomas was eventually confirmed to the Supreme Court on 15 October it was by a narrow margin in the Senate but with a more decisive majority of support amongst African Americans in the polls. Given his well-publicised lack of sympathy with African Americans as a political constituency (see his remarks quoted in the Introduction), such backing was a measure of the degree of investment in symbols of black achievement in the difficult climate of the early 1990s. For historian Manning Marable this was a critical moment in racial politics, when growing class differences and fading memories of the civil rights movement meant that solidarity amongst black Americans was on the wane. Since a collective experience of racial identity was harder to sustain, the emphasis was shifting to role models and images of integration, as if these could carry the burden of convincing Americans that inequalities no longer existed.[11]

If this explains why many black Americans supported Thomas apparently against their own interests, it also provides a context for the traumas of the Rodney King beating and the O. J. Simpson trial, both of which showed how flimsy the rhetoric of overcoming inequality had become. Simpson was in many respects the poster boy for an integrated society, and his downfall saw the return of racist currents in American culture that the myth had hitherto repressed. And the images that Americans saw on their screens on 4 March 1991, showing home-video footage of a man being severely beaten by police on the road two nights before, seemed uncomfortably reminiscent of a pre-civil rights era. Though outrage against the beatings was instantaneous, it took almost a year for the officers involved to stand trial. The California Court of Appeals controversially changed the venue from Los Angeles County to Simi Valley, a predominantly middle-class and white district home to many LAPD officers, and from whose population the court was unable to field a single African American in the jury. During the trial revelations of racist remarks among police

Figure 3.2 George Holliday's video footage of Los Angeles police officers beating Rodney King, 3 March 1991 (© CNN/Getty Images).

officers strengthened suspicions that racism had become institution-alised in the police force, and when the four defendants were finally acquitted of all charges the conclusion that minorities were now utterly estranged from justice was inescapable. On 29 April 1992, only two hours after the verdict was announced, riots spread throughout Los Angeles that were to last six days and cause more fatalities than any instance of civil unrest since the New York Draft Riots of 1863.

The Los Angeles riots exposed the extent to which urban poverty was stratified according to race, even as politicians in the run-up to the presidential elections tried to place the blame on a lack of responsibil-ity amongst the poor or on the usual culprits of moral decline, as with a cross-party campaign led by Dan Quayle and Tipper Gore to indict rapper Ice-T over the song 'Cop Killer'. In particular, what political and media discourse seemed unable to represent was the complex multiracial and interracial nature of the unrest: incidents were not limited to one area but spread across neighbourhoods from Watts and South Central towards Hollywood, affecting black, Mexican, Central American and Korean communities; arrest figures revealed that more Latinos were involved than African Americans; truces amongst black and Chicano gangs and the collective targeting of Korean stores

indicated that economic class played a significant part in the antago-
nisms between racial groups. Media coverage that referred to the
Watts riots of 1965, focused on violence in black popular culture,
or replayed images of black youths attacking a white truck driver
reduced the riots to a recurrence of a long-established (and implicitly
insuperable) opposition between black and white, and proved unable
to acknowledge the new conditions of a multicultural America.

Watching the Watchmen: the Rodney King video

George Holliday's recording of LAPD officers beating motorist Rodney
King on 3 March 1991 is one of the most consequential pieces of home
video footage to date, and can be seen as a forerunner to the counter-
surveillance that was to become a key tactic of political activists and
grassroots news movements. Not only did it promise to expose the racist
police treatment that many African Americans experienced; it also offered
a glimpse of the power that could be retrieved by citizens who turned a
watchful eye back on the authorities.

How, then, did the Simi Valley jury manage to acquit the accused police
officers? Critics attributed the verdict to a predominantly white and middle-
class jury more predisposed to accept the use of force, or to the prosecution's failure to give sufficient weight to the racist abuse and physical harm
that King suffered; some suggested that the prosecuting attorneys were
reluctant to convict members of a police force they had to work with from
day to day. But the possibility of reading the videotape differently lies at
the heart of the trial's enigma and outrage: fifty-six blows in eighty-one
seconds, most of which were dealt while King was lying down on the
ground – how could this be anything other than brutality?

'We got the jurors to look at the case not from the eye of the camera
. . . but from the eyes of the officers,' remarked defence attorney Michael
Stone.[12] This involved questioning the documentary status of the images
themselves, exposing and subverting the codes that allowed them to be
read as truth. Where the prosecution played the tape in its entirety, implying that it stood as testimony in its own right, the defence subjected it to
extended scrutiny, replaying it to the jury to deaden the shock of the violence, and then slowing it down or freeze-framing for a dissection of each
movement and gesture. At this level the sequence of cause and effect was
so stretched that any impact was hard to recognise as such, and it could
now be claimed that the relations of force were reversed, making King the
aggressor. Thus Stone claimed at one point, with skilful abuse of syntax,
'In the hundredths of a second between this photograph and this one, Mr
King is again coming up off the ground, and he charges Officer Powell.'[13] As
Marita Sturken points out, both interpretations are validated by appealing
to certain generic conventions: the defence relied on video realism's look of

authenticity, created by the shaky camera, poor focus and low-grade image; the prosecution called upon a 'clinical gaze', with its own history dating back to nineteenth-century chronophotography, to reveal a truth hidden by the passage of time.[14] But we should also note that it is in the corruption of video into photograph that the expert opinion supplants the amateur testimony, allowing the 'official' viewpoint to prevail over the citizen's. The separation of the image from its temporality is Stone's greatest trick, since it enacts nothing less than the isolation of the event from the historical contexts that made it meaningful as a watershed moment in race relations in America.

Those histories were not just the abandonment of the urban poor over the 1970s and 1980s, nor the lamentable record of the LAPD under its chief Daryl Gates (who had once suggested that blacks were more likely to die in choke-holds because their arteries were inferior to those of 'normal people'), but also the racial politics of the so-called War on Drugs that framed the officers' fears that King was out of control on PCP, and even the recent police action of the Gulf War. The scandal of Holliday's footage was the way it called to account those occasions where violence was committed in the name of maintaining order, and threw into relief television's complicity in the logic of policing in the conflict of the previous year.[15]

If the video meant the interruption of reality into the broadcast, normal service was quickly resumed. As rioting spread through Los Angeles Mayor Tom Bradley petitioned NBC's local station Channel 4 to show the final episode of The Cosby Show, landmark of liberal black programming, rather than live coverage of the unrest. Soon after, the LAPD commissioned its own documentary series LAPD: Life on the Beat to repair its public image. Video cameras were installed on the dashboards of police cars, not just for the purpose of gathering evidence but also to encourage discipline amongst the officers themselves; this would of course provide the lucrative footage for future clips shows such as Police! Camera! Action![16] Thus the apparatus of television was mobilised once again to ensure a seamless delivery of the scripts of policing, civil order and race.

Media theorists have long been aware of the dialectic of rupture and flow in television. Since the experience of constant interruption (ad breaks, channel hopping) becomes its own continuity, eventfulness must always appear as a further interruption, with ever-diminishing returns: thus the newsflash is degraded into rolling coverage that itself needs to be interrupted by another newsflash from elsewhere; thus the regular scheduling of entertainment broadcasting falls victim to the compulsion to produce the 'special event', the 'must-see' episode. This dialectic became evident in the spectacle of the King incident, where politics became a matter of resisting the media's drive towards closure. Senator Bill Bradley's remarkable speech to the House on the day after the verdict was one such instance: taking a fistful of pencils, he banged the podium fifty-six times, shouting 'pow!' with each blow, in an attempt to return the reality of pain to the now over-familiar images of violence. In a similar way, the riots can be seen as a disorganised but collective attempt to insist upon the persistent rupture of race in the fabric of the nation.

In 1994, the arrest of O. J. Simpson on a double-murder charge gave Americans another spectacle of race. Media interest was phenomenal: over its nine months' duration the trial received more coverage on network news than the Bosnian War and the Oklahoma City bombing combined, making stars of the judge and jury as well as the accused. When the verdict was finally announced on 3 October 1995, 42 per cent of American homes were tuned in. As George Lipsitz noted, what made the story such a sensation was its congruence with central elements of television discourse. Simpson's connection with advertising and conspicuous consumption of luxury items (Rockingham houses, leather gloves, Bruno Magli shoes, Ford Broncos) 'allowed journalists to report the news and talk about shopping at the same time'; details of drug use, sexual promiscuity and violence gave viewers the opportunity to enjoy the usual prurient thrills of television in a more legitimate context, while the main theme of the tragic destruction of an ideal middle-class family, central to television ideology, led inevitably to a sense of a nation in crisis.[17] But equally significant was the way that the case helped to establish live coverage of criminal trials as a key element of television programming.

Television cameras had been permitted in courtrooms since 1981, following a Supreme Court judgment that they did not necessarily obstruct due process and could in some instances aid public understanding of the law.[18] Ten years later, Steve Brill's cable channel Court TV went on air, featuring live coverage of selected trials. Brill shared the idealism of the Supreme Court, believing that television could 'bring back to the people' what had become an arcane profession priced beyond the reach of many Americans. At the same time, of course, the televised trials provided unscripted and therefore cheap drama – in many respects a precursor to the incipient reality TV genre. Restrictions in the 1981 ruling had stipulated that there should be no more than one camera and one technician, and no additional lighting or sound recording facilities: what resulted was a kind of television *vérité* whose primitive look added to its realism. Journalist Jeff Goodell described the viewing experience as follows: 'You get hooked on Court TV because of the medium. The bad lighting, the bad sound. The slow pan and focus of the single camera . . . The closer you look, the more nuance is revealed. The nervous tick of a defence witness. The finger-tapping of a judge. Nothing escapes notice. In the courtroom, the camera becomes the unblinking eye of God.'[19]

Goodell's celebration of a world re-enchanted by the continuous gaze of a camera places Court TV in an interesting lineage which includes the unedited films of Andy Warhol such as *Sleep* (1963) or *Empire* (1964), while also marking the arrival of surveillance as a new televisual style. The assumption that television could be a transparent medium offering direct access to truth was a key part of the appeal of trial coverage, and it was shared by Judge Ito when he ruled in favour of cameras at the Simpson trial:

> The problem with not having a camera is that one must trust the evaluation and analysis of a reporter who is telling you what occurred in the courtroom . . . Whereas if you have a camera in the courtroom, there is no filtering. What you see is what's there.[20]

Such an idea was soon discredited by the excesses that followed, as the extraordinary scrutiny given to the trial seemed to render it only more opaque. Were Americans watching something of real social significance, or gorging on trivia and sensationalism? Was this the exemplary conduct of a legal system forced to acquit where the evidence could not overcome reasonable doubt, or an illustration of a different standard of justice for the wealthy and famous? Was it yet another case of racial victimisation, or did race have nothing to do with it?

Televising the law had other important consequences for the future of television in the way that it disciplined audiences and created new kinds of viewing pleasures. If trial coverage made aspects of the judicial process more accessible to the public, it also put viewers in a special position from which to judge proceedings. In the aesthetics of Court TV, viewers are encouraged to adopt the position of jurors – an illusion sustained by the fact that filming of the jury itself is prohibited – while at the same time they have a greater knowledge of the trial, not only through general consumption of media coverage but also in the ability to see parts of the process that the jury cannot, such as decisions over the admissibility of evidence or the selection of the jury itself. Hence they become a superior kind of jury, flattered that their views are authoritative even as they displace the idea of the jury as a 'discursive community', representing the diverse values of a society and reaching a judgment through dialogue. In coming years television networks would learn how to cultivate and capitalise on this new relationship with audiences, making telephone voting and the judging of game-show contestants an integral part of television watching.

Post-cinema and New Independents

The conglomeration of entertainment industries that had such an impact on popular music would also come to transform cinema in the 1990s. By the end of the century the field was dominated by huge media companies spanning film studios and theatres, television and radio stations, record labels, publishing, computer games, sports teams, retail outlets and theme parks. The goal of the mergers and acquisitions was 'synergy': integration across different sectors would allow a company to capitalise several times over on the same product and minimise risk in increasingly volatile markets. Thus Sony's purchase of Columbia-Tristar Pictures in 1989 added content to its hardware manufacturing business and helped protect against the kind of disaster it suffered when its Betamax video format lost the battle with VHS in the 1980s. The deal also gave Sony access to a chain of theatres across North America and Europe and a share of national television network CBS, ensuring a broad and repeated distribution for its products. Following suit, the merger of Time International and Warner Brothers brought together film production, cable television channels (HBO, Cinemax) and a range of magazines (*Time*, *People*, *Sports Illustrated*): this was expanded with the acquisition of Turner Broadcasting in 1996, bringing with it the New Line studio and Castle Rock production companies and, most importantly, the libraries of MGM, RKO and Hanna-Barbera. Time-Warner could therefore draw on a rich source of old titles for resale as Hollywood classics while its ownership of different outlets gave it a large range of opportunities for cross-promotion.

In 1990 Japanese electronics giant Matsushita took over MCA-Universal Studios, though it would struggle in the industry and later sell to Canadian drinks corporation Seagram; Seagram would pass Universal on to French-owned Vivendi by the end of the decade. Paramount Pictures was acquired by Viacom in 1994, which also bought Blockbuster entertainment to create synergies between studios, video rental and proprietary cable channels such as Showtime and The Movie Channel. Viacom would go on to merge with broadcast network CBS in 2000 to form a company with an extensive reach in film, television and music production. Of all the major producers of motion pictures, only one did not change hands in this period: Walt Disney Pictures remained under the control of the Disney Corporation, expanding from a relatively minor operation in a company that focused on theme parks and merchandise to take an increasingly central role in the business. Disney had created Touchstone and Hollywood Pictures in the 1980s to allow it to produce films for adult audiences without damaging the brand, but its acquisition of independent distributor Miramax in 1993 and broad-casting/publishing company Capital Cities/ABC in 1996 consolidated its position as one of the five new media conglomerates.

Acquisitions and mergers involving the major motion picture studios, 1985–2001

1985	Twentieth Century Fox bought by News Corporation
1986	Turner Broadcasting Systems buys libraries of MGM/United Artists
1986	Columbia Pictures bought by Sony; Warner Bros. becomes studio division within newly merged Time-Warner Inc
1990	Universal Pictures acquired by Matsushita in purchase of MCA-Universal
1992	MGM/UA sold to French bank Crédit Lyonnais
1993	Disney buys Miramax
1994	Paramount Pictures bought by Viacom Inc.
1995	Matsushita sells 80 per cent stake in MCA-Universal to Seagram Co.; foundation of new studio Dreamworks SKG
1996	Disney buys Capital Cities/ABC; Time-Warner merges with Turner Broadcasting
1999	Viacom expands with acquisition of CBS
2000	Universal under ownership of Vivendi after purchase of Seagram
2001	Merger of Time-Warner and America Online

Conglomeration affected not just the production of films but also their content, most of all in the high-budget blockbusters or 'event movies' designed to generate enough revenue to cover losses on other projects. What made these successful was not the total of box-office receipts but the ability to generate income in ancillary markets. Michael Eisner explained the process in his annual report for Disney in 1993:

Synergy: the inspiration of a classic movie like *Aladdin* to move the entire Disney Company to new heights of co-operative energy. In one year, *Aladdin* inspired thousands of new products in every conceiv-able category including genie and camel dolls and an exciting interac-tive video game for Sega Genesis, a dramatic new ice show touring the world, and major new parades and characters at Disney parks.[21]

The following year *The Lion King* grossed nearly $300 million for Disney in cinemas alone but went on to earn over a billion dollars in subsequent manifestations on video, DVD and Broadway, becoming one of the most lucrative animated films of all time. Even a relative failure of a movie like *Godzilla* (1998), whose audiences plummeted soon after release, was just one part of a franchise including toys, books, games and cartoons which eventually reaped profits in excess of $350 million. Given that it was more important for event movies such as these to perform in secondary spin-off markets, evaluating them as films seems quite beside the point.

The economic imperatives of cinema in an age of conglomeration often showed through in the films themselves, leaving many of the movies of the 1990s with a kind of disrupted textuality – those moments where the film's universe is intruded upon by product placement, a star's catchphrase or a sequence promoting the CD soundtrack, as well as the more obvious cases where a conclusion is contrived to make way for a sequel. Arnold Schwarzenegger's line 'I'll be back' from *Terminator 2* (1991) is a good example of one of these textual intrusions: although it has a narrative justification, its primary function is to circulate in popular conversation outside the cinema as a promotional tool. A more sophisticated example comes from *Jurassic Park* (1993), in a scene that takes place in the theme park's gift shop, where the camera passes slowly across the goods for sale. Here, for the first time, merchandise appears within the film world itself, collapsing the distinction between primary and secondary commodity, original event and souvenir. The film even thematises this move, since it is after all the commercial manifestation of cloning: if the dinosaurs are generated from samples of DNA, the film and its merchandise are also replicated from a code – the 'Jurassic Park' concept. A further incarnation of this code is the theme park ride at Universal Studios, where the folding of actuality into fiction is repeated and the branded experience comes full circle. In the recreation of pre-history the film expresses one of Hollywood's enduring aims to bring the past to life, to make real a 'lost world'; at Universal Studios Theme Parks the ride brings the film to life, allowing visitors to realise it as a personal experience. Thus 'Jurassic Park' as a brand epitomises the logic of the blockbuster in its drive towards totalisation: past and future are collapsed onto each other in the space of the film, while the film itself spills over its own textual limits into other aspects of everyday life.

Paradoxically, the era of conglomeration was also the period in which a new independent American cinema flourished. The reasons

Figure 3.3 Dinosaur meets clone in *Jurassic Park* (Steven Spielberg, Universal, 1993) (© Amblin/ Universal/The Kobal Collection).

behind its emergence are complex, but in many respects it was a reaction against conservative trends within Hollywood in the 1980s: filmmakers whose ambitions did not sit firmly within the mainstream were forced to look elsewhere for support, and audiences increasingly dissatisfied with the formulaic pictures issuing from the major studios began to show up as potential new markets. At the same time, home video had reached such a level of penetration (almost three-quarters of American households by 1989) that new material was needed to meet demand. Video companies began to invest in production, while further sources of capital were opened up by financial deregulation under Reagan.[22] Just as important to the growth of an independent scene was the establishment of a dedicated distribution system through which new films could reach their audiences. In Peter Biskind's account, *Down and Dirty Pictures* (2004), the main characters in the story are Robert Redford, whose Sundance Institute took over the ailing US Film Festival in 1984, and Bob and Harvey Weinstein, founders of distribution company Miramax. Over the course of the decade the Sundance Festival was to become one of the main events in the independent calendar, functioning as a showcase for new works. Miramax, meanwhile, rapidly gained a reputation for picking up specialist pictures and selling them to mainstream audiences. Given the low budgets of many such projects, the profits that could be made were phenomenal: Steven Soderberg's *sex, lies and videotape*, for example, cost the Weinsteins $2 million for theatre rights alone but went on to take $25 million at the American box office in 1989 and a further $30 million abroad. In 1993 they paid $1.5 million for rights to Irish director Neil Jordan's *The Crying Game* and received a quarter of its record $62.5 million gross, but the most spectacular earnings came from *Pulp Fiction* (1994), which cost a mere $8.5 million to produce and recouped over $100 million in the United States and twice as much again overseas.[23]

What counts as 'independent' in these circumstances is by no means clear-cut. An independent film may be defined in terms of finance (receiving the majority of its funding from sources other than the major studios); budget (made for a relatively small sum, such as $20 million or less); aesthetic strategies (using unconventional approaches to narrative, cinematography, picture quality or casting, or distinguishing itself from the mainstream by other means) or ideological position (foregrounding marginalised perspectives or addressing issues that Hollywood would be reluctant to touch). It is certainly true that distance from the majors, low budgets and the label of independence allows a degree of autonomy for producers and helps to bring more idiosyncratic directorial visions to the screen – as the decidedly un-Hollywood works of Todd Solondz attest (see the following Case Study) – but at the same time the story of the independent scene in the 1990s was one of progressive incorporation, when the boundaries between the two sectors were increasingly blurred. Sundance turned from festival to fair, attracting the attentions of the major companies and pushing unestablished film-makers to the sidelines; Miramax and rival distributor New Line were bought by Disney and Turner Broadcasting in 1993, and major studios created their own 'indie' divisions such as Sony Pictures Classics in 1992, Fox Searchlight (1994) and Paramount Classics (1998). The involvement of the majors inevitably led to price inflation, greater financial investment and a more cautious approach to risk. By the end of the decade independent cinema was governed by similar principles to mainstream Hollywood and 'indie' was

Figure 3.4 John Travolta and Uma Thurman in *Pulp Fiction* (Quentin Tarantino, Miramax, 1994) (© Miramax/Buena Vista/The Kobal Collection).

arguably little more than a means of differentiating a certain kind of product in a wider market.

Pulp Fiction stands out as one of the landmarks of independent cinema in the era, epitomising the movement's stylistic self-confidence as well as its crossover commercial potential. Its director Quentin Tarantino became the darling of the industry not only because of his evident creative talent and his genuine, almost grateful embrace of celebrity but because he embodied the sensibility of the fan: his prodigious knowledge of film, lack of discrimination between high and low, and delight in the most basic elements of screen spectacle (suspense, action sequences and violence) was a reminder of what it might mean to love cinema again. As Biskind points out, what was unique about the new generation of film-makers was their familiarity with film history through video: growing up watching films at home meant that tastes could be formed more freely, unrestricted by theatre or television schedules and without the mediation of the high priests of cinema at film school or in the press.[24] The outcome was work like Tarantino's, which paid homage to American genre fodder as sincerely as it exploited European arthouse techniques. Thus *Pulp Fiction* takes stock characters from noir and crime thrillers (hapless hitmen, a gangster's bored girlfriend, a boxer throwing his last fight) but retells the stories in unconventional ways, introducing incongruous non-generic dialogue, placing scenes out of chronological sequence or breaking the fourth wall (as when the heroine draws a dotted line on the screen's surface). To associate these techniques with the avant-garde tactic of defamiliarisation, as if the aim were to disrupt the audience's easy consumption of mass culture, would nevertheless be a mistake. Rather than open up a critical perspective, such features are there primarily to signify sophistication and flatter audiences on their movie literacy. When the two lead characters dance in a nightclub, it is a key scene not because it marks a significant development in their relationship but because the audience is given a moment to enjoy Uma Thurman and John Travolta performing together, unencumbered by their fictional roles. Whether it recalls the musical sequences in Jean-Luc Godard films or the dancing in Travolta's seventies disco blockbuster *Saturday Night Fever*, the primary purpose is to gratify spectators' personal film memories.

Happiness (Todd Solondz, 1998)

Todd Solondz is one of the more resolutely leftfield of directors in contemporary Hollywood cinema, with a distinctive style and subject matter. His films, from *Welcome to the Dollhouse* (1995) to *Palindromes* (2005), are cautionary tales of suburban life featuring teenagers and misfits struggling to come to terms with their world. More expressionist than realist, his characters hark back to the grotesques of Sherwood Anderson's short-story cycle *Winesburg, Ohio* (1919): they are victims of their own fantasies or the expectations of others. But we should be wary of seeing Solondz as an 'independent' director operating outside the constraints of mainstream Hollywood: as the story behind the release of *Happiness* shows, small production companies are not sufficiently autonomous, and the large conglomerates that sponsor them too vulnerable to multiple interests to foster the individual creativity and artistic freedom that the term implies.

American distributors had initially been reluctant to fund the film because it contained, among other things, a storyline concerning paedophilia, and it was only when the script was received enthusiastically by German and Italian companies at Cannes that producers Good Machine were able to secure a deal with October Films, a subsidiary of Universal Studios. This became problematic when the film's content became known to Universal's owner Seagram, which at the time was under pressure from shareholders for its decision to move into entertainment and worried about demands for tighter regulation in the drinks industry, its major concern. Seagram's dilemma was that backing a controversial film could inspire a consumer boycott, but selling it on would both admit bad business and offer an easy public relations victory to whoever 'rescued' it. The solution was to allow Universal to pay Good Machine to distribute the film itself: thus the film ironically achieved a level of financial control beyond most low-budget Hollywood productions, though its 'indie' status was a purely simulated one.

What makes *Happiness* so challenging is that it resists the hysterical representation of paedophilia at a moment when the paedophile had become a new kind of folk devil in the mass media. Instead, it interrogates sexual perversity as part of a wider spectrum of desires and pleasures that threaten to overwhelm American life. As producer James Schamus claimed, 'The average American has too much desire to know what to do with, and it is in the disposition of this excess desire, in the inability of the social structure to absorb it properly, that trouble starts in suburbia. And that's what *Happiness* is about.'[28] Through multiple storylines revolving around the lives of three sisters, the film satirises the most common conceptions of happiness: fulfilment through family (a mother who repeats 'I have it all' with barely suppressed resentment throughout), creative expression (a novelist who longs for rape or some other trauma to make her writing more authentic) and true love (the younger sister, a doomed innocent, who insists on her romantic fantasies of embracing the immigrant even as he exploits her). The story of the psychiatrist who is consumed by his craving for teenage boys and eventually rapes his son's schoolfriends is no different in kind, but serves to show just how wrong the pursuit of happiness defined solely in terms of individual desire can go.

In the movie's most extraordinary scene, the son confronts the father after his arrest with the one truly unspeakable question: *what was it like?* Here the film abandons the customary narrative of child abuse (as well as, one imagines, a realist depiction of police procedures) to make the abuser speak. In replying, the father is obliged to acknowledge not the moral law – which is never in dispute – but the scandalous pleasure of the act itself: 'It was – great . . .' This irruption of obscenity is so severe that it threatens to tear a hole in the entire film, making it hard for the viewer to recover a comic or satirical perspective in the face of such a horror. But Solondz insists on keeping the father talking, prompted by his son's innocent enquiries, and in doing so he is forced to confront the extent of his desire: assuring the boy he will not be raped in turn, the father can only utter, pathetically, 'I'd jerk off instead.' If the source of the panic over paedophilia derives from the idea of a desire that knows no bounds, then this is a remarkable and ultimately affirmative image of the battle for self-control.

In fact, it is masturbation that is the broader motif of *Happiness* – presented as a pathology in the story of a nuisance telephone caller who harasses two of the sisters, but also as a normal part of sexual development for the psychiatrist's son, whose final success in his attempts provides the film with its comic climax. Solondz's aim here is not to condemn autoeroticism outright, but to thematise a tendency towards solipsism in American life as a whole. For if masturbation has become normalised in recent decades as a form of sexual exploration and emancipation (through feminist reclamations of the 'right to pleasure'), it also epitomises the turn in western culture towards technologies of the self, and the redescription of pleasure and freedom as private, individualised goals. Jean Baudrillard, among others, has theorised this shift not just as an abandonment of collective political projects but as a drift towards identity and homogeneity. The revolutions in politics, science and culture undertaken in the name of liberation have resulted, he says, in a sterile existence in which people are free only to reproduce themselves: 'Our society is entirely dedicated to neutralising otherness, to destroying the other as a natural point of reference in a vast flood of aseptic communication and interaction, of illusory exchange and contact . . . No longer the hell of other people, but the hell of the same.'[29] The exclusion of otherness is dramatised in *Happiness* in numerous ways: the nuisance caller unable to speak to his victim in person, the writer unable to imagine material outside herself or the glutton who is disgusted by sex ('the thought of someone inside me . . .').

Happiness is, therefore, a critique of the forms of emancipation inherited from the 1960s, suggesting that the enhanced prospects for happiness in contemporary America have ultimately come at the expense of a diverse and differentiated social life. The rhetoric of this new sensibility, with its aggressive inclusiveness that serves to mask the divisions it creates, is perfectly captured in the final exchange between the writer and her younger sister: 'I'm not laughing at you, I'm laughing with you.' 'But I'm not laughing . . .' The lines also convey the spirit of Solondz's satire which, though comic, refuses comic resolution.

Given a thoroughly incorporated cinema, where at one end of the scale movie-making was driven wholly by marketing initiatives or technology-driven spectacle and at the other end opportunities for genuinely alternative visions were drastically limited, it was perhaps inevitable that a mood of angry disappointment would pervade film criticism on the eve of the millennium. In 1996, a hundred years after the Lumière brothers showed moving pictures to the first paying audiences, Susan Sontag declared that cinema as a cultural force was dead, killed by its over-industrialisation: 'The reduction of cinema to assaultive images, and the unprincipled manipulation of images . . . to make them more attention-grabbing, has produced a disincarnated, lightweight cinema that doesn't demand anyone's full attention.'[25] In part, the idea of the demise of cinema was simply a cry of frustration at the poor quality of Hollywood's output: here Jeffrey Sconce has recently produced an interesting thesis that the revival of interest in trash culture, the celebration of second-rate B-movie directors like Ed Wood (see Tim Burton's film of 1994) and the profile given to a cinema of 'negative guarantees' (the films you go to see in the full knowledge they will be terrible) all testify to a new sensibility amongst audiences whose only option is to celebrate cinema's failure rather than continue to be duped by the industry into thinking that its products constitute entertainment.[26] But the end of cinema also meant something in a Hegelian sense: the end of its internal aesthetic development and the severing of its relationship with history. For the theorists of 'post-cinema', the historical formation that had positioned film as the pre-eminent modern art form was over: going to the pictures was no longer the centre of the rituals of mass entertainment, and the claim it once had as a site of social interaction and source of public meaning was now derelict.[27]

Sean Cubitt designates the primary type of film for this era 'neobaroque': technically excellent but more involved with the architecture of a separate universe than with the concerns of the present day. In neobaroque cinema, narrative is reduced to pattern; characters act out preordained destinies rather than confront real situations or experience uncertainty in the face of what might be possible: hence the compulsively repetitive time of *Groundhog Day* (1993) or the prevalent use of retrospective structures in films like *The Usual Suspects* (1995), *Snake Eyes* (1998) and *Memento* (2000), where much of the action consists of flashbacks contextualising the opening sequence. For Cubitt, the construction of autonomous worlds whose time bears no relation to our own is the expression of a desire to escape politics, to live as if all social and ideological conflicts have been transcended or rendered obsolete: thus 'a specific task of the Hollywood baroque is to bring wholeness, a healed and healing world that runs against the acknowledgement of difference'.[30]

A good example of the kind of cinema that Cubitt is describing is James Cameron's *Titanic* (1997), the film that marked the culmination of the blockbuster in the period. At $200 million it was the most costly moving picture in history: parent studio Paramount capped its spending at $60 million, and work on the film only proceeded after Fox stepped in to provide assurances it would fund completion in exchange for international distribution rights. The gamble seemed extraordinarily risky but paid off when the film grossed almost half a billion dollars in the United States and $1.2 billion in the rest of the world. Along with his contemporary Steven Spielberg, Cameron exemplified the way that the director had evolved into a kind of corporate auteur, where the name signified not so much an individual style or ideological vision but an industrial force, capable of turning large expenditure into larger profits. Interestingly, both directors switched between historical and science fiction subjects in the 1990s – Cameron having made the first two *Terminator* films and *The Abyss* (1989), while Spielberg moved from *Jurassic Park* to *Schindler's List* (1993), *Amistad* (1997) and *Saving Private Ryan* (1998) before returning to science fiction in the new millennium with *AI* (2001) and *Minority Report* (2002) – suggesting that a similar mode of production applies in the two genres. Certainly the representation of the past and of the future both play on the spectacle of totally realised alternative worlds, and both tend to fetishise material details in the *mise en scène* at the expense of narrative. Ideologically, too, they are two sides of the same coin: the science fiction movie seeking a form of reconciliation with a threatening future – the apocalypse ultimately deferred, humanity reaffirmed – and the history film seeking redemption from the past, overcoming trauma by finding the proper form of narrative closure. *Titanic* achieves its own resolution by means of a rich girl/poor boy romance which escapes cliché only by the sheer brazenness of its execution.

The story of the Titanic was of course 'pre-sold' in the sense that it had commanded an enduring fascination both on and off screen ever since the disaster, and it came packaged with a moral so well known that there would be little for audiences to do other than sit back and watch the spectacle unfold. The irony was that the tale of humanity overreaching itself in its hubris was in danger of being played out in production: not only did it involve several dives to film the wreck itself but also the construction of the largest offshore filming tank ever built, where a three-quarter scale model of the ship was equipped with a hydraulic system to ensure it would sink in a manner that resembled the real incident. In many respects the production – with its colossal budget, set construction, archival work, debates over historical accuracy and numerous filming difficulties – is the principal drama of *Titanic*, with the film itself subordinated to the status of documentation (the same may also be said of all those films in the category of 'troubled production', such as Kevin Costner's *Waterworld* of 1995, which audiences go to see primarily because of the story of their making). But if the scale of production is a monument to the contemporary desire for the perfect simulation, the movie's neobaroque qualities become evident in the transition between the time of the present (a salvage operation working on the wreck) and the time of the story, where realism cannot be allowed to get in the way of spectacle. When, at the beginning of the film, the salvage submersible explores the wreck to show us the cabin where the romance begins and ends, it does so without raising any of the silt that would spoil the view; when the surviving lover returns to the site to begin telling her story, it is without a trace of trauma or anxiety.

Figure 3.5 Low-tech artwork from local residents decorates the perimeter wall around the set of *Titanic*, Popotla, Mexico, 1998 (© RTMark.com).

The other 'real' elided in the spectacle of *Titanic* is the global dimension of the industry, which led to the building of the film set in Popotla, a village south of Tijuana, Mexico, in order to benefit from cheap labour. While the project was accompanied by the customary rhetoric of expected benefits to the local economy through increased tourism, there were also reports of damage to local fishing and concerns that it would provide few long-term prospects for inhabitants. For artist Allan Sekula, who photographed the site in 1998, Popotla cast the movie in a different light, exposing the arrogance of a culture which mobilises the 'lesson' of the Titanic as a distraction from the ongoing crises of globalisation: 'We peer morbidly into the vortex of industrialism's early nosedive into the abyss. The film absolves us of any obligation to remember the disasters that followed. Quick as a wink, cartoon-like, the angel of history is flattened between a wall of steel and a wall of ice. It's an easy, premature way to mourn a bloody century.'[31]

Quality TV and Reality TV

By the 1990s the landscape of television was also undergoing change. The traditional assumption that television was not just a commercial enterprise like cinema but also sustained an element of public interest was on the wane, as a more business-oriented attitude in the 1980s brought a wave of deregulation in broadcasting and famously prompted Mark Fowler, Chair of the Federal Communications Commission, to state that television was nothing more than 'a toaster with pictures'.[32] The main threat at the time came from cable television, which was not subject to the same rules for content and ownership and could therefore expand freely while offering a range of programming denied to the networks. As cable grew, reaching 57 per cent of American homes by the early 1990s and taking 20 per cent of viewers, the old networks ABC, CBS and NBC saw their long-established monopoly slipping away. On another flank, the 'Big Three' were also challenged by the expansion of independent broadcasting and the creation of three new national networks: Fox in 1986, followed by WB and UPN in 1994.

Competition amongst networks and cable channels had a direct impact on programming. In the past, regular profits and reliable audience shares had led the Big Three to settle into a comfortable but bland arrangement in which programmes were rarely innovative and addressed Americans in general rather than catering to specific tastes. Now, splintering audiences forced them to tailor their products to separate markets. Advertising revenue was the key factor: even if the major networks still commanded a greater proportion of the viewing public, sponsors often preferred to buy more targeted spots on cable or Fox, which had cultivated a young and hip audience from the start with programmes such as *Roc*, *21 Jump Street* and *Beverly Hills 90210*. Consequently, production budgets were channelled into new areas: family sitcoms were dropped, children's programming was progressively abandoned to cable channel Nickelodeon and networks battled for the attention of viewers with fresher, edgier material. By mid-decade the idea of a mass audience had been almost obliterated by niche marketing and viewing figures were no longer the sole measure of success: in 1996, for instance, CBS's Christian-themed drama *Touched by an Angel* was the most watched programme in its time slot but the least lucrative in advertising revenue, at $150,000 for a thirty-second spot against $175,000 for ABC's *Lois and Clark: The New Adventures of Superman*, $185,000 for *The Simpsons* on Fox and $225,000 for *Third Rock from the Sun* on NBC.[33] The different values placed on audiences indicated that the idea of television as a unifying force – 'the nation's living room' – was firmly at an end.

The abandonment of the family viewing paradigm meant first of all that programmes could be oriented more specifically to adult tastes:

Figure 3.6 Jerry Seinfeld and Jason Alexander in *Seinfeld* (NBC, 1990–8) (© NBC TV/The Kobal Collection).

hence much of the material that came to be known as 'quality TV' challenged former prescriptions on acceptable language, depictions of nudity, graphic violence and gore, as well as promising a more serious engagement with social issues. Police dramas such as *Homicide: Life on the Streets* (1993–9) and *NYPD Blue* (1993–2005) came with warnings about strong content and brought new levels of realism to the small screen, using innovative techniques such as rapid montage and hand-held camera footage. Sitcoms went upmarket, moving from the bar to the coffee bar and the suburban living room to the urban apartment: major successes like *Seinfeld* (1989–98), *Frasier* (1993–2004) and *Friends* (1994–2003) spawned numerous imitations that commonly featured the lives of aimless, childless, white middle-class professionals in flight from the normative family unit of traditional sitcom-land. Interestingly, where regional and working-class settings were abandoned by the format, the terrain was reclaimed in the emergent trend of animated sitcoms such as *Beavis and Butt-Head*, *The Simpsons*, *King of the Hill* and *South Park*, all of which situated themselves in opposition to hip metropolitan life.

A third major category of quality programming was the cult TV series, typified by programmes like *The X-Files* (1993–2002), *Buffy the Vampire Slayer* (1996–2003) and *Ally McBeal* (1997–2002). Born of a fiercely competitive marketplace, this was the most innovative of all formats in the 1990s, as the battle for audiences demanded increasingly distinctive visual styles and unusual textual variations. A series would commonly consist of serial and episodic elements – a long narrative arc to reward continuous watching, punctuated by stand-alone instalments designed to give more immediate gratification and hook occasional viewers. Thus in *The X-Files* agents Mulder and Scully spent each week investigating a government conspiracy to hide evidence of alien contact, but in one-off episodes the premise could be suspended to allow for a more playful interrogation of textual boundaries: as for instance when the pair find themselves in an episode of the real-life police show *Cops*, or on a film set watching the dramatisation of their own lives.[34] Cult shows were often noted for their loose and hybrid form, mixing horror and suspense with comedy or interrupting narratives with non-diegetic elements such as song and dance routines; while this paralleled postmodern tendencies in other fields it also had the simple practical function of identifying viewers as a sophisticated audience that no longer tolerated traditional formulae. But what made the genre especially interesting was the way that cult television acknowledged a fan sensibility and folded it into the design of a series: while efforts were made to appeal to a wide audience within the demographic, writers also aimed to give a smaller sector of avid viewers a sense of exclusivity by inserting in-jokes, narrative enigmas and provocative characterisation to be picked up and discussed by devotees. Joss Whedon, creator of *Buffy the Vampire Slayer* and spin-off series *Angel* (1999–2004) became well known for frequenting internet forums and contributing to debates about the direction of the shows. As Sara Jones has observed, the rise of fan-oriented programming marks a significant shift in the way that television is consumed: 'The wide open, producerly texts of these series appeal not so much to their audiences' desire to be entertained as to its need to be imaginatively involved.'[35] As the growth of the internet has tightened the loop even further, making the feedback between producers and specialised consumers ever more immediate, the traditional idea of what a television text is and where authorship lies is also challenged.

Is quality TV a more progressive TV? Does the decline of family viewing also mean an easing of the relatively conservative ideological boundaries that accompanied it? To what extent is the articulation of any new, minority or radical perspective possible within a framework that is, after all, still beholden to the bottom line of revenue from advertising and syndication? Whedon famously moved from cinema to television in disappointment at the way Hollywood had compromised his vision of 'populist feminism' in the original feature film of *Buffy*, but a potentially feminist outlook in the television series is still very much contained within models of femininity suited to selling products, as the deal between its lead actress Sarah Michelle Gellar and Maybelline cosmetics illustrates.[36] Similarly, proponents of *The X-Files* have claimed that the series performs valuable cultural work in alerting its viewers to contemporary issues of late capitalism such as environmental damage and scientific experiment, though to do so while giving credence to a conspiratorial view of government clearly owes more to television sensationalism than political insight. Perhaps the important point here is that no programme is likely to take a specific stance on social issues at the risk of alienating potential viewers when it is more beneficial to support multiple conflicting positions in order to stimulate and capitalise on further debate.

An alternative argument is put forward by Nancy San Martin in her analysis of NBC's Thursday-night scheduling, branded as 'Must-See TV', where she suggests that quality television often works to enforce dominant values even as it appears to entertain difference. Reading the schedule as a block, running from sitcom to drama to the eleven o'clock news, she notes that the ideological thrust of the evening is highly normative: the playful treatment of masculinity and sexuality in a show like *Friends* is subsequently disciplined by the reaffirmation of gender and sexual norms in *ER*. Equally, if *ER* appears to redress the glaring imbalance of racial representation in sitcoms by featuring a number of non-white characters, it only does so within certain constraints; as actor Eriq Lasalle illustrated when he complained of having to play in a mixed-race couple rather than in a relationship between African Americans, an image of multicultural hybridity usually takes precedence over representations of non-white characters leading separate but ordinary lives.[37] Similarly, Ron Becker has examined the growing visibility of homosexuality on American screens, and argues that the inclusion of gay characters and storylines became a central means through which networks established their credentials with a younger and more liberal audience – moving from a time when a scene showing two men in bed in the series *thirtysomething* in 1989 reputedly lost ABC $1.5 million in advertising revenue to the point where the same channel could double its prices for a thirty-second spot to $330,000 for the 1997 episode of *Ellen* in which the star and her character came out as lesbian. Even so, Becker notes that gay people on television were usually white, tended to have no sex life and were solitary figures rather than appearing as part of a larger gay community: 'For the most part,' he concludes, 'gay characters, despite their increasing numbers, continued to exist solely for straight characters to react to.'[38] Thus differences of race and sexuality continued to be circumscribed by norms and often failed to transcend their episodic appearances on television to become part of serial representations of American life.

A second important trend in television in the 1990s was the rise of what is now known as reality TV – a broad category designating programmes that in one way or another make a central feature of the representation of 'real life'. While the genre has its obvious precursors in documentary films and shows featuring members of a 'general public' such as daytime talk shows, talent contests or *Candid Camera* (1959–67), what was distinctive about the period was the massive expansion in non-fiction programming and the proliferation of new formats. In the popular police and emergency services subgenre, shows like *America's Most Wanted* (1988–), *Rescue 911* (1989–) and *Cops* (1989–) offered re-enactments of real-life scenarios or trailed professionals in the actual performance of daily duties; in another, the clip show pioneered by *America's Funniest Home Videos* (1990–) exploited the vast amount of amateur footage produced with the spread of the new technology. Talk shows also evolved into more provocative, unruly and sensationalist forms – the latter exemplified by *The Jerry Springer Show* (1991–), whose episodes could generally not be called a success until the bouncers had been called in to break up a fight between the invited guests. Real court cases were broadcast as entertainment on the cable channel Court TV from 1991, while *Judge Judy* revived the small-claims court show in 1996. But the most important format for shaping current conceptions of reality TV was arguably introduced by *The Real World*, first broadcast on MTV in 1992, which cast a selection of young adults unknown to each other with the purpose of living together under the eye of the camera.

The Real World played an important part in repositioning MTV from the twenty-four-hour music video channel it had been in the 1980s into a more conventional station, and its promotion of diversity helped improve the channel's image after a notorious policy of refusing to broadcast black music. Its first series made race a central issue and featured journalist Kevin Powell, who would go on to acquire a significant profile in politics and black intellectual life. In the third series the casting of activist Pedro Zamora offered a candid portrait of what it was like to live with AIDS: cameras followed him as he underwent medical examination, was refused assistance from private medical companies, started a romance and made a life commitment with his partner. Zamora's death a day after the final episode was screened prompted a public statement from President Clinton in honour of the work he had done to raise awareness about safe sex. But *The Real World*'s liberalism should not go unexamined, and several critics have pointed out that its representation of diversity is limited by the programme's narrative structure. The treatment of contentious issues like race and homosexuality tends to be dominated by stories of cast members overcoming prejudice through friendship; hence a more complex understanding of the way that inequalities are perpetuated by other means, despite anti-homophobic or anti-racist sentiments, is compromised.[39] Nevertheless, within the bounds of American television representation the show's attempt at normalising difference is a relatively progressive one, and it set an important precedent for subsequent reality shows.

Animation

The 1990s also saw a renaissance in animation, both in film and television. It was due in part to Disney's return to studio production in the 1980s, but it was also driven by industrial changes such as the emergence of cheap overseas labour and the development of new technology. Computer graphics interfaces revolutionised production at every stage of the process, allowing more complex effects to be realised at lower cost and challenging traditional techniques such as stop-motion or cel animation. The power of the new medium became evident with the release of *Toy Story* in 1995, the first feature-length movie to be made entirely on computers. On television, cartoons became a useful means of filling time slots and attracting audiences in the more competitive marketplace that cable had opened up: John Kricfalusi's *Ren and Stimpy Show* (1991–6) was commissioned for Nickelodeon when its new owner Viacom injected funds to create its own content, and later shifted to stablemate MTV to generate audiences for both channels; Mike Judge's *Beavis and Butt-Head* (1993–7) was a means for MTV to diversify the delivery of its music videos. But the resurgence of animation was also a generational matter: creators such as Judge, Kricfalusi, Matt Groening, Trey Parker and Matt Stone came from the first generation to have grown up with Saturday-morning cartoons in the 1950s and 1960s, and therefore were able to look on it as a part of the cultural landscape rather than a 'low' art form meant only for children. Traces of that past can be seen in the parodies of fifties family viewing on *The Ren and Stimpy Show* and *King of the Hill* (1997–2009), or in the way that *The Simpsons* compulsively works over the memory of the sixties.

The Simpsons (1989–present)

The Simpson family first appeared on American screens in 1987 in a series of one-minute shorts on a midweek variety show on the fledgling Fox network. Its creator Matt Groening had originally been invited to develop an animated version of his comic strip *Life in Hell*, but was reluctant to surrender rights over his characters and decided to submit a different idea, first conceived in high school, about the hapless exploits of a family of yellow figures.[40] The full-length show debuted in December 1989, and it proved so successful that Fox made it their flagship programme the next year, pitting it against *The Cosby Show* on Thursday nights in a bid to challenge NBC's claim for 'Must-See TV'. This was the first time an animated cartoon had appeared in the prime-time slot since *The Flintstones* ended in 1970, and the gamble paid off, as *The Simpsons* quickly became Fox's most lucrative programme and established the network as a major player in the industry.

Much of the humour and pathos in *The Simpsons* derives from the family's inability to live up to norms established in the television sitcom, a genre that has traditionally presented an idealised image of middle-class life with its hierarchy of roles, affirmation of patriarchal authority and ethic of self-improvement. Homer, the father, is lazy, incompetent and easily outwitted by his children; mother Marge fits awkwardly into her part as happy housewife, wavering between barely suppressed frustration and a pathological delight in daily chores; son Bart is inventive but belligerent, and in early episodes accepted his educational failures with pride; elder daughter Lisa is incongruously bright but unable to improve the family's prospects; baby Maggie is largely forgotten and left to her own devices. Those who missed the parody believed the show undermined social values: schools banned Bart Simpson t-shirts while President Bush Sr famously called for families 'a lot more like the Waltons and a lot less like the Simpsons' during his re-election campaign in 1992. In fact, *The Simpsons* is no less affirmative of the traditional family unit than other sitcoms but it takes up a resolutely anti-bourgeois perspective, focusing on the specific difficulties facing working-class Americans and refusing the consolations of aspirational television lifestyles. The usual sentimental resolutions of the genre are repeatedly skewered: when, for instance, Homer's attempt to act as an authority figure for Bart ends with him careening off into a canyon on a skateboard, or when Marge tries to conclude an episode in which the family loses all its Christmas presents with the hackneyed 'we still have each other', only for the children to reason 'But we would have had each other anyway!' – 'Yeah, plus lots of cool stuff . . .' Similarly, the sitcom's generally complicit relationship with consumer culture – offering up a fantasy domestic life for the viewer like an extension of the narrative space of the adverts that surround it – is problematised by Homer's extraordinary gluttony, which insists on the infantile, abject and laborious aspects of modern consumption.

Over the course of the decade *The Simpsons* expanded from a mere television series into a wider cultural phenomenon. Bart was appropriated as a black hero on bootleg t-shirts worn by African Americans in the summer of 1990 and released the funk-rap single 'Do the Bartman' (written by Michael Jackson, and rightly jeered by Bart's schoolmates in a subsequent episode), and numerous catchphrases such as Homer's anguished 'd'oh!' entered common speech.[41] While branding was lampooned on the programme through Krusty the Clown's indiscriminate endorsements of dodgy products, Simpsons characters were appearing on all manner of items from lunchboxes and toothbrushes to bumper stickers and air fresheners (which Bart assured purchasers were 'smell-o-rific'): in the first year alone, sales of merchandise netted Fox over a billion dollars. Being drawn as a character on the show gradually became a badge of importance for public figures, comparable to featuring on *Sesame Street* or being caricatured on the British puppet satire of the 1980s, *Spitting Image*: the list included musicians such as Michael Jackson, Mick Jagger and Tom Petty, British Prime Minister Tony Blair (whom Homer mistakes for Mr Bean), reclusive author Thomas Pynchon (with a paper bag on his head) and scientist Stephen Hawking. Co-writer Mike Scully illustrated the political currency of the guest appearance when he noted in 2000, 'Several years ago we tried to get Al Gore on the show and were turned down, very politely. Now he's running for President, he called us . . .'[42] Thus *The Simpsons* epitomised the complex intertextuality of nineties media products – not just because it is saturated with references to other cultural texts and aware of its own status as a television commodity, but also because it is disseminated across a range of cultural sites, spilling over generic and media boundaries.

How, then, should we judge the significance of *The Simpsons*? Can we speak of it as a progressive or critically incisive text given its thorough incorporation into the television system? When Fox's chief executive Rupert Murdoch is persuaded to appear on the show and identify himself unflatteringly as 'the billionaire tyrant', is this an indication of the programme's cultural clout or a sign that corporate media ownership is entirely unaffected by the messages it carries? One response would be to say that *The Simpsons* gains a critical edge by exposing the generic assumptions of the sitcom (as I have suggested above), or in a similar vein that it exploits the conventions of cartoons – anarchic energies, the normalisation of the grotesque, a childish (though not innocent) outlook – to propose an alternative way of looking at the all-too insistent realities of contemporary America. Groening himself has claimed that he tried to turn the logic of television against itself, using the serial format to interrupt its amnesiac tendencies:

> Television touches on an issue then dances away from it and never comes back to it. So it has the illusion of having a strong point of view,

but the real point of television is that nothing matters, because it's going to be replaced in the next millisecond by something different, and then replaced again and again. That's one reason why, in conceiving the show, I made sure that Homer worked in a nuclear power plant, because then we can keep returning to that and making a point about the environment.[43]

Marxist critiques of *The Simpsons*, however, have argued that its capacity to make ideological interventions is compromised by its inability to reflect on its own status as a commodity in a system of global capital. As the increasingly squeezed and speeded-up credits attest, much of the labour of animation is contracted to Korean houses such as Akom Studio in Seoul, at a fraction of the cost of production in the United States. The show cannot represent this dependence on cheap foreign labour without it creating a disturbance in the text: hence any reference to global economic conditions is usually displaced through humour or national stereotypes.[44] Equally problematic is the lacuna in the representation of race, apparent in the ambiguous status of the Simpsons' yellowness which is both race-neutral (the colour of a cartoon universe) and yet white (because of the presence of other racialised characters). Dr Hibbert features as the show's Bill Cosby, and perhaps his habitual inappropriate laughter is to be read as a reference to the disparity between *The Cosby Show*'s comedy and the realities of life for African Americans, but there is no further discourse on race except for the crude and unforgiving stereotyping of other ethnicities, particularly Apu, the Indian supermarket manager, who seems to function mainly as the 'safe' object of race-based humour. Thus for all its welcome attacks on the pieties of American society, *The Simpsons* embodies a liberal outlook with an anxious colour-blindness characteristic of the era.

Disney's successful return to animation was achieved by reassuring audiences that little had changed. Staying close to the old formula, it recycled popular myths and folk tales in a manner that appealed primarily to children and affirmed sentimental truths such as the need to follow personal desires, the virtue of love and friendship, and the importance of duty to one's tribe. The stories it told, however, were sufficiently open to admit multiple readings and were often taken for allegories of contemporary events and issues: *The Little Mermaid* (1989) was received as a comment on the fall of communism, *Aladdin* (1992) as a commentary on the Gulf War, *The Lion King* (1994) as a reflection on a new post-apartheid South Africa, *Pocahontas* (1995) as a response to Native American protests against the recent Quincentennial celebrations and *Hercules* (1997) as a meditation on America's responsibilities as sole global superpower. Even if Disney producers' primary aim was to affirm continuity in the brand rather than to address contemporary cultural concerns, the openness of

Disney texts inevitably meant that social realities intruded on their reading as 'innocent' children's entertainment: hence the use of black voice-actors in *The Lion King* raised an argument over racial stereotyping and *Aladdin* produced an outcry amongst Arab Americans who objected to the description of a land where, in the lines of the film's opening song, 'They cut off your ear if they don't like your face; it's barbaric, but hey, it's home!' (The words were subsequently changed.)

Competition in the industry appeared in the form of two new studios specialising in animation, Pixar and Dreamworks SKG – though the degree of mutual investment in stimulating interest in the medium is signalled by the collaboration between Disney and Pixar, first agreed in 1991 (Pixar was bought by Disney in 2006, although it continues to operate relatively independently). Dreamworks productions departed visually from Disney animation but returned to similar approaches such as the theme of the individual against the crowd in *Antz* (1998) and the remaking of popular myth in *Prince of Egypt* (1999), which told the story of the Israelites' exodus and provoked further complaints about cultural insensitivity (to the extent of getting banned in Malaysia and the Maldives). The most important creation of the period, however, was Pixar's *Toy Story*. Released in 1995, the film's entirely computer-generated manufacture announced the new possibilities of the medium, while the narrative cleverly articulated relationships to an American popular cultural past, since its two toy protagonists, a wooden cowboy and a plastic astronaut, recalled different eras of film history as well as different manifestations of the country's obsession with the frontier. As a film which both enacts and thematises the impact of new technology in mediating experience of the world around – our excitement with the virtual worlds of computing mirroring the child's delight with his new Buzz Lightyear – *Toy Story* is unusually complex and ambitious.

What it means to be 'only a toy' is central to the irony and metaphorical richness of both *Toy Story* and its 1999 sequel, *Toy Story 2*. While the first film deals with Buzz's growing awareness that he is nothing but a toy – just a mass-manufactured object with no unique identity and no superpowers – the follow-up explores the wider economic context in which toys circulate, making Woody the subject of a captivity narrative in which he is stolen from his child's home and returned to the original family of licensed products as a collector's item. For Paul Wells, the plots work as potent analogies of the conditions for identity in a posthumanist and late capitalist context, a world in which we have awoken to discover we are no more than playthings of corporations or effects of language and information flows.[45] On another level, the films are thoughtful meditations on the nature of fantasy life. The fact that the toys 'come alive' as nothing but toys plays not only to children's fantasies that their playthings are 'animated' with their own personalities, but to their deeper knowledge that they are only fantasies after all. Thus the films address the adult in the child, rather than the child in the adult – a welcome relief in a consumer society that is increasingly oriented towards the infantile.

Chapter 4

Art and Architecture

During the heyday of the Young British Artists it was common to
hear claims that the centres of power in the art world were shifting
away from their usual loci in the United States. The group's success
in defining British art in the 1990s was attributable to an alignment
of interests among artists seeking a more commercially appealing
version of conceptualism with a collector (Charles Saatchi) wishing to
establish his cultural status and a press eager to capture a new national
mood after a change of government. Irreverent, assertive and accessible, their work became the ideal vehicle for the 'Cool Britannia'
brand, finally coming to America in the form of the Sensation exhibition of 1999, where the controversy it attracted in New York granted
it just the right kind of publicity.

It is an exaggeration to say that the UK 'stole the idea of modern
art' during this period, but the case of the YBAs does offer a useful
contrast to the situation in America, which was unable to produce
any equivalent movement. Rather than serving as the expression of a
new kind of national confidence, art in America throughout the 1990s
was a more fragmented terrain, characterised only by its diversity and
ongoing anxieties about a loss of direction and critical force. At the
beginning of the decade it constituted one of the main battlegrounds
in the culture wars, where struggles over the meaning of the nation
were fought out and public funding of the arts became a political issue.
With the resurgence of the economy and revival of the art market in
the mid-1990s such political tensions subsided, but new concerns
arose over the relation between art and its institutions, questioning
its complicity with commercial values as well as the interests of galleries and museums. By the decade's end, the impact of globalisation
on the art world had made the idea of a specifically 'American' art all
the more problematic: if there was such a thing as a distinct national

tradition, it had to be defined within (and in opposition to) a context in which artists, exhibitions, audiences and critical discourse circulated increasingly freely across the world.

However difficult it might be to determine the boundaries of American art in the period, it is still possible to pick out a set of general trends. Broadly speaking, we can say that the 1990s saw an expansion of the field and a proliferation of artistic practices: new communities sought representation, new spaces opened up for exhibition, new materials were introduced into artworks. As the political currency of identity-based art diminished with the waning of the culture wars, artists turned their attention to formal concerns once again: the activist art of the Whitney Biennial in 1993 was succeeded by Whitney 1995's more academic theme of 'metaphor', a show that some accused of abandoning the idea of political commitment. Many found new ways to explore the world of objects, combining a pop sensibility and an awareness of minimalism in their examination of the stuff of everyday life. The installation became a favourite mode of exhibition, in part because it enabled artists to engage in heroic contests with the grand spaces of the new museums springing up across the world, but also because it offered a means of accommodating a wide range of artefacts in non-hierarchical arrangements. Urban ruins were reappropriated as art spaces; white cubes became cluttered with junk; stories of gallery cleaners mistakenly sweeping up parts of an artwork became legends.

At the same time, traditional forms of art-making also prospered. Talk of the 'return of beauty' was prevalent in the latter half of the 1990s when painting combined contemporary subject matter and classical techniques, and photography abandoned the rigours of the previous decade's conceptual work to make sumptuous, compelling images. Video achieved a growing recognition in the mainstream in work that engaged with cinema rather than television: high production values and a command of increasingly large spaces signalled not only the new ambitions of its artists but the intensified levels of competition amongst different sectors of the leisure industry at the end of the century. Meanwhile, the internet offered artists a radically new medium for experimentation and exhibition – the 'virtual gallery' raising hopes (and fears) of an art entirely liberated from existing institutions.

Given the range of artistic activity, the lack of distinct movements or groupings, the flourishing of both traditional and experimental work, and the simultaneous occurrence of high- and low-end production techniques, the decade seems to throw notions of dominant

currents in art history into question. As a result, one of the themes
in the art criticism of the period is how to understand the legacies
of modernism and the concept of the avant-garde which it saw as
the engine of cultural progress. Is this a moment of crisis for art, in
which it becomes entirely coopted by its commercial and ideological
functions, where the proliferation of activity betrays a lack of critical focus? Alternatively, is it a moment of possibility where art is no
longer beholden to its former duties of subversion and critique? If my
chapter is ultimately unable to answer such questions, I shall at least
try to present some of the work that provoked them: first in a survey
of art produced in relation to the theme of identity, then in an examination of new media and art-making practices, thirdly in a discussion
of the ways that artists addressed a culture of spectacle, and finally
through an account of themes of migration and displacement in an era
of globalisation.

Art and Identity

Two incidents of 1989 indicate the way that the problem of the public
sphere impacted on American art, setting the stage for what was to
come. In March, Richard Serra's sculpture *Tilted Arc* (1981) was
removed from its site in Federal Plaza, New York after a protracted
battle that pitted a community of artists, critics and cultural institutions against government officials. The large slab of rusting steel,
cutting across what was a bleak expanse in a way that refused to adorn
or soften it, had provoked angry debate between supporters who saw
it as an intervention into the alienating effects of state and corporate
architecture and detractors who claimed it was an imposition of elite
taste and an offence to the workers in the surrounding offices. Its
subsequent destruction became a landmark in art history because it
captured the declining stature of the arts in public life at the same time
as it revealed the dilapidation of the public realm itself. At the hearing,
protests that played on fears of deviants haunting the plaza (arguing
that *Tilted Arc* was a barrier to surveillance) spoke volumes about the
lack of confidence in the public after years of neglect.

The pressure on the arts was further evident in the furore over art
deemed blasphemous and obscene by conservative groups seeking to
extend their cultural influence into new territories. In May, Senator
Alfonse D'Amato ripped up an exhibition catalogue on the floor
of the Senate to protest against Andres Serrano's work *Piss Christ*
(1987), a photographic print of a plastic crucifix immersed in the

artist's urine. This sparked a campaign against 'taxpayer-financed obscenity' (in the words of the National Republican Congressional Committee) that next turned its attention to Robert Mapplethorpe's photographs of nudes and gay sado-masochists, some of which were due to be shown in the retrospective exhibition *The Perfect Moment* in a Washington gallery. When this was cancelled by the curator on the dubious grounds that the artist deserved the right to exhibit in an atmosphere free from political controversy, it again highlighted the low levels of confidence amongst arts administrators in the face of such attacks. The show was later restaged elsewhere, but the weakness of the arts was confirmed when the House of Representatives voted to cut the NEA's funding for the following year by $45,000, this being the sum received by the two exhibitions. A series of further cuts and constraints were to follow, to the extent that by the end of the decade the NEA's budget had been nearly halved.

The art controversies in this period were, of course, only superficially about public morality. More concretely, they were struggles to establish a leaner form of government, shifting the burden of social and cultural expenditure onto the private and voluntary sector while limiting the demands made by minorities at a time of considerable social change. Correspondingly, activist artists sought to contest the suppression of identity groups and force a way back into the public arena. In the early years of the AIDS crisis, for example, the coincidence between infection and homosexuality had compromised the government's response to the extent that the public visibility of gay Americans was literally vital: as the campaign group ACTUP put it, 'Silence = Death'. Or as artist David Wojnarowicz explained in a catalogue essay for Nan Goldin's 1989 exhibition *Witnesses: Against our Vanishing*, 'It is a standard practice to make invisible any kind of sexual imaging other than white straight male erotic fantasies . . . So people have found it necessary to define their sexuality in images, in photographs and drawings and movies in order not to disappear.'[1] While numerous groups – Gran Fury, Group Material, VisualAIDS and others – formed to contest the misrepresentation of homosexuality and AIDS, their opponents fomented outrage amongst Christians and conservatives to create a new constituency of voters and claim authority as the true representatives of the mainstream.[2]

Activist and identity-based art fell out of favour in the mid-1990s as museums' increasing reliance on private money made the art world more risk-averse and led to a preference for formalism above cultural politics. Felix Gonzalez-Torres is one of few artists from this moment whose work attracted sustained critical interest throughout the decade, in part because it brought the two approaches into a dynamic relationship. Nancy Spector has described his art as a 'queering' of formalist traditions, questioning the machismo of the minimalist cube or the terms of visual mastery implicit in the documentary photo, and complicating the exploration of space and form with elements that resonate with a personal or political context.[3] His best-known works are his candy spills and paper stacks: arrangements of endlessly replenished sweets and printed sheets that visitors are invited to take away with them. The forms they take evoke the 'specific objects' and gestures of minimalism – the blocks of Donald Judd, the floor sculptures of Carl André or the molten metal splashes of Richard Serra – but they never achieve the same integrity or permanence: since they are designed to be given away, such works are 'complete' only when someone removes a part.

More than just a playful reworking of high modernism, the giveaway technique is also a provocation directed at art's institutionalisation: the act of generosity opposes the system of museums and galleries that have traditionally been sites of restricted property. A 'piece' can be used, consumed, discarded, given away or treasured as a souvenir, but it is of little worth as an artwork in the usual sense – a hallowed object passing from artist to collector. In addition, the technique is important for challenging traditional distinctions between public and private spaces, something that was central to the cultural politics of the AIDS crisis. By encouraging viewers to take something away, Gonzalez-Torres's work creates an image of public interaction as an exchange of intimacies, rather than a place from which private life should be withheld. In the 1991 candy spill *Untitled (Lover Boys)*, for instance, the visitor is invited to take from a pile of silver foil wrapped sweets equivalent to the combined weights of the artist and his partner Ross Laycock. As Gonzalez-Torres explained in 1995:

> It's a metaphor. I'm not pretending it to be anything other than this – I'm not splashing lead on the floor. I'm giving you this sugary thing; you put it in your mouth and you suck on someone else's body. And in this way, my work becomes part of so many other people's bodies. It's very hot. For just a few seconds, I have put something sweet in someone's mouth and that is very sexy.[4]

As a memorial to his lover, who died that year, the piece is eloquent in its refusal of physical representation. This resistance to the monument's traditional form gives it some affinities with earlier public work – from Maya Lin's Vietnam Memorial (1982) to the German Counter-Monument movement – but it should also be placed in the context of concerns amongst activist groups that the continuing urgency of the AIDS crisis was in danger of becoming lost in rituals of mourning. Gonzalez-Torres's art of expenditure refuses to appropriate the lives of AIDS victims or appeal for some sort of closure to the crisis; instead, rather than accept the consolations of art as a form of substitution (the aesthetic object for the absent body), Gonzalez-Torres recreates the sense of loss through a further act of abandonment.

In a range of different contexts, artists of colour were also conducting political interventions and critiques of representation. In *Two Undiscovered Amerindians Visit the West*, Coco Fusco and Mexican performance artist Guillermo Gómez-Peña sought to challenge the racism implicit in the celebratory narratives of discovery that surrounded the Quincentennial festivities of 1992. Posing as natives of an unknown tribe in various public sites across America and Europe, they offered passers-by a spectacle reminiscent of the anthropological displays of native peoples in nineteenth-century World's Fairs. So embedded in western culture is this mode of appearance (the racial other as cultural specimen) that, in Fusco's own account, the satirical elements of the performance – bizarre costumes, television as 'native custom' – often went unheeded.[5] African American artists such as Renée Green and Fred Wilson also interrogated the forms of authority associated with museum presentation. Wilson's installation *Mining the Museum* (1992) was a re-arrangement of the artefacts in the Maryland Historical Society's collection that recovered a suppressed history of slavery by playing with exhibition conventions: one cabinet labelled 'Metalwork 1793–1880' displayed ornate silverware alongside slave manacles; elsewhere, period furniture was assembled around a whipping post as if ready for Baltimore's elite to take their seats. Such an approach was part of a larger trend that Hal Foster named 'the ethnographic turn', in which critique is oriented towards cultural practices and institutions rather than specific images and objects.[6] But as Wilson asserts, his own work is also motivated by a desire to explore a kind of racial uncanny, revealing the traces of oppression latent in familiar historical narratives or popular culture.[7]

Other black artists sought forms of resistance to the colonising gaze through critiques of racial stereotypes, especially those around the representation of the black body. Lorna Simpson and Carrie Mae

Weems produced photo-text montages that undermined the body's transparency by emphasising the particularities of black lives as well as the inadequacies of word and image as descriptive systems. Simpson extended this procedure into installation format with *Hypothetical?* (1992), in which a blow-up section of a black man's mouth is hung facing a wall of mouthpieces from brass instruments, while a newspaper cutting recalls the Rodney King verdict. Beyond the immediately obvious references to anger and riot, elaborated as a tension between disorder and control, the piece is also an eloquent questioning of what is absent when signs of blackness are visible. Differences between visual and textual histories of blackness were also explored by Glen Ligon: in *Notes on the Margin of the Black Book* (1991–3) he re-exhibited Robert Mapplethorpe's controversial photographs of male nudes alongside texts on art and race so that the highly aestheticised images of the black body had to be seen as part of a contested cultural history rather than as autonomous artistic products. In his best-known pieces Ligon painted fragments of text onto canvas – famous literary statements or Richard Pryor jokes – so that the emphasis on the material qualities of language defamiliarised the discourse on race.

In all of this work, we can follow a transition from an earlier phase of identity politics seeking to build solidarity through affirmative expressions of race towards more critical examinations of blackness as a cultural construct. As Fusco put it, such artists 'shift black art practice away from "representing the race" to representing what it means to be raced by offering their own bodies as subjects and objects'.[8] Similar re-examinations of identity were occurring amongst gay artists and women artists.

Abject Art

The Whitney Biennial of 1993 proved to be a watershed moment for American art, since it simultaneously bore witness to the range and force of identity-based work and marked the beginning of a backlash in the mainstream and art press. A common criticism was that the curators had favoured the representation of social groups above any other criteria: for Arthur Danto of *The Nation* it was 'a bean-counter's dream show', while Peter Plagens of *Newsweek* called it, even more scathingly, 'as close as a museum can get to a Salon of the Other without becoming an outsider art festival'.[9] The show gave early exposure to artists like Simpson, Ligon, Wilson and Green, but it was Daniel Martinez's admission tags that set the tone for the exhibition, forcing visitors to wander round the rooms wearing sections of the statement I CAN'T IMAGINE EVER WANTING TO BE WHITE. Seen as an act of institutional critique, these are a witty assault on the traditional humanist aspirations of the museum, since they demand that spectators look at each other – and in a racially divisive way – rather than enjoy being part of a public unified in aesthetic contemplation. But it is easy to see how the badges also created an antagonism between art and spectator that carried over to the show as a whole, and contributed to the sense that identity was the dominant ground for artistic production and response rather than something to be examined or contested. In a round-table discussion for the journal *October*, Hal Foster worried about 'a turn to autobiographical identity . . . in the very moment of its questioning': a preference for personalised narratives of oppression that also marked a retreat from the work modern art had historically undertaken on the 'politics of the signifier'.[10] Certainly, the show's inclusion of George Holliday's video footage of Rodney King – which surely depended for its cultural significance on the fact that it was *not* a work of art – suggested an eagerness to embrace social issues as the specific meaning of art (what the *October* group called a 'rush to the signified'), and a loss of confidence in art's ability to engage audiences on the level of its own internal histories and formal practices.

The problem that identity politics faced, especially where it intersected with avant-garde cultural practices, was how to make interventions into the public sphere in the name of specific groups while at the same time acknowledging that the identities around which those groups mobilised were themselves highly fluid and constructed. For instance, from the point of view of gay victims of AIDS or physical abuse – people who received little legal or cultural recognition at all – the poststructuralist critique of the subject seemed politically debilitating and an intellectual luxury. And yet, as Foster and his colleagues noted, the opposite danger was that the political articulation of identities tended back towards essentialism and exclusion. This tension between the affirmation and deconstruction of selfhood was displaced onto a psychoanalytical register in what came to be known as 'abject art', which focused on the body and its basic drives, exploring states of being that lay beyond or prior to the formation of identities themselves.

For Julia Kristeva, whose theories in *Powers of Horror* (1982) were central to much of the debate, *abject* designates a degraded condition or substance of indeterminate form, occupying a troubling region between person and thing. Neither subject nor object, it poses a threat to the basic processes of identification on which language and the social order is built. Artists explored this condition through figurations of disarray, waste matter and bodily excretions, seeking to produce the emotions associated with the abject's appearance and repression such as disgust, squeamishness, fear and morbid fascination: thus Rona Pondick's hairy balls of teeth, John Miller's simulated piles of shit, Janine Antoni's gnawed blocks of chocolate and lard, or Robert Gober's violated body parts. Of course, an interest in the debased and the formless has been integral to modern art throughout, from Duchamp's urinal to Andy Warhol's pissed-on 'oxidation paintings'[11]; but it took on a renewed oppositional force in the early 1990s, where abjection became a metaphor for social crisis and the work's visceral impact served as an antidote to the blank, affectless art of the previous decade.

Artists deployed the tropes of the abject body for a range of different purposes. Antoni addressed the strictures of femininity, sustaining a tension between lyricism and horror by turning sensuous activities into forms of labour, often with obsessive connotations: the chewed morsels of lard and chocolate in *Gnaw* (1992) are fashioned into lipsticks and candy box trays; busts made of soap and chocolate are reworked by intimate bodily contact in *Lick and Lather* (1993–4); paint is daubed across the floor with the artist's own hair in *Loving Care* (1992). Her later work moves away from the solitary female self to explore contact and interaction, but it still questions the limits of the body and the senses: *Mortar and Pestle* (1999), for example, is a photograph of a tongue touching an eyeball, blown up to such a degree that the viewer cannot help but recoil. The image subtly articulates a tension between violence and intimacy while the overly literal attempt to sense another's vision – what Antoni has called 'a wilful misunderstanding of how to know something' – turns playfully on the male gaze.[12]

Gober, on the other hand, was concerned with the physical integrity of the body and psychic relationships to inanimate objects. Much of his work of this period involved artificial body parts manipulated to produce uncanny effects: a candle rises in a phallic manner from a section of hairy, creamy-white flesh; drains are inserted into legs that protrude from the wall; in *Man Coming Out of Woman* (1993–4), a man's foot, clothed in a sock and shoe, emerges from a vaginal opening in a rudimentary torso. The resonance with the losses of AIDS is clear, given the associations of drains and wasted bodies and the metonymic chain that links candle, wax and death, but what makes these works compelling is the way they go beyond a purely memorial function to question the processes of sexual differentiation and the formation of sexuality itself. In the latter piece, the shock lies not just in the disruption of scale or the corrosion of child/adult boundaries but in the contrast between the male shoe and the torso as fixed and barely determinate signs of gender.

On the West Coast, artists developed the trope of abjection in other directions. Their work continued to signify within an avant-garde tradition – the interest in the uncanny, for instance, harked back to European surrealism – but its loose, downbeat aesthetics were also rooted in an American vernacular. Paul McCarthy created a vision of a Disneyland gone crazy: toys took on monstrous pro-portions; theme park creatures engaged in orgiastic frenzies, crudely animated mannequins humped barrels and trees, and the abstract-expressionist artist-hero acted up like a spoiled, soiled child. McCarthy's world, in which the dominant subjective states are the perverted adult fantasy and the infantile tantrum, is a place of gleeful transgression as much as a source of horror, and can be read as an assault on various aspects of the social order from its norma-tive family structures to its modes of consumption. Friend and occa-sional collaborator Mike Kelley dealt with similar themes, though his treatment of the abject was more melancholy than grotesque: his 'craft morphologies' of 1990–1 feature stuffed toys in formal or dramatic arrangements – bound in clumps according to colour, or sitting beside each other in conversation. Hand-made, worn and discarded, the toys are doubly abject, first as hapless imitations of their pristine mass-produced counterparts and then as abandoned objects of affection.

On one level, then, the widespread interest in the abject can be read as an expression of outrage at the crises of the late 1980s – the neglect of marginal groups under conservative social policies which was most starkly revealed to gay victims of AIDS. But on another level abjec-tion is a response to the dead end of identity politics, the recognition of its failure to transform the cultural realm. Ultimately, the desires mobilised by identity politics were aimed at expanding, and there-fore confirming, the social order; and as the rise of 'lifestyle politics' would suggest, they were all too easily oriented to the sphere of con-sumption. In their various explorations of regression and infantilism, Kelley and McCarthy make explicit this link between the formation of identity and the penetration of the commodity, in double defiance of capitalism's colonisation of the young imagination and the sentimen-tal myth of childhood innocence.

Figure 4.1 Kara Walker, *Slavery! Slavery! Presenting a GRAND and LIFELIKE Panoramic Journey into Picturesque Southern Slavery or 'Life at "Ol' Virginny's Hole" (sketches from Plantation Life)'. See the Peculiar Institution as never before! All cut from black paper by the able hand of Kara Elizabeth Walker, an Emancipated Negress and leader in her Cause* (1997). Cut paper and adhesive on wall, 11 × 85 feet. Installation view: 'Kara Walker: My Complement, My Enemy, My Oppressor, My Love', Hammer Museum, Los Angeles, 2008 (photo: Joshua White. Courtesy of Sikkema Jenkins & Co.).

The irony for Kelley was that his deployment of abjection as an interrogation of mass culture was hard to extricate from a context in which it would inevitably be read in autobiographical terms. His treatment of regression and the visual tropes of abuse were understood as signs of his own childhood traumas, prompting him to abandon abject imagery and turn his attention to the operations of 'trauma discourse' itself. Thus in *Educational Complex* (1995) he fabricated a traumatised past, or more precisely evoked a history that both displayed and withheld traces of trauma. The work is a recreation from memory of all the educational buildings of Kelley's life, amalgamating them into one sprawling architectural model so that it initially resembles the stylistic composites of contemporary urban regeneration but on closer inspection reveals sections that are little more than abstract blocks, marking where memory has failed. These architectural blocks/memory blocks inevitably take on a more charged significance as the places of trauma, where long-forgotten abuses may have occurred, but they are equally (if not absolutely) the effects of an imperfect mental process, which itself is governed as much by the desires of the present as the scars of the past.[13] And then again: if we *are* to take them as signs of trauma, might they not also signify the harm caused by the artist's formalist training, with its emphasis on the rigours of conceptualism and its own repression of 'lowbrow' popular culture?

Kara Walker

In Kara Walker's work the tropes of abjection are used to explore the legacies of America's racial history and the persistence of racism in the present. Her medium is the silhouette – a minor nineteenth-century middle-class art form in which figures and landscapes are traced in black on a white background. Walker combines this with another archaic form, the panorama, to produce large mural-sized installations depicting satirical scenes from a mythical antebellum South – perversions of the plantation romance in which slave girls copulate with animals or old soldiers, children play with Klan regalia and an air of decorum is vainly maintained amid a riot of violence and muck.

In the piece *Slavery! Slavery!* (1997), for instance, the dominant motifs are monstrosity and scatology: a young woman whom we assume to be white from her hooped skirt holds a baby upside-down to smell its behind, but a second glance reveals that legs protrude at both ends; a lady dressed for a masquerade is attended by a boy in North African pantaloons spray-ing perfume behind her while she approaches a cloud of flatulence emitted from a man prostrate before a fountain which either resembles or actually is a girl perched on a monkey, spraying fluid from all orifices. Further on, a boy impossibly suspended from the finger of a young squire urinates or ejaculates back onto him. We might read this as a Rabelaisian vision of a world turned upside-down, or a world in which the libidinal exchanges fostered under slavery are no longer hidden beneath the veneer of respect-ability, but what makes these works compelling (and problematic for some) is the way that Walker emphasises our own continued immersion in the taboos of race and desire. The cyclorama, surrounding the viewer's field of vision, is an obsolete visual technology (one of the precursors to cinema, we should not forget) but it illustrates her insistence that there is no place outside this melodrama. The point is reiterated by the absurdly lengthy title, which blends the rhetoric of an abolitionist text with that of a Barnumesque freakshow. In drawing attention to the voyeurism latent in nineteenth-century representations of race and the mutual investment in the spectacle of black suffering that liberals appear to share with their opponents, Walker offers a caution to those who might consider that America has put such forms of racism behind itself.

As might be expected, Walker's enthusiastic reception amongst art institutions and collectors has been accompanied by fervent criticism over her use of racial stereotypes. Following the award of a MacArthur Foundation Fellowship in 1997, artist Betye Saar circulated a petition for its withdrawal on the grounds that Walker perpetuated imagery that damaged African American political efforts; Howardena Pindell warned audiences at the Johannesburg Biennial that Walker and others working with stereotypes (such as Michael Ray Charles and Robert Colescott) were acting as 'a contemporary form of minstrel', catering to white fan-tasies of black degradation even as they allowed their patrons to appear progressive by exhibiting black artists.[14] Notwithstanding these important concerns about the unequal distribution of power and capital within the art world, it seems obvious that Walker's images are subversions rather than affirmations of stereotypes: the silhouettes are, after all, not the profiles of actual heads but the shadows cast by caricatures under the spotlight. As Mark Reinhardt has pointed out, stereotypes are normalising devices that support the social order by containing and masking ideological contradictions (thus the happy slave, or the potent black male): Walker, however, takes them to such an excess that they can no longer be considered normative, generating 'a powerful centrifugal force at the very places where white supremacy's forms of racial and sexual identification are held together'.[15] Thus any attempt to read the scenarios in Walker's work forces a viewer to confront the way stereotypes have colonised the imagination of all Americans – herself included.

The dispute over Walker's work and success highlights a general shift in cultural strategies for addressing race. If critics like Saar and Pindell find the playful or transgressive use of stereotypes damaging, it is because they hold to the principles of the cultural activism of the 1960s for which 'positive' representations of black community were central. As Cornell West has noted, the consensus around this approach was on the wane from the 1980s: what he calls 'the new cultural politics of difference' emerging in its wake was more attentive to different forms of black subjectivity and more sceptical of idealised notions of blackness and community.[16] Walker's own scepticism is clear – not just in her scorn for positive images, but in her desire to challenge notions of authenticity that plague racial politics. In particular, what comes under scrutiny is the role that the memory of slavery plays in the construction of contemporary black identity. At a moment when trauma had a special moral currency in America, Walker warns that the tendency to identify with slavery risks perpetuating a psychological attachment to victimisation, something she refers to as the 'inner plantation': 'this grand place where . . . one is whole . . . and knows what to fight against, or what not to fight against, or who to obey, or how to hold oneself in the face of oppression'.[17] Refusing the consolations of an authentic black subject, she insists that identity is always partial, divided against itself, and that solidarity is a matter of alliances rather than exclusions.

In the catalogue for her 2003 exhibition Walker imagines a macabre, Delacroix-inspired Civil War scene as if the sketch of an installation not yet realised: on a devastated battlefield emancipated slaves loot the corpses of defeated Confederate troops, 'too hungry, as it were, for that blood-thirsty new power you've heard tell of . . . too hungry to rethink desire'.[18] The significance of her work lies in this observation – that the urgency of the demand for social equality subsequent to the abolition of slavery and ongoing into the twentieth century has left the forms of racial and interracial desire that it left behind relatively unattended to. The legacy of this failure to rethink desire is evident in the perpetuation of racism in popular culture and in the infatuation with race, which paradoxically defined the culture of the 1990s at a moment when the politics of colour-blindness vainly offered the promise of closure.

The Art of Stuff

Interest in the stuff of everyday life did not stop at abject art, but continued in sculpture and installation throughout the decade. From the 'craft morphologies' of Kelley to the suspended junk pieces of Nancy Rubins and the ramshackle constructions of Jason Rhoades and Sarah Sze, artists appropriated found objects, refashioned them, placed them in unexpected combinations and displayed them in defamiliarising arrangements. Others explored the qualities of ordinary materials as artistic media: Vik Muniz used chocolate as a medium for reproducing images of old masters; Al Souza pasted fragments of jigsaws into wall-pieces reminiscent of abstract expressionism; Tara Donovan produced postminimalist sculptures from household materials such as fuse wire and Styrofoam cups. The impact of all of this work depends on its articulation of a tension between art and non-art qualities – the way a particular piece produces reflection on its formal properties or its relationship to art history, but at the same time evokes the real world, through references to the artist's personal life or the ordinariness of the commodities on display. Souza's *The Peaceful Kingdom* (1998), for instance, might recall the scale and aggressive individuality of gestural painting, but it is undercut by the inescapable fact that these are jigsaw pieces, assembled in a far less expressive manner, and with far less heroic connotations of thrift shops and Sunday afternoons.

A key theme in this work is amateurishness. As with the artist who works 'in jigsaw', the traditionally prized mastery of a medium is played off against the value or pleasure of working in an uninformed manner with lesser materials. If Gonzalez-Torres was partly responding to the high seriousness of modernists like Richard Serra when he produced his candy spills, then there is a similarly casual sensibility in Nancy Rubins, a West Coast sculptor whose monumental assemblages of trailers, old kitchen appliances, boats and broken aeroplanes are bound together in a manner that is highly artful yet quite devoid of expertise: 'I kind of engineer by the seat of my pants,' she confided in 1999.[19] Jason Rhoades, another California-based artist and occasional collaborator with Paul McCarthy, also used the amateur as a means of approaching one of his central concerns: the relation between fine art, professional work, personal creativity and mass production. His *CHERRY Makita – Honest Engine Work* (1993) was a makeshift shed filled with a jumble of objects signifying various types of imaginative and manual activity: photographs, drawings in motor oil, screws, nails, bits of shelving, tools modelled in tin foil and plaster, a large drill and a running motor engine connected to a long exhaust pipe snaking through the gallery. Faced with what was a poor reconstruction of a suburban workshop displaying few traces of design or skill, a viewer was forced to consider the power of the institutional apparatus that nevertheless made it art – while at the same time acknowledging other forms of labour in daily life that go unseen or undervalued. In the installation *My Brother / Brancuzi*, exhibited at the Whitney Biennial in 1995, Rhoades expressed his relationship to modernism in a way that was inspired by seeing his artistically untrained brother's arrangement of his own work in his room at the family home: 'I was curious about how he took my old artwork from high school and put it against stuff in the room that was already there. I tried to understand his formalism.'[20] Here the unconscious formalism of the non-artist is the mirror image of the artist's ongoing struggle to be 'informal' – to find new ways of addressing historical antecedents and new ways of speaking to audiences.

The art of stuff also seemed motivated by a new sensibility with regard to the realm of mass production – one that aimed not to add to the glut of commodities with new creations or differentiate itself by creating 'pure' objects, but to present alternative means of sorting and ordering what was already there. Rhoades spoke of 'making sculpture disappear', and often recycled parts of artworks in later installations so that the integrity of any individual piece would be permanently undermined.[21] Throughout the decade and into the next century (until his untimely death in 2006) his installations continued to expand to the point of taking over the spaces they inhabited, transforming them into factory, warehouse, storeroom, showroom, shop floor or cabaret, always evoking the circulation of commodities and the human drives they put into play. In a piece like *Meccatuna* (2003), the organising principles are sex, faith and consumption: neon signs displaying slang terms for the vagina are strewn around a room amongst tawdry donkey figurines, camel saddles, boxes of Ivory Snow detergent featuring Marilyn Chambers (a model who moved from soap advertising to pornographic films in the 1970s) and cans of tuna, bought in Mecca and shipped to New York as souvenirs from a pilgrimage. In the centre, a million Lego blocks are assembled to form a scale model of the Kaaba, the focal point of Islamic worship. The combination (and perhaps trivialisation) of sacred and sexual experience suggests the endless deferral of desire and the lack of satisfaction or redemption, but the exuberance of Rhoades's work is enough to overcome any melancholy in the subject.

Rhoades's approach bears comparison with that of Sarah Sze, a New York-based artist who came to prominence in the late 1990s and is also known for her use of everyday objects in large-scale installations. In her work, the most minor household items – cotton buds, pen lids, pills, buttons, chewing-gum strips, packaging boxes, mugs, kitchen utensils, electric fans and potted plants – are redeemed from their insignificance by their incorporation into delicate structures rising from the floor or suspended from the ceiling. Matchsticks are glued together to make ladders and towers, plastic straws and wires loop around the assemblages like painterly flourishes; lamps cast occasional elements into relief while magnifying glasses invite the spectator to peer into imaginary depths. The difference between the two artists might be read in terms of gender, Rhoades's unashamedly masculine imagery against Sze's meticulous ornamentation of interior space – but this would be to impose uninteresting identity categories on work that is more usefully talked about in terms of the colonisation of the gallery space and the desire to manage the clutter of everyday life. Both artists invoke the gallery as a frail, permeable place, no longer able to prevent the intrusions of a world of stuff outside. But where Rhoades's sensibility is governed by libidinal investment and abandonment, Sze's tends towards mastery. Her constructions are a display of technical skill and exhaustive labour (with traces of the obsessive), but they also play with scale, giving viewers an impression of power over miniature worlds even as they suggest the autonomous life force of a household ecosystem.

It is easy to see why Sze's art has become so rapidly popular (she achieved critical notice even before graduating from her Masters in 1997, exhibited at the Venice Biennale in 1999, and received a MacArthur Fellowship in 2003): after the limited pleasures afforded by conceptualism and the more visceral impact of abject art, her works bring a long-absent sense of wonder back into the gallery. At the same time, their sprawling extrusions through space offer the welcome illusion of art overcoming the institutions that house it. That this is only ever an illusion is emphasised by a piece such as *Second Means of Egress*, first exhibited in the Berlin Biennial of 1998: matchstick bridges, rails and towers rise from floor to ceiling, appearing to break out through a skylight, indulging fantasies of adventure and escape but also recalling the museum's control of visitors' transit through its rooms.[22]

Installation art flourished during the 1990s, incorporating video,

Figure 4.2 Sarah Sze, *Second Means of Egress* (1998): installation view, Akademie der Kunst, Berlin Biennale (courtesy of the Artist).

audio and performance elements as well as found objects and sculptural forms. In part it showed artists' growing interest in staging environments within which spectators could construct their own set of narrative associations or become participants. No doubt it also reflected their effort to rise to the challenge of the new spaces of exhibition: amidst spectacular museum architecture and exotic festival locations, the artwork itself faced competition for people's attention. The trend towards installation was treated with scepticism by some critics, who worried about the absence of commitment to a specific medium or the fetishisation of interactive experience at the expense of critical reflection. Others, however, saw it as the ideal format for the eclecticism of contemporary art, in that it created a space from which no object, medium or dimension of lived experience would be excluded.

Mass Media and the Visual Archive

Expansion, eclecticism and the love of spectacle was evident in other art forms too. In painting, a key tendency was the return of traditional fine art values set against contemporary subject matter. John Currin, for instance, carefully pastiched the anatomy and gestures of Renaissance nudes but gave his portraits the faces of present-day models and film stars. Lisa Yuskavage went further to create jarring effects by taking the lowest kinds of imagery – kewpie doll figures with inflated breasts in coy soft-porn poses – and rendering them in a gorgeous and highly painterly manner. Visual pleasure was also a feature of new photography and video art – indeed, to the extent that 'the return of beauty' became a common topic of conversation in the art world toward the end of the decade.[23] If practitioners in previous eras had tried to resist spectacle, or treated its constituent elements (such as detail, illusion and glossy reproduction) as the objects of critique, then artists of the 1990s often sought ways of incorporating it into their work. The question, of course, was whether they were playing with fire – if the sensory appeal of the art overdetermined its critical impact, and made it no more than just another instance of the culture of spectacle propagated by mass media and entertainment industries. If this was indeed true of some works (and any judgment has to be the outcome of interpretation on an individual basis), others found ways of engaging viewers in critical reflection on the mediated image, through and not despite its seductiveness.

Two photographers worth considering in this respect are Gregory Crewdson and Philip-Lorca diCorcia. Both of them produced work in the 1990s which was explicitly 'artful' – carefully staged images, dramatically lit, charged with narrative. Opposing themselves to realist traditions, they asserted the role of photographer as author rather than witness, and the photograph as the outcome of a predetermined concept rather than the submission to experience. Furthermore, rather than stress the uniqueness of an image, both referred to a world already saturated by visual culture: their pictures recalled other images from art history, movies and television, and drew resources from advertising and fashion photography. What needs to be decided is how they mobilise such references, whether to establish a critical relationship to the industries of visual culture or to achieve some form of accommodation. Crewdson takes the uncanny as his main mode of enquiry, imagining ruptures in the fabric of ordinary suburban life: his evocation of a Middle America, with its tension between the virtues it affirms and the desires it necessarily represses, recalls the American Scene painters of the 1930s and 1940s as well as later B-movies and TV sitcoms. His work has been enthusiastically received in part, one suspects, because of its resonance with these other sources, the way it reassures viewers that this is a familiar world despite the glimpses of the extraordinary. Smoke pours from an overturned school bus on the street while sunset falls on the hill behind the houses; a man caught in a spotlight from the night sky reminds us of alien abduction scenes or the epiphanies of religious leaflets. We have seen it all before: even if the photographs depict horror, loss or death, we are reassured by our sense of inclusion in the histories of these images.

Crewdson's better-known work is probably the *Twilight* series (1998–2002), but the previous series *Hover* (1996–7) is just as indicative of his affirmative sensibility. Black-and-white aerial shots of a semi-rural suburb offer visions of life redeemed through ritual, the merit of small aspirations, the presence of authority as an ornamental motif, all presented through the consolations of a bird's-eye perspective. In one of the scenarios the neighbourhood looks on while a man begins laying turf in the middle of the street, as if to join up the lawns and recreate a common ground. It is a tremendously nostalgic vision, a realisation of the desire for an unalienated world, and the image might have achieved some critical insight had it turned on the absurdity of the enterprise and registered more clearly the anxieties that such a sentimental view of nature masks. But Crewdson's reflections show how little interest he has in the disruptive energies of the uncanny after all: 'So we sodded the street closed and I got in the elevated crane, and I was lifted and floating over this scene. It's the most beautiful thing in the world to hover.'[24]

DiCorcia, on the other hand, offers fewer consolations, even if his photographs are just as visually alluring. His signature approach is to use techniques borrowed from commercial photography – strategic lighting, rich colour and dramatic composition – and apply them in contexts previously the domain of documentary realism. Thus for his *Hollywood* series of 1990–2, he sought men on the streets around Santa Monica Boulevard, an area frequented by male prostitutes and drug users, but rather than photograph them *in situ* he invited them to pose in tableaux prepared in advance. In dingy motel rooms, twilit parking lots or by the light of illuminated fast-food restaurant signs, these men feature simultaneously as casualties of the Dream Factory and leading players in stories of their own. DiCorcia acts the part of the objective realist photographer by recording each subject's name, age, place of birth and appearance fee in the title, but of course there is no guarantee the details given are true: if the men are prostitutes (and there is no reason to believe this either), then they will already be in their own business of artifice and fiction. Hence diCorcia calls attention to the photograph first as a series of performances and secondly as a transaction, one in which the viewer is implicitly involved. Complicating the transaction further is the fact that the project was funded by a fellowship from the NEA for which, in the wake of the Mapplethorpe controversy, diCorcia would have had to sign an agreement promising not to make work that might be deemed obscene. In a subtle act of protest, the appearance fee records what happened to the grant money.[25]

In subsequent work diCorcia extended the technique of combining realism and artifice, collapsing street and stage set onto each other. In cities across the world he rigged up concealed flash lighting in public spaces that would illuminate unsuspecting passers-by at random intervals for a long-lens camera. Captured in sharp focus with dark shadows, people appear detached from their surroundings – wandering around in a dream, walking an imaginary catwalk or acting out a drama they themselves are unaware of. In some respects these photographs take the realist aim of objectivity to excess: the photographer's artistry (the mythologised 'eye' for a good picture) is subordinated to a set of automated constraints, while the oblivious subjects are unable to compose themselves for the shot. But the theatricality and glamour of the images make it impossible for us to read them as 'real'. As with a lot of the art of the decade, we cannot take diCorcia's use of the materials and techniques of mass culture as straightforwardly critical: he embraces the glossiness of commercial photography, and as much as his work stresses subjectivity as performance (in an avant-garde tradition) it also shows us an everyday world infused with the aura of transcendence (in the tradition of advertising). But at least we know the latter to be a falsehood, merely a trick of the light.

Video's expansion as an art form was due in part to the availability of new digital techniques that gave artists a richer palette and grander ambitions. Production costs increased, picture resolution improved, and more and more works demanded to be screened in separate, darkened spaces. If this meant that video art was tending towards cinema, some crucial differences in presentation usually remained such as the absence of fixed seating and a less dogmatic insistence on watching from beginning to end. As Brandon Taylor has pointed

Figure 4.3 Philip-Lorca diCorcia, *Head #1* (2001). Fujicolor Crystal Archive print, 48 × 60 inches, 121.9 × 152.4 cm (courtesy David Zwirner, New York and Monika Sprüth Philomene Magers, Berlin and London).

out, the resulting mode of viewing – lying somewhere between the upright contemplation of the gallery and the submissive repose of the cinema – occasionally created an uncertainty over whether to read a piece experientially as installation or textually as film, one that was not always resolved in the works themselves.[26] The cinematic turn in video art also prompted new explorations of the visual archive, as artists became progressively interested in the ways that film and television images circulate in contemporary culture and affect individual lives. Film could be treated as a found object or used as raw material for digital manipulation: Scottish-born Douglas Gordon, for instance, projected the famous 'talking to me?' scene from *Taxi Driver* onto multiple screens for *Through the Looking Glass* (1999), and in *24 Hour Psycho* (1995) slowed Hitchcock's movie down to a point of near stasis, its original running time stretched out to an entire day.

Not everyone has been convinced that defamiliarising techniques such as these do much to challenge or provoke reflection on the entertainment industry – in fact, it is quite easy to argue that rescreening Hollywood films in the gallery is more likely to enhance their status. More successful at interrogating the power of screen images is Paul Pfeiffer, who began exhibiting installations, prints and video pieces at the end of the 1990s using horror films and sports television footage. His 1999 piece *Fragment of a Crucifixion (After Francis Bacon)* is a short looped sequence of match coverage featuring a basketball player screaming in triumph to the crowd from which key elements such as kit markings and other players have been digitally erased. Thus isolated, trapped within the loop and never allowed to finish screaming, the player stalks the confines of the court as if measuring out the extent of his prison. In other works Pfeiffer removed the boxers from footage of a prize fight and the players from a victory celebration, leaving only the cup dancing around the court on its own like a perfect fetish object. The combination of loop and erasure allow Pfeiffer a greater purchase on media culture than Gordon's more reverential treatments: erasure parses the constituent elements of the event to isolate the source of affect while the loop, by denying closure, emphasises the eternal continuity of the mass-produced image. 'That's the promise of advertising and that's the promise of the spectacle,' he remarked in the PBS documentary series *Art: 21* (2003). 'That things will go on forever . . . no one will die, and things will be beautiful and glamorous for eternity.'[27]

We could think of Pfeiffer's approach as a structuralist one to the extent that he takes samples of media culture and dissects them to understand how the spectacle penetrates everyday life. In the same category we could also place Tony Oursler, whose sculptural installations (often faces projected onto rudimentary dolls) examined the relation between the immateriality of images and individual lives in the real world. At the other end of the spectrum, artists like Matthew Barney and Bill Viola adopted the language and forms of spectacle, as if rising to the challenge of media culture to produce art that competed on an affective as well as intellectual level. Foregrounding high production values and addressing grand themes, they set out to produce visually compelling work and, perhaps unusually in an age of digital reproduction, recover the aura of uniqueness surrounding the art object. Both were accused of succumbing to the blandishments of spectacle: Viola for his uncritical treatment of sacred and sublime experience, Barney for his extravagant set pieces that borrowed heavily from mass entertainment and populist politics.

Bill Viola

Video is often treated as the principal postmodern art form, not simply because it uses recent technologies but because its main means of communication is the image on a screen, and its main object is a world mediated through television. Theorists of video claim that its key role has been to comprehend the impact of TV on culture and individual perception and equip viewers with the tools to resist its hegemonic tendencies: thus, since the late 1960s, it has played with the sculptural properties of the TV set to reflect on its intrusion into the home, operated on the flow of disconnected images to see how meanings can be produced or altered and dissected its common narrative and generic elements to examine its role in the construction of identity. For Fredric Jameson, writing in 1991, video allows us to understand what television distracts us from thinking about – the way the continuous flow of images arrests the processes of memory and undermines critical faculties, turning viewers into helpless spectators and little more than components of a general system of production and consumption. By resisting the minor comforts of narrative closure or the conventions of 'entertainment' and 'information', video exposes the medium's reductive and depersonalising effects; as such it does not explain TV so much as make it shocking again.[28]

How does Bill Viola fit with this perspective on video art? For some, his emergence as one of its stars in the 1990s – representing the US at the Venice Biennale in 1995, and the subject of a large touring retrospective in 1997 – is an indication of the maturity of the art form; for others, however, it is a sign of video's disappointing incorporation into the nexus of media and cultural institutions that it once promised to critique. His work is a long way from the lo-fi introspective recordings of early artists like Bruce Nauman and Martha Rosler or the visual overload of a Nam June Paik installation, and in many respects it appeals to traditional aesthetic values which suit, rather than challenge, current forms of consumption. Viola deals with the grand themes of what some would call 'the human condition': birth, death, states of consciousness, and the relation between material and spiritual worlds. Works can be monumental in scale and often insist on austere surroundings – the darkened, hushed spaces of museums and churches – as if wishing to recapture the aura of sacred art: for instance, *The Messenger* of 1996 was installed in Durham Cathedral in England where visitors could see it having already been prepared to feel something like momentousness or transcendence. Finally, the works demand a different mode of viewing to that of the distracted, exhilarated and bored spectators of video that Jameson characterises: subtle modulations of light and colour, a play with illusions of depth within the frame and a use of dramatically slow motion all seem to evoke the kind of extended private contemplation characteristic of painting.

In *The Greeting* (1995), three women meet in a street and soundlessly act out gestures signifying welcome, introduction, the communication of news, and reactions. The piece refers explicitly to an Italian Renaissance painting and would be merely a pastiche were it not for its dazzling technical properties, a playback time so slow that the forty-five-second-long scene is stretched to ten minutes, and without the usual jerking from frame to frame (achieved by filming at high speed and replaying at the normal rate). This smooth, almost imperceptible motion creates an uncanny effect: on the one hand it lulls the viewer into a dreamlike state, allowing him or her to forget the presence of the camera; on the other, it insists that this remains an inhuman form of vision, able to capture a reality that is not available to perception. Under the machine's gaze the slightest movement of the body or clothing is endowed with intensified significance while the meaning of the scene as a whole, the actual exchange of the greeting, disappears.

In this and later extreme slow motion works that focus on expression as well as gesture, the temptation is to believe they reveal a truth of the person or event underneath appearances (much in the way that Muybridge's chronophotography of the 1870s revealed for the first time the way a horse gallops): 'the unconscious body language and nuances of fleeting glances and gestures become heightened,' Viola writes in his own notes on *The Greeting*.[29] But these pieces play on the difference between human and mechanical forms of perception, rather than represent an objective reality or interpret the unconscious. The mastery of slow motion techniques is highly seductive, but ultimately the limitations of the technical apparatus show through; however mesmerising this world of infinitesimal movement is, the camera cannot disclose any truth, only present us with the banal fact of existence.

Viola has been preoccupied with the nature of experience in a highly mediated world from the outset. Earlier works examined the formal qualities of the medium (different types of screen, the perceptive and reflective properties of the lens, the reproduction of time), and in this respect he can be placed firmly within a modernist avant-garde tradition. But his focus here on the distinctive properties of human subjectivity harks back to an older romanticism, as does his attraction to notions of the sacred and the sublime. Agreeing with Mircea Eliade that 'the sacred is an element in the structure of consciousness and not a stage in the history of consciousness', Viola sets out to awaken it, and thus appeals to desires for a re-enchanted world, for artistic images reinvested with the aura of the icon.[30] This expressly ahistorical outlook, with its emphasis on individual, spiritual forms of liberation, goes some way to accounting for the success of his work in the 1990s.

If Viola was interested in addressing the relation between video and painting, Barney was working predominantly with the language of Hollywood film. In the early 1990s he broke onto the art scene with installations involving strenuous physical performance and disconcerting biomorphic objects – clambering round the walls of the gallery and sculpting weightlifting benches with Vaseline. This became the foundation for the epic *Cremaster* series (1994–2002): a cycle of five feature-length films that articulated his highly idiosyncratic vision of the relation between human biology and culture. Blimps float above a football stadium while ballroom dancers trace diagrams of sexual organs on the pitch below; a male satyr dressed like a dandy tap-dances on a pier while TT bikers speed round the Isle of Man with balls in their pockets; hybrid creatures chase each other across the ceiling of the Guggenheim Museum in New York; forties saloon cars smash into each other in the foyer of the Chrysler Building while revellers use the spire above as a maypole. The imagery is deliberately arcane, and the copious amounts of exegesis it has produced have undoubtedly helped cement *Cremaster*'s status as an important work of art; but a discrete set of themes is iterated throughout, concerning sexual differentiation, hybridity, bodily prosthesis and creative or competitive activity (sport, song and dance). The title itself refers to a muscle that controls the height of the testes, which we can think of as the point where biological and psychological processes meet, or desire is translated into physical action. The dominant motif, therefore, is possibility and the beginnings of change: 'it's about how you can get back to that place where things aren't complete, ideas are fertile, forms aren't yet defined,' Barney has said.[31] Perhaps this is reminiscent of the old modernist preoccupation with the regenerative forces of spring, but the idea of potentiality also had a special significance at the millennium, in the aftermath of twentieth-century political ideologies.

Barney's ambition to create art that matches up to the visual impact of Hollywood film should be recognised, but whether it opens up fruitful angles for critical intervention needs to be questioned. In *Cremaster*, spectacle is not just a theme but a basic constituent element of the work, from the extravagance of production to the fetishisation of the DVDs that play the films, which are displayed as relics and rumoured at a million dollars apiece. Regardless of the costs involved, filming a sequence in which dancers use the Chrysler Building's spire as a maypole does nothing if not make a spectacle of permission, inflating the conception of the artist as a heroic figure to whom all access is granted. His treatment of scale is contentious too: when Barney comments that he chose the Isle of Man for *Cremaster 4* because it was 'small enough that it could be understood as a single form', we get a sense of his attempt to find a cosmic perspective from which to view the world, but at the same time his desire to see individual activity as part of a larger pattern bears an uncomfortable resemblance to the aesthetics of the mass ornament that linked Busby Berkeley dance routines with political rallies in the twentieth century.[32] But perhaps the biggest problem with the work is that its representation of universal forms and processes in all things from the human body to art and culture is at once amazing and banal – a revelation of a fundamental pattern to life that allows no significance in difference other than the fact that it is biologically necessary. Hence all the aspects of culture that *Cremaster* refers to – football games, gangster movies, heavy metal, opera, dance, bagpipes – fall back into equivalence as variants of an endlessly creative life force.

Critical Histories/New Directions

This brings us to the heart of the matter: how to plot the developments of the 1990s in relation to the broader history of modern art in the twentieth century. Does the range and variety of output indicate a lack of consensus about what is to be done in art? If all things are now possible and all practices have equal value, on what grounds should individual artworks be judged? Amongst critics there was a prevailing sense of a break away from avant-garde movements of the past: 'This new art doesn't fit the old criticism,' observed Johanna Drucker.[33] Hal Foster, in another round-table discussion with his *October* colleagues, concurred:

> Today the recursive strategy of the 'neo' appears as attenuated as the oppositional logic of the 'post' seems tired: neither suffices as a strong paradigm for artistic or cultural practice, and no other model stands in their stead; or, put differently, many local models compete, but none can hope to be paradigmatic.[34]

If the work of the 1990s and beyond could no longer even be described as 'post' modern, it raised the possibility that the entire project of modernism, premised on the idea of cultural renewal through avant-garde experiment, had run its course.

Museums across the world testified to this post-historical animus by anxiously rearranging the furniture, displaying their collections in new configurations designed to appeal to wider audiences and dispensing with former historical categories in the process. The rehang at the Museum of Modern Art in New York City in 2000 saw works grouped around general themes such as 'Actors, Dancers, Bathers' or 'Seasons and Moments'; the British museum Tate Modern took a similar approach when it opened in London in the same year with headings such as 'Nude/Action/Body'. In the eyes of the institution this was an attempt to stimulate new responses to modern artworks, but as Franco Moretti pointed out, it happened at the expense of attention to technique – the very thing that had made modern art significant in the first place. At MoMA, Picasso was now to be looked at for the guitar, not the cubism or the collage. 'The citadel of modernism in the visual arts has raised the white flag,' Moretti announced.[35]

For advocates of modernism the stakes were high, since embedded in the practice of technical innovation was the possibility of seeing the world differently and taking up critical positions on things as they are. Amidst the welter of new art being produced, left-wing critics found disappointingly few alternative visions of society and worried that artists had become too deeply involved with the interests of the market, if they hadn't sold out entirely. Julian Stallabrass argued in *Art Incorporated* that 'the most celebrated contemporary art is that which serves to further the interests of the neoliberal economy, in breaking down barriers to trade, local solidarities, and cultural attachments in a continual process of hybridization'.[36] Benjamin Buchloch was similarly pessimistic about the opportunities for radical opposition:

> The post-war situation can be described as a negative teleology: a steady dismantling of the autonomous practices, spaces, and spheres of culture, and a perpetual intensification of assimilation and homogenisation, to the point today where we witness what Debord called the 'integrated spectacle'. . . Are there still spaces situated outside that homogenizing apparatus? Or do we have to recognise that many artists themselves don't want to be situated outside it?[37]

Buchloch may be right that a distinctive feature of late twentieth-century culture is the penetration of the market into all aspects of life, further constraining the always limited autonomy that art may have enjoyed in earlier periods. But his narrative offers little room for manoeuvre and no way of evaluating artists' different approaches to a culture of spectacle. A more satisfying way of conceptualising 1990s art, I think, can be found in Johanna Drucker's book *Sweet Dreams* (2005), where she advances the notion of 'complicit formalism' – the idea that artists are not looking for spaces of autonomy but acknowledging their own personal and professional implication in capitalist society, struggling to mediate demands for critical integrity with an interest in the pleasures of art-making, the attractions of mass culture and the necessity of economic survival. This does not mean that such art has no critical value: Drucker's argument is that a playful reworking of materials, forms and historical references has the potential to shift culture 'out of phase', opening up new relationships to the mass media representations that already structure our consciousness. As she says of Karen Kilimnik, whose paintings look like the work of a teenager copying pictures of favourite celebrities from magazines:

> Her transformation isn't meant to undo the operations of these mass-mediated artefacts but rather to embody a commentary upon them that breaks the unified surface of mass culture into a dialogue. The space of splitting, of reflection and refraction through an individual subject, is one space of aesthetic criticality, but the affirmative sensibility of Kilimnik's work is equally charged with a sense of longing, belonging, and engagement with the objects of her own desire.[38]

For some, Drucker's claims for art's potential as a radical political force will be disappointingly modest. But in the context of an expanding art world – a booming market, the integration of exhibitions into a wider leisure industry and an increasingly global circulation of artists and their audiences – to think about artists' complicit relationships with their own institutions and the wider world will ultimately be more productive than continuing the search for autonomy.

One sign of art's expansion was the number of museums springing up in America and across the world. Many of these in the United States were showcases for leading architects from overseas: Renzo Piano's Cy Twombly Pavilion in Houston (completed in 1995) and Nasher Sculpture Centre in Dallas (2003); Tadao Ando's Pulitzer Foundation building in St Louis (2001) and Modern Art Museum at Fort Worth (2002); Rafael Moneo's Davis Museum in Wellesley College (1993) and addition to the Museum of Fine Arts in Houston (2000) and Santiago Calatrava's Milwaukee Art Museum (2001). American architects also built commissions abroad, such as Richard Meier's Museum of Contemporary Art in Barcelona (1995) and Frank Gehry's Guggenheim Bilbao (1997). While they were not always public commissions, such buildings were often associated with the regeneration of a city or region – the idea being that a great work of architecture could enhance the prestige of a particular location and even revitalise its economy. The most remarkable case is Gehry's Guggenheim Museum, which turned a blighted port city into a major tourist destination almost overnight.

Figure 4.4 Guggenheim Museum, Bilbao (Frank Gehry, 1991–7) (photo: Owen Harrison).

Frank Gehry

'Now we are left with a world without urbanism, only architecture, ever more architecture,' lamented Dutch architect Rem Koolhaas in 1994.[39] He was suggesting that the new excitement over architecture was the outcome of a disappearing faith in the ability to shape the city as a whole. Ideals that once motivated modernist planners no longer seemed credible in the face of expanding and increasingly heterogeneous urban populations, and in their absence it was falling to architecture to sustain what hopes there might be for social renewal.

Nowhere is this situation better illustrated than in the phenomenal success of Frank Gehry, who became one of America's foremost architects at the end of the twentieth century and whose construction for the Guggenheim Foundation in Bilbao initiated a wave of enthusiastic museum-building across the world. The 'Bilbao effect', as it became known, symbolised the belief that outstanding architecture could transform an ailing city's fortunes by boosting tourism and restoring its self-image. Gehry was also a leading proponent of the use of computer-aided design, which allied him with another kind of hope: that computers could liberate architects from Euclidian geometry and produce new relationships between people and space. His irregular, warped structures, looking in varying degrees like giant misshapen toy blocks or folds of fabric laid over the terrain, began appearing across America and Europe as signs of a new exuberance in architecture, and an attitude to modern life that was simultaneously optimistic and uncertain.

Gehry worked almost exclusively in California for the most part of the 1980s, and it was here that key elements of his vocabulary were developed: the use of low-grade, DIY materials such as plywood, corrugated iron and chain-link fencing; a delight in incongruous juxtapositions revealing his affinities for pop art and minimalism, and a scattered distribution of spaces that announced his repudiation of modernist principles of coherence and functional utility. Admirers of his work saw it as a bold attempt to make the chaos of the modern city somehow habitable, while sceptics thought it too acquiescent with dominant power structures. In *City of Quartz* (1990), the well-known tirade against the disenfranchisement of the citizens of Los Angeles, Mike Davis went so far as to accuse Gehry of 'turning away from the street' and aestheticising the city's oppressive surveillance culture.[40] But by the end of the decade Gehry was receiving commissions from further afield, and it was at this point that his designs shifted from geometric to biomorphic forms, facilitated by the use of computer software originally developed for aircraft manufacturing. Tested out on a large fish sculpture made for Barcelona's Olympic Village in 1992, its first full architectural application was for the Guggenheim Museum in Bilbao (1991–7), and Gehry would use it thereafter in buildings such as Seattle's Experience Music Project (1995–2000), the DG Bank Building in Berlin (1995–2001) and the Walt Disney Concert Hall in Los Angeles (1987–2003).

The immediate advantages of computer-aided design are that it makes complex structures cheaper to build: a digital model can produce highly accurate templates for structural components that eliminate waste at the manufacturing stage. But at a time when architects often saw their work compromised by the necessities of finance and consultation, the new tool also allowed Gehry to retain a degree of control over the project which bolstered his status as an individual artist. The claim was spectacularly realised in Bilbao, which turned Gehry into a world celebrity and established the style that would become his signature. The Guggenheim's curved, flowing volumes appeared to erupt out of the surroundings: titanium cladding produced constantly changing light effects while giving an integrity to the structure as a whole; the abandonment of conventional markers such as visible entrances or clear distinctions between walls and roof made it seem more sculptural than architectural.

The project was billed as a collaboration between the Guggenheim Foundation and the Basque government, but with the majority of funding coming from Basque taxpayers it is not surprising that it was received in some quarters as a form of cultural imperialism – the promotion of an American art brand at others' expense. Critics also complained that the building's architectural extravagance was at odds with its actual purpose as an art gallery: visitor pathways were made unnecessarily complicated and the scale of its interior spaces threatened to dwarf anything but the most monumental of works hanging on its walls. In response, Gehry himself scorned the idea that an art museum should be little more than a background for artworks, and the undisputed boost to tourism that the museum gave the city (recouping its costs within a year of opening, according to official reports) dampened much of the original resentment.[41] Leaving aside the larger questions about the way art and culture were being conscripted to urban regeneration schemes in this period, it was clear that Gehry was particularly adept at creating architecture for a burgeoning leisure industry – combining technical innovation with an unapologetic appeal to the pleasures of spectacle. This approach was again evident in the Experience Music Project in Seattle, a large complex built on the site of the 1962 World's Fair in a way that allows the old monorail to pass through it, piercing its outer skin. The result is a kind of mutual tourist promotion: passengers get a glimpse of the EMP's attractions while the monorail is reconceived for the centre's visitors as an architectural feature.

Whether the use of irregular, curvilinear forms marks a productive departure in architectural design is a further matter for debate. In an age of apparently boundless mobility and global capital and information flows, where the forces acting on people and societies were increasingly immaterial, such architecture seemed more appropriate than previous classical or modernist traditions. Inspired by Gilles Deleuze's concept of the fold, some theorists hoped that notions of flexible, liquid or warped space could help develop more positive ways of thinking about difference: Greg Lynn, for instance, spoke of 'formal integrity through deformations which do not internally cleave or shear but . . . connect, incorporate and affiliate productively'. On the other side are those critics who see Gehry's work as merely cosmetic, plastic without being functional, or at its worst, an alibi for a neoliberal economy that represses signs of manual and mechanical labour in its celebration of the miracles of the digital age.[42]

Another factor in the breakdown of former critical paradigms, especially those of national traditions and movements, is the globalisation of the art world. Often connected to wider regeneration agendas, international art fairs and biennial festivals multiplied during the 1990s and became increasingly important both to the circulation of ideas and to the production of reputations. If the barometer of national art since 1932 had been the Whitney Biennial, the centres of the new international context were biennials in places such as Venice, Sao Paulo, Istanbul, Johannesburg and Gwangju, or branded exhibitions like Documenta and Manifesta. Here, national identity was reproduced in a relatively abstract sense – artists would 'represent' their home country like athletes at sporting contests without representing specific national concerns – while the festival as a whole generated the sense of a global art community engaged in conversation around common themes. A list of participating artists in the American Pavilion at the Venice Biennale gives a good indication of the way that the idea of a single story of American art breaks down in the 1990s, as individual artists give way to group shows:

1990   Jenny Holzer
1993   Louise Bourgeois, Andres Serrano
1995   Bill Viola
1997   Robert Colescott
1999   Douglas Aitken, Chris Burden, Jimmie Durham,
       Tim Hawkinson, Ann Hamilton, Jenny Holzer, Zhang
       Huan, Richard Jackson, James Lee Byars, Christian
       Marclay, Bruce Nauman, Shirin Neshat, Jason Rhoades,
       Sarah Sze
2001   Robert Gober, Michael Joo, Do-Ho Suh, Bill Viola

The proliferation of biennials also helped give rise to a new class of artist defined by their mobility, more likely to produce work in different locations across the world than in their own studio. These 'itinerant artists', as Miwon Kwon calls them, would be invited by institutions to act as ethnographers, critics-in-residence or creators of collaborative situations in the hope that their practice would generate new insights into local conditions. Mark Dion, for instance, raised questions about the formation of scientific and historical knowledge by posing as a kind of amateur naturalist or collector of curiosities at sites across Europe and the United States. In 1999 he worked with artefacts from the Carnegie Museum collection in Pittsburgh to reimagine the life of early American ornithologist Alexander Wilson, and conducted excavations on the banks of the Thames outside the two Tate Galleries in London in a project that brought teenage and elderly volunteers together in a search for the meaning of the river's accumulated junk. Site-specific works such as these can certainly be successful in reviving historical sensibilities or performing interventions in an everyday context, but as Kwon points out, they cannot escape the irony that a foreign artist is being hired to facilitate the expression of local identities. If one of the effects of globalisation is the emptying out of local distinctiveness in metropolitan centres across the world, then the kind of strategy that turns to art to emphasise the differences of place is ultimately a compensatory one.[43]

Globalisation naturally became a source for imagery and issues in representation: travel and migration, the spaces of the new economy, the crossing or enforcement of borders, the dissemination of mass culture and its appropriation in local contexts were all common themes. Notable examples were Martha Rosler's ongoing photographic project on the non-spaces of air travel, *In the Place of the Public*; Allan Sekula's *Fish Story* (1995), a series documenting the transit of container ships, making visible the industrial labour that was often repressed in images of the global economy; and Belgian artist Chantal Akerman's video installation *De l'Autre Côté* (2001), which addressed the myths and realities of the Mexican-American borderlands. But the most challenging and innovative art at the turn of the millennium seemed to come from artists for whom mobility and displacement also had a personal dimension. Itinerant in a different sense, they experienced globalisation as a persistent tension between incommensurate cultures: western and non-western, communist and liberal capitalist, developing and over-developed. Shirin Neshat from Iran, Ilya and Emilia Kabakov from Russia, Do-Ho Suh from Korea, Zhang Huan from China and Tehching Hsieh from Taiwan all took up residence in New York in the 1990s, where they produced work that explored relations and contrasts between political and social systems. If conflicts between individual freedoms and restrictive regimes were prominent themes, the art was by no means a straightforward affirmation of American life; instead, being situated between or outside national cultures was treated as a new position from which to examine subjectivity, states of consciousness and artistic practices.

Do-Ho Suh and the Kabakovs sit at opposite ends of the spectrum of installation art, but they are equally concerned with the persistence of communism in a western imaginary and the ways of recovering its potential as a signifier of social alternatives. In pieces like *Public Figures*, *Doormat* and *Bridge*, multitudes of miniature figures are assembled to support the weight of a plinth or passing spectators: though they seem to trivialise revolutionary aesthetics, they nevertheless show Suh attempting to find affirmative images of mass activity. Ilya and Emilia Kabakov's more conceptual work, such as the *Palace of Projects* installation of 1998, presents utopianism as a basic human impulse that should not be dismissed because of associations with discredited regimes. In language that evokes the authoritarianism that forced the artists into exile as much as it parodies the moral didacticism of art institutions, they explain the purpose of the piece thus:

But it is no less important, and perhaps more so, to create a unique museum of dreams, a museum of hypotheses and projects, even if they are unrealizable. In many of them, the visitor to such a 'Palace' will encounter stimulus for his own fantasies, much will prompt him to the resolution of his own tasks, will awaken his imagination and, the main thing, will provide the impulse for his own creative activity in a 'positive direction'.[44]

While representations of globalisation often emphasise its fluid, insubstantial dimensions, many of these artists insist on the very real material impact of a transnational existence. Suh describes his own sense of displacement in the following terms: 'When I first came to the United States my response to the new environment was often physical. I often felt that I was living in someone else's body and I felt like I was dropped from the sky and granted this new body.'[45] The same sentiment appears in the work of Zhang Huan, whose gruelling but nevertheless lyrical performances evoked the difficulty of adapting to the environment with almost absurd levels of literalism. *Pilgrimage – Wind and Water* (1998) featured the artist lying prostrate on a block of ice, surrounded by dogs, in the hope that the heat of his body might melt the ice and bring him into contact with the Luohan daybed that represented his ancestors. In *My America (Hard to Acclimatize)*, he sat motionless while sixty volunteers walked round pelting him with bread, signifying offerings to the destitute; in *My New York*, performed for the Whitney Biennial in 2002, he appeared in a body suit made of raw meat, looking like a bodybuilder whose skin had been torn off, before walking amongst the crowd distributing doves.

Also known for his feats of endurance is Tehching Hsieh, a Taiwanese artist who came to America as an illegal immigrant in 1974 and produced a series of legendary year-long performances in New York between 1978 and 1986: a year in a cage in his studio; a year punching a time clock every hour on the hour; a year without going indoors; a year tied to another artist; and a year without any contact with art whatsoever. Absent of references to national cultures, these works make the passage of time the main object of contemplation and the body – not its capacity for gesture and sign-making, as is usually the case with performance art, but its physical and psychological resources for survival – their medium. At the same time, they cannot escape being invested with culturally specific meanings. On one hand, the pieces signify within western traditions of performance art (Hsieh is often compared with Marina Abramovic and Ulay), while on the

Figure 4.5 Zhang Huan, *My New York* (2002): Performance, Whitney Museum, New York (courtesy of Zhang Huan Studio).

other they invite connotations of imprisonment, torture, homelessness, companionship and religious retreat.

Hsieh ended his career as an artist on 31 December 1999, after a thirteen-year performance in which he imposed the restriction of never showing any of his art publicly, and after which he declared that his main accomplishment had been simply to survive. This would seem a fitting way to end the chapter: with a non-performance that makes the mere endurance of the decade a work of art, while at the same time powerfully evoking the urgent conditions of life at the turn of the century – the failure of communist plans, the suppression of individual expression and the theoretical end-point of a voracious modern art system which colonises all forms of existence as art.[46]

Chapter 5

Digital Culture

'I believe that an essential prerequisite to sustainable development, for all members of the human family, is the creation of this network of networks. To accomplish this purpose, legislators, regulators, and business people must do this: build and operate a Global Information Infrastructure. This GII will circle the globe with information super-highways on which all people can travel . . . From these connections we will derive robust and sustainable economic progress, strong democracies, better solutions to global and local environmental challenges, improved health care, and – ultimately – a greater sense of shared stewardship of our small planet.' Al Gore, 1994

The excitement that accompanied developments in computing at the beginning of the 1990s is difficult to recapture today. Technology that was only just emerging then has now become so thoroughly integrated into social life that many readers will be unable to imagine a time when things took place without it: when friends wrote letters; when passengers navigated road journeys by reading a map; when speaking on the telephone tied you to a designated corner of the living room; when taking a photograph meant a lengthy wait for the end result. Moreover, what we now think of as the primary symbol of the Information Age – the World Wide Web – has become widely colonised by media corporations and commerce, to the extent that recent users will hardly recognise it as a medium that once had a radically egalitarian agenda. 'Free access' was once championed as an end in itself, the mainstay of the internet pioneers' visions of a global online community; now it is often used as a means of growing a market for monetisation at a later stage. Innovations continue, of course, and they are often imbued with expectations that they will increase efficiency or ease the stresses of life. But the earlier period in which computers and information technology were associated with transformations of mythic dimensions – bringing social renewal, improved democracy, the end of scarcity and peace between nations – has receded as quickly as it appeared.

To see how dramatically the field has changed let us return to the beginning of the 1990s and review the extent to which new technology would shape everyday life over the course of the decade. About fifty million computers were in use in the United States at this time: most of these were in the form of the desktop unit, and only a few were connected to the internet. By 1995 there would be ninety million computers, equivalent to one for every three Americans, while the networked population increased at an equally astonishing rate – from between five and ten million users to fifty-four million in 1997. This would reach 134 million in 2000, by which point the United States was hosting a third of the world's traffic.[1] Mobile communication was still in its infancy: in 1990 cell phones were bulky analogue machines carried by five million people, and it was not until the middle of the decade with the widespread adoption of cheaper and more functional digital models that their profound impact on personal interaction and social space would begin to be perceived. (One early instance anticipating those changes is Robert Altman's film *The Player* (1992), whose opening sequence shows the protagonist talking on a cell phone to his wife while spying on her from outside the house. Four years later, the same routine is played for suspense in Wes Craven's spoof horror *Scream* – a movie in which, notably, it is still plausible for a teenage suspect to claim not to own one.) Digitisation had taken place a little earlier in recorded music, and in 1990 most music was consumed on compact disc: record companies were still enjoying the boost to revenues that came from reselling analogue recordings in digitally 'remastered' versions, and the threat of the mp3 was not yet on the horizon. Computer games had shifted from the public arcade to the home console, but they were still largely based on rudimentary two-dimensional graphics and key genres such as the first-person shooter were only just beginning to emerge.

Subsequent developments in digital technology and its applications occurred so rapidly that it is easiest to present them in the form of a separate chronology (see the beginning of the book for a more extensive chronology where these events can be placed in a wider context):

Key developments in digital technology and culture

1990

- Launch of Windows 3.0, beginning Microsoft's dominance in operating systems
- Dycam (Logitech) Model 1, first consumer digital camera, goes on sale
- Photoshop 1.0 released for Apple Mac, a tool for the creation of composite images that soon becomes indispensable in design, advertising and publishing

1991

- Tim Berners-Lee publishes details of the protocol for the World Wide Web (declared a permanently free resource in 1993)
- Release of Apple's QuickTime, an application allowing video images to be run on a computer screen
- First webcam – Cambridge University's Coffeecam – goes online
- GNU/Linux, an open-source operating system to rival Microsoft Windows, established

1992

- Word-processing package WinWord challenges WordPerfect, exemplifying Microsoft's strategy of aggressive competition for industry standards

1993

- Publication of Mosaic browser (becomes Netscape in 1994)
- *Doom*, the original first-person shooter game, released as shareware (installed on ten million computers by 1995)
- First issue of *WIRED* magazine, a key source of cyberculture discourse
- First 'spam' message sent (by accident)

1994

- Foundation of search engines Netscape and Yahoo
- White House website goes live
- First commercial transaction using encrypted credit card details
- Launch of Amazon.com, setting the standard for web commerce
- Visible Human Project publishes its first set of data allowing users to inspect and explore the body of a dead American man

1995

- AuctionWeb founded, later renamed eBay
- Netscape Communications goes public in the largest stock market flotation in history, raising $12 billion and signalling the beginning of the 'dotcom' boom

1996

- Adventure game *Tomb Raider* makes its avatar Lara Croft the first 'virtual celebrity'
- Communications Decency Act passed in response to concerns about pornographic content on the web
- BackRub, a search engine evaluating backlinks, runs on Stanford University's web server; relaunched in 1997 as Google

1997

- Release of *Ultima Online*, the first game to popularise the MMORPG genre (Massively Multiplayer Online Role-Playing Game)
- Microsoft releases Internet Explorer 4.0, whose bundling with Windows prompts a government investigation into the company's business practices
- Activist Jody Williams receives the Nobel prize for her work with the International Campaign to Ban Landmines – one of the first organisations to use email for activist purposes

1998

- eBay and Google go public
- Portable mp3 players appear on the market
- Political blog The Drudge Report breaks news of Clinton's improper relations with White House intern Monica Lewinsky

1999

- Music file sharing software (Napster) becomes freely available

2000

- Fears of a 'millennium bug' – that the turn of the clock to zero will destabilise computer systems worldwide – are disappointed

2001

- Foundation of Wikipedia, the best-known example of large-scale networked user-generated content

From this limited selection we can pick out a number of key trends. First, there is the transition from stand-alone software loaded on individual computers to internet-based applications: a move made possible with increasing bandwidth and processing power, but most of all with the arrival of the World Wide Web, which entered popular consciousness in 1994. While the internet has a history dating back to the 1950s, it was the invention of the web, a simple system of hypertext with text input, that realised its potential for mass networked communication and established a new medium. At this point the utopian ideals of the internet's early users came up against state and commercial interests, and the web was increasingly conceived as a space for economic development. Microsoft played a central role in this story, reinventing itself in 1995 to focus its energies on net-based activities: browser Internet Explorer was coupled with Microsoft Network (MSN) and news service MSNBC. The growing concern over the corporation's potentially monopolistic practices was part of an ongoing struggle between business, government and social groups to shape the internet's evolution – something that will be explored in the following sections.

A second trend to note is the emergence of social applications. In the 1980s, individual users socialised on bulletin boards and in multiuser domains; as the decade progressed these were joined by other communities organised around specific leisure interests, from fandom to gaming to music file-sharing. Auction sites appeared for a moment to offer a powerful alternative to retail, conjuring an image of the ideal marketplace where demand alone determines the price of goods. Activism also thrived online, the relative cheapness of the medium and the speed of communication allowing for groups to mobilise rapidly around a particular issue and create independent forms of news distribution. The mainstream press itself was slower to take advantage of the web, and it was the more informal aspects of news – rumour, opinion, subscriber forums – that flourished first. This became acutely evident in the scandal of President Clinton's affair with Monica Lewinsky, in many respects a story that both lived and died on the net, ignited by speculation amongst political bloggers and extinguished soon after the online publication of federal investigator Kenneth Starr's report. Such examples show that internet technologies do not necessarily displace traditional public spaces, but they do have special qualities that help to foster new forms of interaction. On the one hand, net exchanges tend to be governed by a principle of instantaneity which determines not just the content but the tone of communication: the informality of email, the trivialities of chat rooms or the preference for breaking news in journalism.[2] On the other hand, they are determined by the low cost of copying and distributing information, something that fuels a myth of universal access to knowledge at the same time as it threatens to undermine existing markets and concepts of property.

Thirdly, the spread of digitisation in the 1990s had a significant impact on visual culture. The introduction of the digital camera to general consumers prompted an explosion in popular photography and an opening of the field of everyday subject matter, as the elimination of the costs of film and developing allowed users to be more prolific, even experimental with their snapshots. At the same time, the rise in the domestic use of the digital camera was paralleled by its adoption in bureaucratic and disciplinary contexts. No longer restricted to the limited storage capacities of tape, video surveillance evolved from filming to scanning: the continuous, real-time supervision of environments and behaviour. The data it produced could be put to use in various policing contexts such as traffic regulation (number-plate recognition systems), crime detection (facial recognition) or border control (iris detection as a form of ID). Such developments have made fears of 'surveillance society' and 'the end of privacy' an ever-present concern, although one of the ironies of the period is that intrusions into private life are resisted and embraced in equal measure, with the use of webcams and the display of personal information on social networking sites quickly becoming a popular form of entertainment.[3]

Digital visual technologies also had more general implications for prevailing beliefs about representation. When an image is the manifestation of digital code, rather than a physical record of light falling on objects, the link between the visual sign and what it signifies in the real world is broken down. The traditional assumption that the celluloid or photographic image refers on some level to an external reality or event (*something* taking place, even if the image is created in a studio with a high level of artifice) is therefore severely undermined. The repercussions of this development were evident in controversies over the doctoring of press photographs, in courts' reluctance to accept photographic evidence and in cinema where concerns were voiced over the digital manipulation of documentary film. The most obvious example is Robert Zemeckis's film *Forrest Gump*, which played with the film record for comic effect, altering archive footage frame by frame to make President Kennedy speak lines written for a contemporary audience in 1994. Such a profound paradigmatic shift naturally produced anxieties about the loss of authenticity and authority in representational practices, but for film-makers it meant an array of new creative possibilities. Thus film theorist Sean Cubitt sees digital production as a continuation of cinematic principles rather than a traumatic rupture, and speculates that 'at some point in the near future . . . historians [will] recognize that the photochemical cinema is a brief interlude in the history of the animated image'.[4] Critics of photography have similarly argued that the artificiality of the digital image merely offers a lesson that pictures have always relied on a set of codes to establish their claims to truth – that 'realism' was only ever a special effect.

Digital culture, then, denotes the range of experiences, practices, expressions and representations that emerge under the conditions outlined above. Such a broad definition encompasses not only the integration of the personal computer into society but the shift from analogue to digital that has occurred across the field of media, affecting the reproduction of text, images, speech and other types of sound, as well as sensory and spatial experiences. Even the human body has been subject to digitisation: its physical form is dissected and 'captured' by imaging techniques (most dramatically in the Visible Human Project, discussed below); its substance is broken down into genetic code, and its activity is monitored by a host of surveillance tools and converted into datasets. The impact of these changes has been such that for many observers digital culture constitutes an epistemological shift – an 'information revolution' in which the circulation of abstract data takes precedence over the circulation of material goods. Under the digital turn, the world becomes code, with all phenomena potentially translatable into a common language of ones and zeros. The spread of this logic of information influences conceptions of reality, biological life, human subjectivity, economics and politics.

Virtual Subjects and Virtual Communities

The myth of the frontier dominated digital discourse from the late 1980s into the 1990s. Borrowing from its original source in Jacksonian America, the frontier captured the sense of uncharted territory and boundless opportunity, but it also gave the early practitioners of networked computing the chance to see themselves as pioneers in a very traditional national enterprise: the remaking of a more just and equal society away from the interference of the state. Thus Howard Rheingold, champion of computer-mediated communication, spoke of online networking as 'homesteading on the electronic frontier' at a time when his contemporaries in the Electronic Frontier Foundation were busy lobbying for the freedoms of net users and protesting against government intrusions.

Of course, the mythic freedom of the frontier is inevitably bound to the history of its incorporation, and the same was true of the internet in the 1990s. As computer networks were integrated with the national economy, the frontier metaphor was gradually displaced by that of the road: Bill Gates spoke of 'The Road Ahead' in his memoir of 1995, while Al Gore worked hard to popularise the phrase 'information superhighway' in his attempt to build support for developing the net's infrastructure. As the quotation at the beginning of this chapter indicates, the phrase is intended to suggest ease of access to information and open communication across the globe, but it also establishes a very different vision of the net's social applications, one that is more individualised than communitarian. In a later phase of development the superhighway would be replaced in its turn by ecological models emphasising the naturally self-regulating properties of communications networks, but as Andrew Ross has observed, for a period it was a versatile metaphor that tellingly connoted state subsidy of private enterprise.[5]

Equally important for the way that internet activity was first conceived was the language of virtuality. Virtuality has been a part of the lexicon of computing since the 1980s, though the concept of 'virtual reality' can be traced further back to the development of military and aircraft simulators in the 1960s. In the 1990s, virtual reality devices were being used in fields from medicine and marine research to architecture, as well as fuelling all sorts of fantasies of armed combat and remote sex. Headsets, datagloves and tactile suits were all part of the paraphernalia of virtual reality, designed to create the illusion of bodily presence in a simulated environment. Over the decade, however, the concept of the virtual was generalised to include any kind of online or computer-mediated activity, until it ultimately took on the properties of a new order of representation, successor to the real, surreal and hyperreal of previous epistemological paradigms. Indeed, the abbreviation of virtual reality to VR and the corresponding relegation of reality to its other half (RL: Real Life) expressed something of the excitement with which the dreams of the new technology were embraced – the delight in entertaining the idea that reality was only one of several possible states of existence, and that it might not even be necessary to live there. (The nightmare version of this fantasy is given in a film like *The Matrix*, of course, where the virtual and the real have become indistinguishable.)

Virtual communities proliferated as public access to the internet grew. In the 1980s common forms were the bulletin board system (BBS), which allowed users to participate in discussion forums on specific topics of interest, and multi-user dungeons (MUDs), adventure game environments featuring quests and combat with fantasy creatures or other players. Greater processing power meant that these became more sophisticated in the 1990s: new 'object-oriented' MUDs (MOOs) allowed users to manipulate objects or create their own architecture, changing the playing experience for other users and helping the environment to evolve independently of the original programmers. With the development of image-based interfaces and 3D modelling, these would spawn 'massively multiplayer online role-playing games' (MMORPGs) and other virtual environments such as Second Life by the end of the decade. While many people questioned whether user groups in such activities deserved to be called 'communities', MUDs and MOOs were nevertheless of great interest to social scientists studying the impact of new media on social interaction.

An interesting example is Habitat, an early graphic MUD created by Chip Morningstar and Randall Farmer for Commodore 64 users in 1985, and often seen as the precursor to MMORPGs such as Ultima Online (1997) and Everquest (1999). From the outset, the pair realised that a complex interactive environment was impossible to plan and should be left to evolve according to the actions of its participants. Furthermore, they determined that interaction had to include the potential for moral behaviour, meaning that they allowed for the existence of weapons, crime and even death (though this usually involved a form of reincarnation, the user's avatar being sent home where it would be reborn without all the wealth and special features it had acquired in its previous 'life'). In their own account of the game's development, such rules produced a pattern of behaviour that began with users forming gangs to 'rob' and 'kill' other players and ended with collective demands for policing, the building of city walls and the establishment of a church to minister to those users who longed for a common code of moral conduct. Thus Habitat appeared to act out the narrative of frontier settlement to the letter: society and government arising in response to a threat of disorder and a fear of the wilderness.[6] The story poses important questions for those who would see the net as a laboratory of social behaviour. If the temptation is to read it as a confirmation of a Hobbesian truth about the need to exchange freedoms for a guarantee of protection, it may simply be that early users came to the net with ingrained affection for myths of the Old West that they acted out, consciously or not, in cyberspace.

Another case of antisocial conduct which became central to thinking about online communities was an incident that took place on the site LambdaMOO in 1993, described by Julian Dibbell in a well-known *Village Voice* article, 'A Rape in Cyberspace'.[7] Operating under the pseudonym Mr Bungle, a member created an application that allowed 'him' to take possession of other avatars, controlling their speech and making them act out violent and humiliating acts of self-abuse. Ultimately the member was ejected from the MUD, but not before his actions had provoked a fierce debate across the whole community about permissible speech and individual rights out of which a new system of self-government eventually emerged. For

Dibbell, what was being exposed in the furore was the way in which the internet's hallowed principles of free speech and limited regulation came into conflict with the particular qualities of the medium, where words were not merely speech but also a form of action – what he calls 'incantation'. The fact that words on the net can also be code, shaping the environment in which they exist, calls into question the distinctions between material and symbolic realms that he saw as being fundamental to post-Enlightenment liberal societies. Dibbell concurs at this point with a number of other scholars in the field who have highlighted the peculiar configuration of the rational and the mystical in cyberspace: see, for instance, Margaret Wertheim's *The Pearly Gates of Cyberspace* (1999).

Howard Rheingold, *The Virtual Community* (1993)

Published in 1993, *The Virtual Community* was an important volume that captured the idealism of the pioneers of the internet and gave online activity a history. Howard Rheingold was a contemporary of the founders of the first networks of internet users – figures such as Larry Brilliant and Stewart Brand from the San Francisco counterculture who had adopted the technology as a cultural experiment and a means of disseminating their ideals. His book chronicled the formation of the first bulletin board systems (BBS), analysed the newer forms of interaction in MUDs and on Internet Relay Chat (IRC), and offered his own story of what it was like to take part in 'computer-mediated communication'. Hence it was both memoir and manifesto, motivated by a desire to assert the value of online interaction (commonly dismissed as juvenile or escapist behaviour) and rally readers to sustain the net's democratic potential.

Rheingold's main focus was the Whole Earth 'Lectronic Link, or WELL: a large assembly of bulletin boards and conferences organised around specific topics of interest from leisure and wellbeing to planning. He noted the diversity of members as the networked population grew – from the post-hippies, computer technicians and Deadheads of the early days to the 'symbolic analysts' of the 1990s, the self-employed in search of knowledge and skills, and the isolated homemakers in search of wider spheres of influence. In addition to mapping these forums, Rheingold noted how the new multi-user dungeons offered chances for identity play and how chat services created new possibilities for cross-cultural dialogue: his account of IRC communication amongst different nationalities during the Gulf War of 1991, for instance, argues that despite the chaotic and fiery nature of the discussion some kind of tolerant exchange could be achieved. Throughout, Rheingold emphasises the radical potential of online communication: for him the value of the WELL is its ability to foster principles of reciprocity and resist the commodification of information ('the people who have the information are more interesting than the information alone'), and the power of the internet in general is its challenge to hierarchical and centralised modes of organisation.[8]

One of the most interesting aspects of *The Virtual Community* is its attempt to chart behaviour on the net at a moment when the norms of conduct were only just beginning to form. Rheingold observes, for example, that the FAQ (Frequently Asked Questions) feature – now an omnipresent component of website design – emerged from the ways in which bulletin board systems welcomed newcomers to their conferences in order to minimise repetition in the discussion. He also considers the psychological effects of online communication, characterising BBS discourse as a mixture of conversation and performance (since only a small fraction of the group members contribute a majority of posts[9]), and MUDs as spaces in which individuals can expose, explore and invent different facets of their personality: 'Masks and self-disclosures are part of the grammar of cyberspace, the way quick cuts and intense images are part of the grammar of television.'[10] While Rheingold acknowledges the problems that such identity play might entail as well as the dangers of excessive internet use, his emphasis is generally on the affirmative and transformative possibilities of the net – the way it liberates the multiple selves latent in all of us, dissolving fixed identities and challenging the power relations that operate around them.

Rheingold's idealism does need to be questioned, and many commentators have been less enchanted with the potential of computer-mediated communication. After all, online chat can produce just as much hostility as tolerance (as the persistent concern over the practice of 'flaming' shows); groups of like-minded users may be mutually supportive but not necessarily for the good of others (witness the enthusiastic embrace of the net by extremists); and for every story of virtual relationships leading to real-life marriage there is a story of a person ill-equipped in social skills whose net habits render him or her less able to function in the everyday world. But the main criticism surrounding the book in the years following its publication centred on the meaning of Rheingold's use of the term 'community': to what extent do networked users deserve to be called a community when access to computers is still only available to few, or when association is based on a shared interest rather than a common predicament? Are these networks not too weak, too easy to leave and too transient to constitute community in any real sense? For Kevin Robins, the key problem was that visions of virtual community often reinforced conservative ideas of society as a set of intimate relationships rather than a means of addressing differences between people: 'the system works to expel all that is uncertain, unknown and alien – all the qualities of otherness that may attach themselves to distance'.[11]

Despite these criticisms (many of which he acknowledged in a 2000 postscript to the book), Rheingold deserves credit for taking online activity seriously and exploring its possibilities as a new medium. He showed how the net can be a place for emotion and sentiment, no less authentic than in relationships that exist elsewhere. In the story he tells of a dying WELL member who remains online up to his final moments with a laptop by his hospital bed; his image of 'hundreds of people around the world sitting in front of computer screens with tears in their eyes' is a powerful evocation of the affective possibilities of computer-mediated communication.[12] Most important of all, though, the value of the book lies in his insistence that the internet's particular structure – its critical difference from the centralised broadcast paradigm of television and radio – gives it a democratic potential worth defending against the encroachment of media monopoly.

Social scientists were also interested in the effects of online communication on identity formation. Sherry Turkle, one of the principal ethnographers of digital culture, spent the 1980s and 90s interviewing participants in various spheres of computer activity and put the question this way:

The Internet has become a significant social laboratory for experimenting with the constructions and reconstructions of self that characterise postmodern life. In its virtual reality, we self-fashion and self-create. What kinds of personae do we make? What relation do these have to what we have traditionally thought of as the 'whole' person? . . . Is it an expression of identity crisis of the sort we traditionally associate with adolescence? Or are we watching the slow emergence of a new, more multiple style of thinking about the human mind?[13]

Along with many other observers Turkle acknowledged the net's emancipatory potential, noting that the adoption of different personae could help people develop facets of their personality that were otherwise repressed, but by the end of the decade she was more equivocal about the lasting value of such identity play. The key issue was the extent of feedback between the virtual and the real: self-reinvention might be possible on the net, but the repercussions on social relations elsewhere might be minimal. Nor was behaviour on the net necessarily free from dominant ideologies and pressures on identity. For instance, if it was undeniable that gay people often found safe spaces for coming out in chat rooms and MUDs, it was also found that heterosexual play amongst homosexuals was more common than vice versa. Thus experimentation and border-crossing did not take place in all directions, and the normativity of heterosexuality remained largely unchallenged.[14]

The same tension between identity play and the reassertion of norms is evident in a story like the one below, originally posted on a WELL conference on internet sex in 1992:

'The other night a "woman" was accused by another "woman" of not being a woman. She thought the "woman" in question was too aggressive to be a woman. The "woman" in question gave her phone number to several people so that they could call to hear her voice. After doing so, a "man" verified that "she" sounded like a female. The "woman" who had raised the allegations was not impressed. "She" said that lots of TVs sounded like women. Someone then asked "her" how we were to know that SHE was a woman. "She" said that there were images of her available for downloading.'[15]

Even if 'masks and self-disclosures are part of the grammar of cyberspace', as Howard Rheingold put it (see case study above), the incident shows how the internet can produce just as much anxiety about boundary-blurring as it provides opportunities for individual transgression. Once the collective will to sustain fantasies is shaken, the desire for the immediacy of face-to-face contact returns in force, and with it the demand to fix identities according to physical attributes like voice and appearance. Despite the fact that this is a space where people go to enjoy experimenting with gender and sexuality, there is nevertheless a residual longing for the stability of clearly defined and unmediated identity categories – mirrored here in the way that the qualifying quotation marks create a visual disturbance that the reader's eye longs to do without.

Gender and sexuality were the dominant topics of critical discourse on net behaviour in the early 1990s – to a large degree reflecting the way that digital culture tended to repress discourses on race and class. Racial stereotypes such as gangsters and ninjas predominated in digital popular culture alongside the ideology of colour-blindness in chat rooms and online forums: 'if you don't want to be racially abused, don't reveal your race' was a widely used means of policing race which left the implicit hegemony of whiteness intact.[16] Such inequalities also existed at the level of access to technology, with black Americans sustaining significantly lower levels of internet use.[17] The repression of class and racial differences was equally operative in the way that the net, and later the web, was promoted as a space of zero-cost exchanges and perfect free markets to the neglect of attention to the real-world labour that went into creating it. Hidden from sight, 'digital sweat' took the form of the 'microserfs' working for software corporations at a lower average salary than in television and publishing industries, voluntary labour supplied by young apprentices at dotcom start-ups and web design companies, the manual work of hardware manufacturing and recycling, and the large markets of cheap labour outsourced to developing countries that would be opened up by the internet in the years to come.

Ecommerce, Government Regulation and Public Space

> Governments of the Industrial World, you weary giants of flesh and steel, I come from cyberspace, the new home of Mind. On behalf of the future, I ask you of the past to leave us alone. You are not welcome among us. You have no sovereignty where we gather.[18]

Thus begins John Perry Barlow's 'Declaration of the Independence of Cyberspace', widely distributed on the internet in reaction to the passing of the Telecommunications Act of 1996. What enraged him were the restrictions placed on net communications in the form of the Communications Decency Act, which had been incorporated within the Telecommunications Act. An early attempt to control the circulation of obscene and indecent material online, the Act had received widespread support in Congress but Barlow and others saw it as an infringement of civil liberties. Former lyricist for the rock band The Grateful Dead and leading member of the Electronic Frontier Foundation, Barlow was very much a part of the internet's pioneering generation and his declaration is one of the liveliest expressions of its anarchic spirit. But the manifesto also marks the next phase of net culture emerging in the mid-1990s, after the establishment of the World Wide Web and the opening of access to users across the country, in which the utopian fantasies of cyberspace ceded to demands for regulation and the putative separation of real and virtual worlds began to break down.

As mentioned in Chapter 2, the Telecommunications Act was heralded as the most extensive restructuring of media and communications for over half a century. Its central aim was to promote economic growth in the context of expanding global markets and rapidly developing technological capabilities. Hence restrictions were lifted on corporate ownership to allow for new synergies between entertainment industries, broadcasting, communications and computing; measures were also introduced to encourage the influx of private finance for the construction of a national broadband network. A number of commentators at the time noted the irony that of all the protests against the Act, far more objections were raised to its infringements of free speech than to the implications of privatising the net, something that would arguably have more serious consequences for its potential as a space for all American citizens. Tirades like Barlow's expressed nothing if not the angst of West Coast libertarians who despised the state but embraced the free market, and were disappointed that liberalisation could go hand in hand with greater government regulation.

The crucial factor in this second phase of net culture was the development of commercial applications on the web. Here an instructive example is Amazon.com, originally launched as an online bookseller by Jeff Bezos in 1994. Amazon became the model of a successful 1990s dotcom business – although, significantly, its success was better measured in terms of stock price than real profits, since the company lost over two and a half billion dollars in its first seven years before it ever turned a profit.[19] What made Amazon distinctive was its combination of scale and computing power: selling books exclusively on the internet meant that the costs of acquiring and running stores were eliminated while the stock, held in large automated warehouses, could be increased by a factor of ten or more. An online database enabled customers to search the catalogue directly, but it also created new possibilities for cross-referencing and feedback. If, as traditional book lovers complained, the website lacked the tactile pleasure of browsing a bookstore's shelves, Amazon found ways to compensate by adding features such as sample pages, readers' reviews and personalised recommendations based on the customer's former visits and aggregated sales data ('Customers who bought this also bought . . .'). Thus it helped to popularise the phenomenon now known as 'crowdsourcing', in which new value is realised from the amassing of data from large numbers of individual interactions. Such a principle underpinned many of the most popular sites on the web – such as music preference site Last.fm (2002) and travel review site TripAdvisor.com (2000), as well as the back-link evaluator Google (1997). As the scientist James Gleick remarked in the *New York Times Magazine*, one of the strange effects of its application on Amazon was the way it reconceived the idea of personal taste. Once recommendations were being made by a machine, taste could no longer be thought of as a property unique to each individual: instead it became merely a mathematical function, a motif in a broader pattern of statistics.[20]

eBay.com was another phenomenon of early ecommerce. First launched as AuctionWeb in 1995, it became a publicly traded company in 1998 and a year later was already hosting over two million auctions. Its success came from mobilising the web's networking potential to put private buyers and sellers in direct contact with each other without the usual limitations of geography. Niche goods could therefore find a market more easily: an unwanted toy soldier collection might be worth nothing in the neighbourhood, for example, but a posting on eBay would make it available to interested buyers in all parts of the country or across the world. eBay's popularity raised new questions about ecommerce's potential for transforming economies by reducing costs and inefficiencies: was this an example of the perfect free market, where price was determined by a direct relationship between supply and demand? Or was it a place which generated and profited from irrationalities in people's behaviour, such as the desire for junk or the impulse to collect?[21] For many amateur sellers it was clearly a useful tool for recycling unwanted items, but its additional appeal as a form of entertainment was also evident in the rhetoric the site used with buyers ('Congratulations! You have won . . .'), and its rapid fame as a place to go for a glimpse into the oddities of human economic activity suggests that it was always more than a model of economic rationality.

Such commerce was not without its real-world implications. Amazon's much-criticised treatment of its workforce served as a warning that capitalism on the internet might be no less unforgiving than in any other sector of the globalising economy: when in 2001 employees in Seattle began organising a union, the company responded by relocating its customer-service facility to India and creating over a thousand redundancies.[22] But an equally important, if less noticeable, consequence was that the growth of ecommerce produced a general demand for security on the web, which led in turn to a proliferation of forms of authentication and identification. While this was unquestionably to the benefit of the web's shoppers, it was a clear sign of the ongoing territorialisation of cyberspace and the disappearance of a principle of anonymity that had been integral to its earlier, more experimental phase.

Nevertheless, the growth of commercial enterprises on the web did not occlude alternative and non-commercial uses. 'Blogging' emerged out of attempts to chart the novelties of the web (such as the *What's New?* and *What's Cool?* pages of early browsers Netscape and Yahoo), and by the end of the decade it had evolved into one of the most popular forms of web authorship. Blog historian Rebecca Blood distinguishes two types: the collection of links with added personal commentary, first developed by web enthusiasts and media specialists with a knowledge of html code, and the online journal that flourished when user-friendly blog-writing sites such as Blogger.com (1999) made the practice available to all. Both show how online communication was changing modes of self-expression: the blogger-editor constructs a personal identity not by narrating his or her own life, but by assembling found materials in creative ways and adding commentary in a witty or idiosyncratic style. The blogger-diarist perhaps resorts to a more traditional form, but the strangely indeterminate space of the 'blogosphere' in which levels of privacy and publicity are confused means that the intimate discourse of the web journal is always disciplined by a potential mass audience, even if it will turn out to be one of the many that may never find a single reader. In either case, the blog epitomises the web's informality and spontaneity: it offers a means of responding instantly to breaking events while it also promotes highly particular, situated perspectives on everyday or specialised matters. Such qualities quickly led to expectations that the web would eventually revolutionise journalism by foregrounding opinion, diversifying perspectives and subjecting the mainstream press to continual scrutiny. As Blood puts it, blogging 'reminds us to question the vested interests of our sources of information and the expertise of individual reporters as they file news stories about subjects they may not fully understand'.[23]

Alternatives to mainstream media have come from both ends of the political spectrum, and the potential freedom from institutional authority that the web offers can be either enabling or obstructive to the democratic process in different circumstances. Right-wing political blog The Drudge Report, which started as an email newsletter in 1994, presents itself not as a news service but a source of rumour, though it is often rumour that makes news. In 1998 it was the first to break the story that became the Clinton–Lewinsky scandal, with the revelation that magazine *Newsweek* was holding information about the President's liaison with a White House intern that it was reluctant to publish. During the presidential elections of 2004 it was a key vehicle for pushing the story from campaign group Swift Boat Veterans for Truth that cast doubts on Democratic candidate John Kerry's war record and arguably contributed to his defeat. On the left, the networking capabilities of the web have offered journalists and activists a forum for producing news that escapes the controls of mainstream media channels and the corporate interests with which they are often allied. One notable organisation is the Independent

Media Centre (or Indymedia), which emerged from the anti-corporate globalisation demonstrations in Seattle, 1999 and has since grown into a global network of grassroots news coverage. Web-based agitation – known as electronic civil disobedience or 'hacktivism' – has also thrived: hacktivists commonly engage in hijacking mainstream spaces in order to propagate their message or disrupting the flow of traffic to sites deemed ideologically objectionable. Thus on 'Jam Echelon Day', 21st October 1999, hacktivists attempted to block the server at the National Security Agency to protest against its Echelon programme – a covert operation monitoring European email and phone traffic for signs of terrorist activity.

Commercial and non-commercial uses have also proliferated else-where on the internet, outside the client-server relationship of the web. The late 1990s saw the rapid growth of peer-to-peer applications that allowed users to pool resources and share files: while some of these – such as music file-sharing programs Napster and Gnutella – created conflicts over intellectual property rights that have yet to be resolved today, others used the collective power of networked com-puting for public non-profit motives. The project SETI@home, for example, was established in 1999 to mobilise a global effort to search for extra-terrestrial intelligence. Since then, millions of volunteers worldwide have downloaded software that enables an individual user to extract a portion of the data gathered by a radio-telescope at the University of California and process it on their own computer before sending back the results.[24]

Debates concerning the governance of the web in this second phase covered a range of issues, of which four key areas are isolated here:

Free Speech: The idea that the net should be a place of free speech with minimum constraints has been central to computer-mediated communication from the outset. With the increasing access that the web provided to non-technical users, popular fears grew over the avail-ability of unsuitable materials such as pornography, and the demands for regulation that they fuelled (of which the Communications Decency Act is an example) were a driving factor in the gradual zoning of the net. Aside from the matter of determining when sexu-ally explicit material should be considered 'without redeeming social value' and therefore obscene, the attempt to regulate the content of communications raised other questions about legal responsibility and the reach of a particular jurisdiction into cyberspace. Should speech on the internet be subject to state laws – and if so, which state's laws? What if, for instance, a user in Tennessee views web pages which are hosted entirely legally on a server in California but fall in violation of local obscenity laws in his or her home state?[25]

Copyright: The general aim of the concept of intellectual property which governs protections such as patents and copyright is to foster creativity by giving an individual the right to benefit from a product or invention for a limited period until it is released into the public domain. This function is put under substantial pressure by the virtual nature of digital objects, which can be copied without cost or loss and are inherently the outcome of collaborative labour. Is file-sharing theft, or a legitimate way of redistributing information? If software evolves over time (as users provide feedback on its design, bugs or functional limitations) at what point should the process become protected and commodified?[26] And what part of a computer application is covered by copyright? In cases where parties were accused of copying a program (such as the suits against clones of the game Pacman in the 1980s, or the *Lotus* v. *Borland* case of 1996 in which rival spreadsheet designers battled over the copyright of drop-down menus), courts often struggled to find the balance between protecting the software code and allowing the replication of design features or user experience.

Two outcomes emerged from these debates. On the one hand, companies' fears of lost revenue from file-sharing drove attempts to reassert property rights and punish infringements: the case against Napster in 2000 and the development of anti-pirate encoding (or Digital Rights Management) exemplify this response. On the other hand, and largely in response to the growing awareness that unlicensed copying and sharing would be ultimately impossible to restrict, there began a search for new ways to rethink property relations on the net. Esther Dyson, then head of a committee on intellectual property convened by Vice President Al Gore, argued in 1995 that value would have to shift from actual content to the reputation of the provider and the quality of the interaction:

> The trick is to control not the copies of your work but instead a relationship with the customers – subscriptions or membership. And that's often what the customers want, because they see it as an assurance of a continuing supply of reliable, timely content.[27]

Surveillance and Privacy: Concerns for individual freedoms and the extent of the supervisory powers of the state have existed since the Enlightenment, but the data-processing powers of computers and their penetration into all aspects of everyday life made surveillance and privacy central problems of governance in the 1990s. On the web, issues involved the policing of communications for national security, the surveillance of employees in the workplace and the use of information on individuals' surfing and shopping habits. In 1998, Congress passed the Children's Online Privacy Protection Act which prohibited companies from gathering personal information on sites aimed at minors; in 1999 users were scandalised to find that company RealPlayer had been distributing free copies of its music-player software which concealed data-collection devices that harvested profiles of users' listening habits and even details of the music stored on their hard disks. Again, there are two divergent reactions: a resurgence of privacy claims on the one hand, in which data encryption and anonymising software play a key part; on the other, a reconfiguration of the nature of privacy. Since the mid-1990s the older model of surveillance which posits a conflict between autonomous individuals and intrusive powers has gradually shifted towards a more differentiated set of relationships in which privacy is less of an inalienable right, and more of an exchangeable asset. Many users today are happy with the bargain by which they concede rights to privacy or anonymity in return for the benefits of Web services.

Territorial Sovereignty: If the apparent borderlessness of the internet allowed fantasies of the global village to propagate, it also posed problems for the exercise of state authority. This should not be seen as an unequivocal good, despite the aspirations of the net libertarians: to take a mundane example, the lack of application of sales tax laws to internet commerce meant that its expansion not only put high-street businesses under threat but also took revenue away from local government. Thus poor Americans could be doubly disenfranchised by the Information Revolution: once by the prohibitive costs of access to the internet, and twice by the stripping of public resources which was an all-too common side-effect of neoliberal economics.[28] On a macroeconomic level, the more fundamental threat to state sovereignty came from the rise of global financial digital networks, entirely separate from the internet and beyond state supervision, yet able to have a real impact on national economies. Saskia Sassen notes that by 2000 capital flows in foreign exchange markets already exceeded the total GDP of the countries making up the OECD, which included many of the richest industrial nations in the world.[29]

Regulating the Net

The emergence of a radically new medium posed a series of challenges for state and federal authorities. While the overwhelming consensus was that the internet was of benefit to society and the economy as a whole, opinions differed over the best way to manage its growth. Should existing laws and values carry across into cyberspace? Or should it be left as much as possible to generate its own procedures? Three landmark cases of the decade illustrate the different ways that corporations, government and the courts tried to impose controls on the internet during its period of rapid development. The lawsuit against Napster in 2000, which was central to establishing ideas about digital property, has been discussed in Chapter 2. This case study deals with two others in which government intervention in the internet's development is at issue: the Communications Decency Act of 1996 and the antitrust suit against Microsoft beginning in 1998.

The spectre of pornography loomed over the internet in the mid-1990s. Individuals had been quick to exploit the possibilities of anonymous networking on bulletin boards for circulating images, and the adult industry soon flourished on the web, becoming a driving force for developments in design. But the popular misconception that the internet was saturated with pornographic content that intruded on ordinary users at every opportunity – a view promulgated by articles such as *Time* magazine's 'Cyberporn' cover story of 3 July 1995 – was clearly an expression of deeper anxieties about the unruliness of the new medium and the loss of authority over a younger generation who already seemed much more skilled in using it.[30] The Communications Decency Act was a consequence of these anxieties: proposed to Congress by Democrat Senator James Exon in 1994 and passed in 1996, it made it a crime to allow users under eighteen to receive any material that was sexually explicit and 'patently offensive as measured by contemporary community standards'. For a president seeking re-election, signing the Act was a way of affirming family values and aligning government control with parental control.

Free speech advocates rose up against the Act. The Electronic Frontier Foundation was joined by the American Civil Liberties Union, the American Libraries Association and numerous AIDS organisations who feared that the new legislation would jeopardise the dissemination of safe-sex messages or further marginalise minority sexualities. Websites turned their background colour to black in protest. When a Philadelphia court blocked enforcement of the law on the grounds that it placed unfair restrictions on speech between adults, the case was submitted to the Supreme Court where the judges upheld the original decision, ruling that the Act defined indecency poorly and that standards previously applied to television and radio should not be applied to the internet. In words quoted by Justice John Stevens, 'the level of discourse reaching a mailbox cannot be limited to that which would be suitable for a sandbox'.[31]

Ultimately, *Reno* v. *ACLU* was significant for two reasons. First, it showed that the struggle to control communication on the internet involved a deci-sion as to what kind of medium it was – to what extent it resembled broad-casting (in which all material is easily available and therefore more strictly regulated), and to what extent it resembled publishing (where material is less likely to be accidentally encountered and free speech is more strongly supported). In addition, the case also highlighted the obsolescence of obscenity laws which appealed to the standards of a single community, a concept which seemed entirely inapplicable to social relations in the 1990s and especially on the net.

The second case pitted the government against America's most pow-erful software company, Microsoft. From the beginning of the decade federal authorities had been worried that the company was using its pre-eminence in operating systems to stifle competition in other markets, but it was with the release of the web browser Internet Explorer 4.0 in 1997 that the Justice Department sought to hold Microsoft to account, instigat-ing an antitrust lawsuit on 18 May 1998. The specific charges were that Microsoft had violated business agreements and unfairly disadvantaged rival browser company Netscape Communications by bundling Explorer with its Windows 95 operating system. In addition, it was accused of withholding essential Windows code that made it difficult for software developers to compete on other middleware products such as webmail, chat software or media players. But the root of the matter was the extent to which the government could or should intervene to direct the precipi-tous growth of a new industry. Was Microsoft's dominance an obstacle to free-market practices, or the result of them? Did its monopoly in operating systems create benefits for consumers, as the company claimed, or was it a threat to the rules of fair competition on which American business depended?

After a protracted trial in which Microsoft's lawyers were criticised for being obstructive to the legal process and owner Bill Gates achieved some notoriety for his churlish behaviour during testimony, the presiding judge ruled the corporation guilty of having illegally maintained a monopoly and ordered it to be broken up into different companies to separate the oper-ating system from middleware products. The order was overturned on appeal, and in 2002 a lighter settlement was agreed that required Microsoft to share technical information for a five-year period and allow PC manu-facturers to hide, but not remove, bundled software. While many critics believed these to be extraordinarily lenient sanctions, a court review at the end of the five years concluded that they had ultimately been effective in opening up competition: Firefox, Opera and Safari now challenged Internet Explorer in the browser market, cross-platform media devices like Flash, Quicktime, iTunes and Acrobat Reader flourished, and alternative operat-ing systems such as Linux had started to gain market share.[32]

Aside from what it reveals about the shifting centre of gravity within the industry from desktop applications to internet services, *United States* v. *Microsoft* also offers an insight into the climate of opinion surrounding market capitalism in the 1990s. When the *Wall Street Journal* commented that the company 'should have argued that we have a monopoly because our customers want us to have one', it was voicing what Thomas Frank called 'market populism', a widespread belief that unregulated capitalism worked best and corporations could be more trustworthy than government. The danger inherent in this ideology is, of course, the equation of citizens with consumers, and the assumption that what counts in every instance are lower prices rather than economic opportunity or the right to decide who controls access to the world's networked information.[33]

Posthumanism

Technology is by definition a means of extending human capacities, and has always been associated with fantasies of escape from the limitations of the human condition. Hence any attempt to argue for the emergence of a new paradigm has to do so against claims that this was ever the case. But in the 1990s the speed of change in digital culture and applied science intensified the feeling that human beings were on the verge of a radical transformation. New forms of communication and information processing were matched by advances in genetics, biotechnology and surgery, which together raised fundamental questions about the nature of the self, the relation between human beings and human bodies, and the blurring boundaries between humans and machines. For some, 'posthuman' literally meant anticipating a point at which machines would become self-replicating and autonomous, or where technology would be so extensively incorporated into the formerly human sphere that a new species category would be needed. As the manifesto of techno-utopian movement Extropianism declared, 'We will co-evolve with the products of our minds, integrating with them, finally integrating our intelligent technology into ourselves in a posthuman synthesis, amplifying our abilities and extending our freedom.'[34] Others used the term to designate a critical reaction to humanism in which the concept of the individual subject had, they believed, been too dominant for too long.

What is often at stake in debates about the posthuman is the degree of control people are thought to have over the environments they inhabit. Do science and technology free us from the limitations of our biology, psyche and society? Or do they help us further to understand the ways in which we are inescapably 'embodied' – that is, situated within natural and social systems? Addressing such questions from the 1980s into the 1990s were Australian and French artists Stelarc and Orlan, who gained some notoriety for the extreme ways in which they treated the body as the object of technology. Claiming 'The Body is Obsolete', Stelarc sought to expand its potential by adding electronic appendages such as a robotic third hand, or by networking its sensory capabilities: in *Fractal Flesh* (1995), for example, he wired himself up to a system that allowed participants in different cities to become the authors of his movements. Such performances evoked the image of a body that was endlessly malleable and upgradable, and therefore no longer even beholden to a single universal structure: as he proclaimed in a 1991 essay, 'Once technology provides each person with the potential to progress individually in its development, the cohesiveness of the species is no longer important.'[35] What was human in people would no longer reside in immutable, god-given flesh, or even in a form given by the slow processes of biological evolution; instead, it became entirely independent of its physical existence, a pure function of will. The problems with such an attitude should already be plain and were levelled at Stelarc's work in numerous critiques, but Mark Dery's observations are instructive: this is a melancholy post-Fordist view of the body, which celebrates efficiency and increased capacity in a system of modular, replaceable parts, but from which the scenes of production and the labour of the real bodies that make the technology are wholly absent.[36]

Orlan, on the other hand, made the point that Stelarc missed – that practices of self-remaking through technology cannot escape the historical and ideological circumstances in which the body is situated. Between 1990 and 1993 she undertook a series of surgical operations in which her facial features were remodelled along the lines of female icons in western art. *The Reincarnation of St Orlan* showed the artist in an operating theatre-cum-television studio, dressed in various costumes from harlequin to Madonna, performing to the camera as the operations took place; bloodied rags and morsels of waste flesh were later offered for sale in a literal commodification of the artist's body. The art, Orlan claimed, was to be seen as a critique of the cosmetic surgery industry and the suffering to which women have customarily subjected themselves in order to conform to standards of beauty not their own. By introducing traces of culture and a spirit of play into the aseptic sphere of the operating theatre, she sought to deflate the aura of authority surrounding medical science and expose it for the power game that it was.

By the end of the decade, the cyborg had lost the aura of science fiction and the integration of new technology with the human body was increasingly normalised. Boosters spoke of enhanced capabilities rather than human-machine interfaces, and focused their attention on the promise of biotechnology and genetic engineering. Joel Garreau, chronicler of emergent trends in America, looked back on the 1990s as the decade in which the groundwork was laid for advances that would come to mean nothing less than the transcendence of human nature:

> The inflection point at which we have arrived is one in which we are increasingly seizing the keys to all creation . . . It's about what parents will do when offered ways to increase their child's SAT score by 200 points. It's about what athletes will do when encouraged by big-buck leagues to put together medical pit crews. What fat people will do when offered a gadget that will monitor and alter their metabolisms. What the aging will do when offered memory enhancers. What fading baby-boomers will do when it becomes obvious that Viagra and Botox are just the beginning of the sex-appeal industry . . .'[37]

Such use of prosthetics and biological enhancements complemented other medical technologies that in their continuing development challenged traditional conceptions of the human, of life, family and individual identity. For instance, note how the everyday use of medical equipment allowed the concept of the human lifespan to expand into the realms of the non-human and non-living: at one end, improvements in the resolution of ultrasound scans brought the foetus further into the domain of the human as an individual being (to the advantage of pro-life groups who displayed the images in anti-abortion campaigns); at the other end, life-support systems forced a redefinition of what it meant to be alive or dead, separating the activity of the brain from the functioning of the organs. Similarly, IVF treatments and surrogacy practices diffracted the notion of motherhood across the different events of egg fertilisation, gestation and birth, and childcare; sex reassignment therapy made sexual identity a matter of psychology and will rather than physiology. This is not to say that all these practices are new to the 1990s, of course – only that they acquired a new significance and cumulatively produced anxieties about the drift away from humanist certainties.

Two major scientific projects of the decade illustrate the ways in which the quest for knowledge of the human body had the paradoxical effect of producing, rather than resolving, uncertainties about the human being. They also show incidentally that epistemological paradigms never quite supersede one another in a procedural fashion but exist instead in an overlapping relationship, driving or being driven by the application of new technologies. In this instance, the new science of genetics looked from the inside out, as it were, focusing attention on the body as a manifestation of biological code; at the same time, looking from the outside in, new digital imaging techniques were being adopted by the far older science of anatomy.

Body Maps: The Human Genome Project and the Visible Human Project

The Human Genome Project was initiated in 1990 by the Department of Energy and the National Institutes of Health. Its aim was to 'map the human genome', which meant identifying the type and position of the thousands of genes populating the twenty-three strands of DNA inside each cell of the human body. A mammoth task that would eventually cost over $3 billion, it was hailed as one of the most significant scientific projects of the century. Myth-makers claimed that it would reveal the key to human nature, or answer existential questions about the difference between humans and other species. More realistic hopes were that the new science of genomics would bring insights into the spread of diseases and better knowledge of genetic disposition, and would even lead to personalised drug treatments.

Research into the human genome was not free from controversy. For many, it summoned the spectre of eugenics, a nineteenth-century discipline that sought to engineer human traits through selective breeding and helped legitimise beliefs in superior and inferior persons. The application of predisposition from disease to behaviour – the idea that there might be 'a gene for' X or Y conduct – disturbed critics who imagined the misuse of genetic information to police individuals or groups (something of this fear is present in the 2002 film *Minority Report*, in which potential criminals are arrested before they get to commit a crime). In addition, there were concerns about the potential threat to privacy – where, for instance, insurance companies might demand access to personal genetic information before providing life cover. A further issue was the ownership of genome knowledge. While the HGP was a government project whose results belonged to the public domain, throughout most of the decade it was in competition with a private company, Celera Genomics. Under the direction of scientist-entrepreneur Craig Venter (who had developed his own technique of 'shotgun sequencing', aptly continuing the tradition of western metaphors at the frontiers of science), Celera used the NIH data for comparison while keeping its own results secret, prompting rumours that it might be planning to 'patent the human genome' or charge researchers for use of the data. Motivated by such concerns (and the mounting costs of the HGP), President Clinton intervened to force a collaboration between the two organisations in 1999.

On 26 June 2000 the partnership announced a working draft of the human genome, with three major discoveries. First, the genome was found to consist of far fewer genes than expected – only 30,000, rather than the 100,000 that had been forecast. Just as surprisingly, almost half of the DNA was waste matter: sequences derived from foreign bacteria, or fragments of genes that might have had a purpose at previous stages of evolution. Finally, it seemed that humans had much more in common with other species than expected – sharing a significant number of genes with simpler organisms such as mice, fruit flies and yeast. While the implications of these findings are still being explored, a key observation was that there are 'not enough' genes to account on their own for the diversity of human traits or the differences between humans and other species. What matters, therefore, is accounting for the circumstances under which genes are switched 'on' or 'off', or work together to produce proteins that affect cell growth. The conclusion that environmental conditions are involved at a sub-molecular level is central to challenging popular (and often ideologically charged) misconceptions of genes as causes.[38]

The Visible Human Project sought a very different knowledge of the human body, and produced cultural anxieties of its own. Based at the National Library of Medicine in Maryland, its aim was to produce a series of digital representations of a male and female body which would be made freely available over the internet. The primary applications for the archive lay in education, medical diagnosis and treatment planning, but the NLM encouraged uses from all quarters, and by 2009 nearly two thousand licences had been granted in forty-eight countries, in fields from computer programming to mathematics, industry and art.

Creating a digital human body was a combination of three different techniques: Computerised Tomography scanning (used to capture solid objects like bone), Magnetic Resonance Imaging (for the more fluid internal organs) and Cryosectioning. For the latter, the selected cadavers were frozen in dry ice, stabilised with gelatine and ground down from one end to the other, with high-resolution photographs taken at intervals. The VHP's male specimen was photographed at intervals of 1mm, producing a dataset of fifteen gigabytes which was released in 1994. A dataset of forty gigabytes for the Visible Human Female, containing images at 0.33mm, appeared a year later. A sample of images is currently available on the NLM website, where it is also possible to view an 'animated trip' through the male body cryosections.[39]

While the project is framed as a neutral contribution to science, the presentation of images in the form of a 'trip' through the body indicates that non-scientific factors are also in play. First of all, we can see it as part of a broader historical moment in the late twentieth century in which the body is presented as a spectacle for mass consumption, and in which everything is increasingly subjected to the gaze – from live births and live surgery on television to internet pornography. But the VHP is also emblematic of the way that matter and human subjectivity are reconstituted in the age of digital technology. These Visible Humans appear to have lives of their own – an 'uncanny vitality', in the words of Catherine Waldby – born into existence through the destruction of their real counterparts, and reanimated by computer simulations across the world: virtual hearts can be made to beat, nerves to tense, limbs to move.[40] At the same time, what is most startling about the cryosections is the way they disclose the body as meat: since the 'slice' pays no respect to separate organs, it violates the traditional ordering of anatomy and produces images that confront the viewer with the less than sublime fact of their own corporeal reality. Thus the VHP both dematerialises (body as data) and rematerialises (body as mere flesh and bone) – both operations posing a profound challenge to humanist beliefs in the body as a hallowed vessel of the spirit.[41]

A further reality haunts the bodies of the VHP, and that is the individual identity of the medical subjects. Soon after the initial release of data it was revealed that the male donor had been Joseph Paul Jernigan, a convicted murderer executed by the State of Texas in 1993. This fact had been unknown to the selection panel, though it was very much in keeping with the history of anatomical science which had dissected criminals' bodies for centuries. Equally, the likelihood of involvement in the VHP would have been unknown to Jernigan when he decided to donate his body before execution – a fact that sparked an ethical debate within the medical community and beyond about the nature of a prisoner's consent and how far rights to bodily privacy extend into death. Visible tissue damage at the site of lethal injection serves as a potent reminder that the embodied person, as opposed to the abstract individual, is always subject to control.

The posthuman condition is often referred to in negative or apocalyptic terms – a loss of human sovereignty to machines, an abandonment of the Cartesian model of consciousness, a threat to the idea that we hold something in common as a species or a dangerous hubris that loses sight of the limitations which make us 'all too human'. Jean Baudrillard, writing in 1990, voiced some of these sentiments in an elegy for the liberation projects of the latter part of the twentieth century:

The cybernetic revolution, in view of the equivalence of brain and computer, places humanity before the crucial question, 'Am I a man or a machine?' The genetic revolution that is taking place at the moment raises the question, 'Am I a man or just a potential clone?' The sexual revolution, by liberating all the potentialities of desire, raises another fundamental question, 'Am I a man or a woman?' . . . As for the political and social revolution, the prototype for all the others, it will turn out to have led man by an implacable logic – having offered him his own freedom, his own free will – to ask himself where his own will lies, what he wants in his heart of hearts, and what he is entitled to expect from himself. To these questions there are no answers. Such is the paradoxical outcome of every revolution: revolution opens the door to indeterminacy, anxiety and confusion.[42]

In Baudrillard's entropic vision, revolution is manifested as the desire to overcome and transgress all limits, and leads ultimately to the loss of distinctions between things. The demand for liberation is seen as a flight from conditions previously thought of as given or fated, whether by nature or society. Thus equality tends towards equivalence: 'That is how we became . . . politically indifferent and undifferentiated beings, androgynous and hermaphroditic.'[43]

Such a view, inattentive to real differences and eager to proclaim a general cultural drift, is quite characteristic of the twilight discourses of the end of the millennium. However, a more positive rendition of the posthuman came from N. Katherine Hayles, who saw in it a critical potential and a chance for generating new intellectual projects for the twenty-first century. For Hayles, previous epistemologies of the subject have privileged individual consciousness and bodily sovereignty at the expense of a more nuanced and situated understanding of the relation between humans and their environments. As a consequence, they have been too intimately connected with the more destructive enterprises of the modern age.

> If . . . there is a relation among the desire for mastery, an objectivist account of science, and the imperialist project of subduing human nature, then the posthuman offers resources for the construction of another kind of account. In this account, emergence replaces teleology; reflexive epistemology replaces objectivism; distributed cognition replaces autonomous will; embodiment replaces a body seen as a support system for the mind; and a dynamic partnership between humans and intelligent machines replaces the liberal humanist subject's manifest destiny to dominate and control nature.[44]

Thus posthumanism need not mean the end of humans – only the end of the politics that derives from thinking about humans as discrete and autonomous beings.

Towards a New Millennium

One of the quintessential themes of American movies of the 1990s is the problem with reality. In a number of films cutting across genres from thriller to satirical comedy and science fiction, reality was not simply a ground in which events unfolded but an unstable quantity often at odds with the human beings that inhabited it. The theme was elaborated in a variety of ways – reality as a set of staged scenarios by an unknown adversary in *Cube* (1997) or *The Game* (1997), reality served up as television entertainment in *The Truman Show* (1998) and *EDtv* (1999), reality as the manifestation of a traumatised mind in *Memento* (2000) or *Nurse Betty* (2000) – but one of the most enduring treatments is Andy and Larry Wachowski's 1999 film *The Matrix*. Here, on a future Earth, everyday life is no more than a computer simulation fed to human beings who have been reduced to a vegetable existence in bio-pods, functioning merely as living batteries for the machines that have enslaved them. The task for the hero, a computer hacker named Neo, is to awaken to the truth by witnessing 'the desert of the real' – as his mentor Morpheus introduces it to him – and learn the ways of the Matrix in order to fight the machines.

While the film was influential for its cool, neo-noir style and the incorporation of computer game aesthetics into mainstream Hollywood, it is this battle to escape the simulation that offers us an insight into the way history was imagined at the end of the millennium. If Neo represents our hopes for emancipation from an existence which is no more than biological, then there is an uncertainty about the type of historical change he represents, one that can be conceived as a split between messianic and revolutionary time. As the anagram implies, Neo is either 'the One', blessed with special powers that will enable him to bring salvation, or he is 'one of us', an embodiment of the coming multitude.[1] At the close of the film Neo issues a warning

to the powers that be, leaving audiences with no doubt that the struggle is to be continued outside the cinema:

> I know you're out there. I can feel you now . . . I didn't come here to
> tell you how this is going to end. I came here to tell you how it's going
> to begin . . . I'm going to show these people what you don't want them
> to see. I'm going to show them a world without you. A world without
> rules and controls, without borders or boundaries. A world where any-
> thing is possible.

Whether the struggle is one of faith or politics is ultimately unclear.

John Gray has suggested that the theme of revolt is in fact a distraction from the deeper anxiety that, when faced with the real, most
people would willingly choose the illusion; like the character who
takes the blue pill for oblivion, we recoil at the sight of real suffering
and opt for the false comforts of the status quo.[2] It is in this respect
that *The Matrix* functions as an allegory of American culture under
the conditions of late capitalism, with its proposition that fantasy
and spectacle have permeated into all aspects of life, limiting the possibilities of thinking alternatives as they protect its participants from a
more terrifying real world. A component of this vision is the fear that
such a system has colonised the spaces of resistance to the extent that
struggle against it no longer constitutes a threat, since all gestures of
rebellion are reabsorbed as signs of its vitality.

Looking back on the decade we can see such a fear expressed in
the knowing nihilism of Kurt Cobain, the anxieties of young writers
about the purpose of fiction and the despair of the *October* art critics.
In a different context Thomas Frank named it 'the commodification of dissent', arguing that the subversive energies of the 1950s and
1960s had been appropriated as the signature of American business
in the 1990s. The powers that be no longer look like the enemy, he
warned:

> They're hipper than you can ever hope to be because *hip is their official
> ideology*, and they're always going to be there at the poetry reading
> to encourage your 'rebellion' with a hearty 'right on, man!' before
> you even know they're in the auditorium. You can't outrun them, or
> even stay ahead of them for very long: it's their racetrack, and that's
> them waiting at the finish line to congratulate you on how *outrageous*
> your new style is, on how you *shocked* those stuffy prudes out in the
> heartland.[3]

Frank's idea that there are no remaining means of dissent is taken up in the later films in the trilogy, *The Matrix Reloaded* and *The Matrix Revolutions* (both 2003), where Neo will discover that his resistance is anticipated and even programmed into the simulation from the start.

Between the two positions outlined by these quotations – the gesture of defiance with its appeal to a world without borders, and the sense of being entirely contained within a system that incorporates all dissent – lie much of the cultural politics of the 1990s. If it is easy to be sceptical of the comic-book sentiments of the original movie, its undeniable impact upon popular and critical audiences can arguably be attributed to the way it captures an authentic desire for change through its representation of a reality that is no longer self-evident or inevitable. By way of a conclusion to this book, I will review some of the contexts in which that desire for change was manifested and how the energies that took shape at the end of one millennium began to define the next.

Post, Neo, Trans

Elements of the transition can be observed in the commerce of pre-fixes in the period, which give notice of a general awareness that existing paradigms were breaking down and new ones were yet to appear. If postmodernism was already losing its currency by the beginning of the decade, it was not because the sense of a radical break from the past was no longer there but because it had splintered into different spheres of culture for which the idea of a common origin was no longer sufficient. Sometimes the driving force was more scientific and technological than economic, as with the concept of posthumanism; sometimes it was part of a story about the emergence of new media, as with post-literacy; sometimes it expressed the notion that the former status or function of a cultural form no longer held, as in the case of post-cinema or post-rock. On other occasions it was motivated by political interests in declaring a mode of thinking obsolete, as with post-feminism and post-ethnicity. In all cases, though, an emerging present moment was defined in opposition to what had gone before, implicitly acknowledging that it was not yet independent of it.

Neo, on the other hand, implied difference through repetition rather than opposition, complicating the idea of a radical break with the past. In literature and art scholars spoke of the return of realism, not as a nostalgic reaction so much as a dialectical response to earlier postmodernist strategies: Winfried Fluck, for instance, described neorealism as an attempt to refresh an increasingly self-referential literary field through the reintroduction of experience.[4] Writers such as David Foster Wallace bore this out by insisting that a representation of a highly mediated and consumer-saturated existence was undeniably a form of realism, not just a linguistic game. In film, Sean Cubitt's characterisation of the dominant mode of Hollywood production as 'neobaroque' related it to an earlier period where art was the expression of political power at its limits: thus the 'neobaroque is the stylistic turn of capitalism in the moment of its uneasy triumph, confronted with the completion of its historical destiny without achieving the justice, peace and common-wealth it was intended to bring'.[5] The prefix also circulated in political economy, of course, naming an ideology that achieved supremacy in the 1980s and dominated western governments until the end of the century. Neoliberalism, a revival of economic liberalism which favoured the withdrawal of the state from areas of social provision and the expansion of markets into all spheres of human activity, not only provided a rationalisation for globalisation policies but also had a profound impact on cultural industries within the United States.

However, the breakdown of political and cultural formations also created the conditions for reassembly in new configurations. Hybridity became a central feature of film and television output, meeting the demands of audiences who were tiring of existing generic variations. Elsewhere, the term was used to designate the new spaces of culture and identity that opened up in postcolonial situations, and in a related sense the weakening of national sovereignty under the effects of globalisation was the occasion for the emergence of transnational institutions and social relations. In *Modernity at Large* (1996) Arjun Appadurai looked upon this development with optimism, noting that the former organisation of power in the nation-state had not exactly proved effective in securing freedom and justice for populations across the world.[6] But if the loosening of boundaries and distinctions was invigorating for some, it was also a powerful source of anxiety, and it should not be surprising that the policing of borders became a central motif of the decade. Incidents such as the running aground of the immigrant-smuggling ship *Golden Venture* in 1993 or the Elián González controversy of 2000, in which a Cuban boy rescued from the sea off the coast of Florida became the subject of an international custody battle, placed global migration and the security of borders at the centre of public debate. Policing was also at the heart of the major media spectacles of the decade, from the Gulf War of 1991 – in which the United States posed as global police-man – to the Seattle protests of 1999. Arguments over the legacies of the cultural politics of the 1960s, particularly in race and gender, can also be seen as efforts to police the identities that emerged from them, and a similar movement between liberation and regulation is evident in the history of computer-mediated communication in the early days of the World Wide Web.

Without claiming that there is a common underlying cause to these phenomena it is possible to say that they are all evidence of a profound deterritorialisation occurring at the end of the century, where the collapsing, contesting and redrawing of boundaries became a central concern. *Trans*, therefore, identifies the 1990s as a moment not of opposition or return but of interaction between things, an interaction that may not be resolved in synthesis but remains continually unstable.

Politics of a New Millennium

Three events mark the close of the political configuration of the 1990s and the birth of a new moment. The first is the series of protests that occurred at the meeting of the World Trade Organisation in Seattle between 28 November and 3 December 1999, which came to symbolise new possibilities for political action outside the traditional structures of party politics and organised labour. The WTO had been founded in 1995 as a successor to the General Agreement on Trade and Tariffs (GATT) with the aim of removing obstructions to international trade, but it quickly became the target of criticism from many quarters for its tendency to promote the interests of rich nations and multinational corporations at the expense of smaller economies. At the third round of talks in Seattle, delegates from the 135 participating countries were greeted by demonstrators protesting a wide range of issues from sweatshop labour to deforestation, genetically modified foods, oil company activities and third world debt. Groups such as Global Trade Watch coordinated aspects of the demonstrations and major union bodies were also involved, but what was remarkable about the 'Five Days That Shook the World' was the lack of a common political objective amongst the protestors, which allowed participants to come together on a number of different fronts. In one unusual alliance, for instance, United Steelworkers joined with environmentalists Earth First! in opposition to the Maxxam Corporation's actions in steel and logging industries. For some, this 'participatory discrepancy' offered a glimpse into the future for left-wing politics in an era of globalisation, where no one issue would be sufficient to mobilise support.

Figure C.1 Riot police at the scene of a damaged store in Seattle, 30 November 1999 (© Mike Nelson/AFP/Getty Images).

Tom Hayden, founder member of 1960s organisation Students for a Democratic Society, acknowledged as much when he spoke to the crowd on the first evening: 'What we had was maybe one or two issues we were dealing with. You here, you're dealing with everything.'[7]

Mass civil disobedience successfully derailed the talks, while inside the conference agreements foundered on differences between northern and southern hemispheres as representatives from nations in Africa, Asia and Latin America were increasingly angered by their exclusion from key sessions. But the more lasting impact of the Seattle protests lay in the image of collective resistance that circulated afterwards. When violence erupted out of what many saw as an overreaction from an under-prepared police force, scenes of demonstrators being tear-gassed and riot police defending the property of businesses such as Gap, Nike and Starbucks became powerful symbols of the way that a consensus on supposedly free trade had to be engineered through force.

The second event that signalled the passage into a new era of politics was the election of George W. Bush to the presidency in December 2000. This proved to be one of the most disputed elections in American history, one of the rare occasions in which a president reached office through the electoral college system without winning a majority of the popular vote. Democratic candidate Al Gore received over half a million more votes than Bush across the country but was beaten by five votes in the college, with the final outcome decided by a controversial count in Florida. Here, a series of problems at polling stations led to claims of the disenfranchisement of non-white citizens and widespread distrust of results showing victory for Bush. When the Florida Court ruled against its own Secretary of State that hand recounts in disputed counties should proceed, the decision was challenged by the Bush team and finally overruled by the Supreme Court. In a widely discussed article published in *The Nation*, attorney Vincent Bugliosi railed against the judgment, accusing the five Justices responsible of nothing less than the theft of the presidency.[8] If few commentators went so far as to call it treason (and later analyses of the uncounted votes, it should be said, never confirmed unequivocally that Gore would have won on a recount), the sense that the whole process had severely damaged the authority of American institutions was pervasive. The sombre mood was captured in the dissenting remarks of Justice John Paul Stevens:

> Although we may never know with complete certainty the identity of the winner of this year's presidential election, the identity of the loser is perfectly clear. It is the nation's confidence in the judge as an impartial guardian of the rule of law.[9]

Amongst the fallout from the 2000 elections was the reputation of Ralph Nader, the prestigious left-wing activist who had stood as presidential candidate for the Green Party. Buoyed by the success of Seattle, where many organisations indebted to his politics played a key part, he saw the presidential campaign as an opportunity to publicise the issues of the new movement to a wider audience as well as a platform for his vision of a more participatory democracy. Unfortunately, after such a close election Nader found it difficult to shake off accusations from despairing liberals that the votes he had won had made the difference between victory and defeat for Gore. And in the years that followed the record of the new administration at home and abroad soon gave the lie to Nader's contention that under a corporate-funded two-party system one candidate was as bad as another. As Bush moved to lift restrictions on mining and drilling and opposed international agreements such as the Kyoto Protocol, it seemed clear to many on the left that Nader's candidacy had cost America and the environment dearly.

Bush's term in office may have taken a different course had it not been for 11 September 2001, though all the signs were that he was keen to distance himself from Clinton and pursue a more unilateral foreign policy from the outset. The menace of international terrorism had been on the rise throughout the 1990s, with the bombing of the World Trade Center in New York City in 1993 by a group of Egyptian, Palestinian and Kuwaiti nationals and simultaneous attacks on US embassies in Kenya and Tanzania by Al-Qaeda in 1998. As Derek Chollet and James Goldgeier report, Clinton recognised his failure to combat the problem and in the handover meeting with Bush expressed regrets that he had been unable to capture Osama Bin Laden.[10] But where Clinton had at least understood that the new security issues facing America were a consequence of transnational pressures, Bush was more inclined to think in terms of traditional threats from nation-states. Hence, when Al-Qaeda operatives hijacked four domestic flights and flew two planes into the World Trade Center and a third into the Pentagon (the fourth, destined for Washington DC, crashed in Pennsylvania after the passengers foiled the mission), the attack was unthinkable in any other terms than an act of war from a foreign power. The consequent 'war on terror', with its notoriously vague definition of the enemy, indicated the degree to which global terrorist networks had come to seize the monopoly on mass violence from nation-states, further undermining the idea of national sovereignty.

In the outpouring of responses that followed the attacks a common theme was the unreality of events. Live news coverage of the World Trade Center meant that millions of Americans witnessed the impact of the second plane on their television screens, and shots of New Yorkers running from the collapsing Twin Towers seemed distressingly reminiscent of scenes from disaster movies. Images of sleeping and waking abounded in the press, often to imply that America needed to face up to uncomfortable truths about its stature in the rest of the world. 'This week's nightmare . . . has awakened us from a frivolous if not decadent decade-long dream,' announced Frank Rich in the *New York Times*, while Slovenian theorist Slavoj Žižek likened the smouldering ruins of the World Trade Center to the 'desert of the real' that confronts Neo in *The Matrix*.[11] At the same time, as Lindsay Waters observed, the spectacular nature of the crime threatened to lull Americans back into another slumber – the fantasy that the perpetrators were an absolutely unknowable Other, more of a metaphysical force than a group of criminals with specific motivations that might somehow be addressed. For a brief moment, then, the meaning of the events of September 11th remained suspended in this radical uncertainty: between the unprecedented and the uncanny, the unthinkable act repeatedly thought in popular culture, and between rupture and continuity, where the trauma demanded that history never be the same again, while ideology required that 'the American way of life' go unchallenged. Soon, however, the possibility latent in this uncertainty was to disappear, as Bush committed to swift military action, first in Afghanistan and then Iraq. The new political order begins at this point, with a transformed foreign-policy agenda, a more aggressive and ideologically driven administration, and the imposition of conditions pertaining to a state of emergency at home. In the new climate of manic patriotism – in which, as Bush famously announced, 'you're either with us or against us' – there seemed to be little room for dissent, and the possibilities for resistance that had been glimpsed at Seattle were lost.

Legacies of the 1990s

Any given decade is likely to be claimed by a historian as a period of transition, but the 1990s looks in retrospect to be peculiarly marked by change: the end of the Cold War, the opening of global markets, the frenzied expansion of digital technology, the widening gap between rich and poor, the struggle over national identity and the dismantling of former certainties such as whiteness and masculinity. In this respect it seems remarkable that Bush could look back on the decade in his Second Inaugural Address of 20 January 2005 as if nothing had really happened: 'After the shipwreck of communism came years of relative quiet, years of repose, years of sabbatical. And then there came a day of fire . . .' The words may have been intended primarily as a slight against Clinton's presidency, but they also indicated that September 11th loomed so large in the imagination that it cast everything that went before it into shadow. For historians, too, the danger is that such a monumental event establishes an ending that makes the previous decade appear more coherent than it would otherwise be – the 1990s as hiatus or interregnum prevailing over all other possible narratives. This view is assisted by the perfect symmetry of the moments at either end, where 9/11 is mirrored by the day that the enforcement of checkpoints at the Berlin Wall ceased – 9 November 1989, or 11/9.

In two recent appraisals of the 1990s – Chollet and Goldgeier's *America Between the Wars* and Philip Wegner's *Life Between Two Deaths* – the first is the greater event: 11/9 marks the end of an ideological formation reaching back to World War II after which America has to confront the truly unprecedented question of its role in a world in which it is left as the sole superpower. Chollet and Goldgeier argue that the collapse of communism in Europe exposes a set of issues that will come to define international politics in the next millennium: the instability of global capital, threats posed by failing states, the rise of non-state actors and the possibility for international cooperation on security, humanitarian aid and climate change. For Wegner, September 11th is less of an event in itself than the repetition of the earlier event, the moment that confirms symbolically what had already happened in 1989. The years 'in between' – which is how the 1990s are likely to be remembered from now on – are therefore characterised by a similar kind of suspension and uncertainty as befell the nation in the immediate aftermath of the attacks. The decade appears as a moment of 'openness and instability, of experimentation and opportunity, of conflict and insecurity – a place, in other words, wherein history might move in a number of very different directions.'[12]

If the Berlin Wall and the World Trade Center are destined to become strange architectural landmarks of the 1990s, monumental only in their absence, then we ought to ask what happened to their remains. In both cases, the stories of the rubble can be read as fables of national identity for America at the end of the twentieth century. While most of the Berlin Wall was broken up and reused in the reconstruction of the city's roads, many fragments were removed and went into circulation as souvenirs or artwork. One of the most popular destinations was the United States, where there are now sections on display at over fifty locations from the United Nations in New York City to the cafeteria at Microsoft's headquarters in Redmond, Washington and the men's room of a Las Vegas casino. The debris of the World Trade Center was sifted to remove human remains and shipped to Staten Island's Fresh Kills landfill, which had been closed earlier that year but reopened to receive the materials. Once one of the largest refuse sites in the world, Fresh Kills is now designated to become a public park in a construction project lasting thirty years. The American afterlife of the Berlin Wall shows us how much the country still has invested in its former ideological conflict with communism, as if it needs to remind itself of its freedoms by preserving the signs of the system that once opposed it. The destination of the World Trade Center's remains discloses a similarly fundamental national impulse: the desire for reconciliation with nature.

Notes

Introduction

1. Diane Crispell and Andy Zukerberg, 'The Decade Waltz', *American Demographics* 15.11 (November 1993), pp. 48–50; Andy Aaron, 'Welcome to the '90s', *New Republic*, 7 March 1994, p. 10.
2. See Fredric Jameson, 'Periodising the 60s', in Sonya Sayres et al. (eds), *The 60s Without Apology* (Minneapolis: University of Minnesota Press, 1984), pp. 178–209.
3. Jason Scott Smith, 'The Strange History of the Decade: Modernity, Nostalgia, and the Perils of Periodization', *Journal of Social History* 32.2 (Winter 1998), pp. 263–85.
4. Jean-François Lyotard, *The Postmodern Condition: A Report on Knowledge*, trans. Geoff Bennington and Brian Massumi (Minneapolis: University of Minnesota Press, 1984).
5. Fredric Jameson, *Postmodernism, or The Cultural Logic of Late Capitalism* (Durham, NC: Duke University Press, 1991), p. 25.
6. Andreas Huyssen, *Twilight Memories: Marking Time in a Culture of Amnesia* (New York: Routledge, 1995), p. 100.
7. Svetlana Boym, *The Future of Nostalgia* (New York: Basic Books, 2001), p. 351.
8. Joseph Stiglitz, *The Roaring 1990s: Why We're Paying the Price for the Greediest Decade in History* (New York: Norton, 2003), pp. 49–55; Raymond Tatalovich and John Frendreis, 'Clinton, Class and Economic Policy', in Steven Schier (ed.), *The Postmodern Presidency: Bill Clinton's Legacy in U.S. Politics* (Pittsburgh: University of Pittsburgh Press, 2000), pp. 41–59.
9. Bruce Miroff, 'Courting the Public: Bill Clinton's Postmodern Education', in Schier (ed.), *The Postmodern Presidency*, pp. 106–23.
10. 'It's still the Economy They Say: 62% Dislike Clinton, 68% Like His Policies', Pew Research Center for the People and the Press, Survey Report, 27 August 1998, http://people-press.org/reports/display.php3?ReportID=82.
11. Lauren Berlant, *The Queen of America Goes to Washington City: Essays on Sex and Citizenship* (Durham, NC: Duke University Press, 1997), p. 178.
12. Stiglitz, *The Roaring 1990s*, pp. 92, 250.
13. David Remnick (ed.), *The New Gilded Age: The New Yorker Looks at the Culture of Affluence* (New York: Random House, 2000), p. xi.

14. Richard Sennett, *The Corrosion of Character: The Personal Consequences of Work in the New Capitalism* (New York: Norton, 1998), p. 62. Sennett's point is that the capacity for reinvention may make for a dynamic company image but has more serious consequences for the lower tiers of workers, who are left without foundations or structures around which to build their careers and identities.

15. Bill Gates, *The Road Ahead* (New York: Viking Penguin, 1995), pp. 214–26.

16. Francis Fukuyama, *The End of History and the Last Man* (London: Hamish Hamilton, 1992), p. 42.

17. Project for the New American Century, Statement of Principles, http://www.newamericancentury.org/statementofprinciples.htm.

18. See William V. Spanos, *America's Shadow: An Anatomy of Empire* (Minneapolis: University of Minnesota Press, 2000) for a critique of this 'imperialist' tradition.

19. Richard Crockatt, 'America at the Millennium', in Howard Temperley and Christopher Bigsby (eds), *A New Introduction to American Studies* (Harlow: Pearson Books, 2006), pp. 376–96.

20. Quoted in Miroff, 'Courting the Public', in Schier (ed.), *The Postmodern Presidency*, p. 109.

21. Howard Winant, 'Racial Dualism at Century's End', in Wahneema Lubiano (ed.), *The House That Race Built* (New York: Vintage, 1998), pp. 87–115.

22. E. J. Dionne, Jr, *Why Americans Hate Politics* (New York: Simon & Schuster, [1991] 1992), p. 61.

23. 1998 Declaration of Sentiments of The National Organization for Women, 12 July 1998, http://www.now.org/organization/conference/1998/vision98.html.

24. Claire Renzetti and Daniel Curran, *Women, Men and Society* (Boston: Allyn & Bacon, 1999), p. 195.

25. Irene Padaric and Barbara Reskin, *Women and Men at Work* (Thousand Oaks, CA: Pine Forge Press, 2002), exhibit 6.3; reprinted in Amy Wharton, *The Sociology of Gender* (Malden, MA: Blackwell, 2005), p. 190.

26. Renzetti and Curran, *Women, Men and Society*, p. 278.

27. See the feature in traditionalist magazine *Women's Day*, 30 October 1990, depicting Barbara Bush with the caption 'Women's Lib Made Me Feel Inadequate and Useless', reprinted in Amelia Jones (ed.), *The Feminism & Visual Culture Reader* (New York: Routledge, 2003), p. 317.

28. Carol Gilligan, 'Getting Civilized', in Ann Oakley and Juliet Mitchell (eds), *Who's Afraid of Feminism?* (New York: New Press, 1997), p. 18; Berlant, *The Queen of America*, pp. 221–46.

29. Renzetti and Curran, *Women, Men and Society*, p. 205.

30. Berlant, *The Queen of America*, p. 243.

31. Arthur Schlesinger Jr, *Disuniting America: Reflections on a Multicultural Society* (New York: Norton, 1992), pp. 16–17.

32. Susan Faludi, *Backlash: The Undeclared War Against Women* (London: Chatto & Windus, [1991] 1992), p. 2.

33. Rita Felski, 'The Doxa of Difference', *Signs* 23.1 (Fall 1997), pp. 1–23.

34. This was a theme Faludi developed in her subsequent book, *Stiffed: The Betrayal of the Modern Man* (London: Chatto & Windus, 1999).

35. Robert Hughes, *Culture of Complaint: The Fraying of America* (New York: Oxford University Press, 1993).

36. See Alyson M. Cole, *The Cult of True Victimhood: From the War on Welfare to the War on Terror* (Stanford, CA: Stanford University Press, 2007).

37. Quoted in Carol Swain, 'Double Standard, Double Bind: African American Leadership After the Thomas Debacle', in Toni Morrison (ed.), *Race-ing Justice, En-Gendering Power: Essays on Anita Hill, Clarence Thomas and the Construction of Social Reality* (London: Chatto & Windus, 1993), p. 219.

38. President Johnson quoted in Michael Omi and Howard Winant, *Racial Formation in the United States: 1960s to 1990s*, 2nd edn (New York: Routledge, 1994), pp. 128–9.

39. Peter Schrag, 'Backing Off Bakke: The New Assault on Affirmative Action', *The Nation*, 22 April 1996, pp. 11–14. For an account of the significance of *Richmond* v. *Croson* see Kimberlé Crenshaw, 'Color Blindness, History, and the Law', in Lubiano (ed.), *The House that Race Built*, pp. 280–8.

40. Manning Marable, *Race Reform & Rebellion*, 3rd edn (New York: Palgrave, 2007), p. 222.

41. George Lipsitz records that CNN averaged around 2.2 million viewers over its 631 hours of live coverage of the trial, and boosted the channel's ratings and revenue by almost 50 per cent. Lipsitz, 'The Greatest Story Ever Sold', in Toni Morrison and Claudia Brodsky Lacour (eds), *Birth of a Nation'hood: Gaze, Script and Spectacle in the OJ Simpson Case* (London: Vintage, 1997), p. 11.

42. Census data from http://www.census.gov/main/www/cen2000.html. For a summary, see US Census Bureau, Census 2000 Special Reports, Demographic Trends in the 20th Century: November 2002.

43. Mike Davis, *Magical Urbanism: Latinos Reinvent the US Big City* (London: Verso, 2000), p. 67.

44. Michael Douglas is the archetypal backlash figure, whose career traces the emergence of anxieties around white male identity from *Wall Street* (1987) to *Basic Instinct* (1992) and *Falling Down* in 1993.

45. Meri Nan-Ama Danquah, 'Why We Really Root For O.J: The Superstar Suspect Embodies the Illusion of a Colorblind America', *Los Angeles Times*, 3 July 1994, quoted in Kimberlé Crenshaw, 'Color-blind Dreams and Racial Nightmares', in Morrison and Lacour (eds), *Birth of a Nation'hood*, p. 114.

46. Crenshaw, 'Color-Blind Dreams and Racial Nightmares', in *Birth of a Nation'hood*, pp. 123–4.

47. Christopher Darden with Jess Walter, *In Contempt* (New York: Harper Collins, 1996), quoted in Jeffrey Rosen, 'The Bloods and the Crits', *New Republic*, 9 December 1996.

48. Berlant, *The Queen of America*, pp. 175–220.

49. David Hollinger, *Postethnic America: Beyond Multiculturalism* (New York: Basic Books, [1995] 2005). In a 2005 postscript Hollinger notes approvingly that the Census records a 70 per cent increase in marriage between blacks and whites since 1990, but he never seriously addresses the reasons why so few Americans (2.4 per cent) chose to identify as mixed race when given the chance. *Postethnic America*, p. 234.

50. Robert Reich, *The Work of Nations* (New York: Alfred Knopf, 1991).

51. Benjamin Barber, *Jihad vs McWorld* (New York: Times Books, 1995). John Tomlinson's *Cultural Imperialism* (Baltimore: Johns Hopkins University Press, 1991) continues to be a valuable analysis of the discourse; for an overview of

the debates see Frederick Buell, *National Culture and the New Global System* (Baltimore: Johns Hopkins University Press, 1994).

52. Paul Giles, *Virtual Americas: Transnational Fictions and the Transatlantic Imaginary* (Durham NC: Duke University Press, 2002), pp. 20, 274.

53. Frederick Buell, 'Nationalist Postnationalism: Globalist Discourse in Contemporary American Culture', *American Quarterly* 50.3 (September 1998), p. 553.

54. Alexis de Tocqueville, *Democracy in America* Vol. 2, ed. Phillips Bradley (New York: Vintage, 1945), p. 114.

55. Robert Putnam, *Bowling Alone: The Collapse and Revival of American Community* (New York: Simon & Schuster, 2000), p. 27. Putnam's original article was published as 'Bowling Alone: America's Declining Social Capital', *Journal of Democracy* 6 (January 1995), pp. 65–78.

56. Putnam, *Bowling Alone*, p. 259.

57. See Simone Chambers and Jeffrey Kopstein, 'Bad Civil Society', *Political Theory* 29.6 (December 2001), pp. 837–65, and Barbara Arneil, *Diverse Communities: the Problem with Social Capital* (New York: Cambridge University Press, 2006).

58. Putnam's initiative The Saguaro Seminar counts George Stephanopolous, William Julius Wilson and Barack Obama amongst its members, and he has also consulted with Gordon Brown's Labour government on social capital and immigration. See organisation websites http://www.ksg.harvard.edu/saguaro and http://www.bettertogether.org.

1. Fiction and Poetry

1. *Reading At Risk: A Survey of Literary Reading in America*, Research Division Report #46 (Washington, DC: National Endowment for the Arts, June 2004), p. xiii.

2. James Wood, 'Tell Me How Does it Feel?', *Guardian*, 6 October 2001, pp. 8–9.

3. *Reading At Risk*, p. 7.

4. Frederick Buell, 'Nationalist Postnationalism: Globalist Discourse in Contemporary American Culture', *American Quarterly* 50.3 (September 1998), pp. 548–91; see also introduction.

5. This issue falls somewhere between debates about cultural literacy and the value of the literary canon which raged in the 'culture wars' of the late 1980s and early 1990s. For a recent discussion, see Robert Scholes, *The Rise and Fall of English* (New Haven, CT: Yale University Press, 1999).

6. Cecilia Konchar Farr, *Reading Oprah: How Oprah's Book Club Changed the Way America Reads* (Albany, NY: State University of New York Press, 2005), p. 101.

7. Gayle Feldman, 'Making Book on Oprah', *New York Times*, 2 February 1997, p. 31.

8. Jeremy Green, *Late Postmodernism: American Fiction at the Millennium* (New York: Palgrave Macmillan, 2005), p. 89.

9. Ibid., p. 86.

10. John Young, 'Toni Morrison, Oprah Winfrey, and Postmodern Popular Audiences', *African American Review* 35.2 (Summer 2001), p. 182.

11. Walter Benjamin, 'The Storyteller' (1936); reprinted in *Illuminations*, trans. Harry Zohn (London: Fontana Press, 1992), p. 84.

12. Paul Gray, 'Paradise Found', *Time* magazine, 19 January 1998, p. 64.

13. Quoted in Justine Tally, *Paradise Reconsidered: Toni Morrison's (Hi)stories and Truths* (Hamburg: LIT Verlag, 1999), p. 13.

14. Toni Morrison, *Paradise* (London: Chatto & Windus, 1998), p. 55.

15. Ibid., p. 306.

16. Toni Morrison, *Playing in the Dark: Whiteness and the Literary Imagination* (Cambridge, MA: Harvard University Press, 1992), p. 64.

17. Morrison, *Paradise*, p. 283.

18. See reviews by Louis Menand, 'The War Between Men and Women', *New Yorker*, 12 January 1998, pp. 78–82, and Michiko Kakutani, '*Paradise*: Worthy Women, Unredeemable Men', *New York Times*, 6 January 1998, p. 8.

19. See Chapter 3 for a discussion of this incident.

20. Jonathan Franzen, 'Perchance to Dream: In the Age of Images, a Reason to Write Novels', *Harper's Magazine*, April 1996, p. 45.

21. See Green for an illuminating discussion of several of these writers, whom he calls 'elegists of the book': Green, *Late Postmodernism*, p. 6 and passim.

22. Franzen, 'Perchance to Dream', p. 38.

23. Paul Lauter, *From Walden Pond to Jurassic Park: Activism, Culture and American Studies* (Durham, NC: Duke University Press, 2001), p. 191. For an example of the *Heath Anthology*'s unfavourable reception, see Frederick Crews, 'The New Americanists', *New York Review of Books*, 24 September 1992, pp. 32–3.

24. See Roshni Rustomji-Kerns's preface to Mukherjee, 'A Wife's Story', in Lauter et al., *Heath Anthology of American Literature*, 2nd edn (Lexington, MA: Heath, 1994), p. 3103. Vizenor quoted in A. Robert Lee, *Multicultural American Literature: Comparative Black, Native, Latino/a and Asian American Fictions* (Edinburgh: Edinburgh University Press, 2003), p. 39.

25. Lee, *Multicultural American Literature*, p. 140.

26. Homi Bhabha emphasises the emergence within postcolonialism of 'a cultural hybridity that entertains difference without an assumed or imposed hierarchy' in *The Location of Culture* (London: Routledge, 1994), p. 4.

27. Gish Jen, 'In the American Society', reprinted in *Heath Anthology*, 2nd edn, pp. 2981–92.

28. Gish Jen, *Typical American* (Boston: Houghton Mifflin, 1991), pp. 123–4.

29. Lisa Lowe, 'Decolonisation, Displacement, Disidentification: Asian American "Novels" and the Question of History', in Deidre Lynch and William Warner (eds), *Cultural Institutions of the Novel* (Durham, NC: Duke University Press, 1996), p. 121.

30. Carol Roh-Spaulding, 'Waiting for Mr Kim', *Plowshares* 16.2 and 16.3 (Fall 1990), reprinted in Shawn Wong, *Asian American Literature: A Brief Introduction & Anthology* (New York: HarperCollins, 1996), p. 272.

31. See Frank Chin's essay 'Come All Ye Asian American Writers of the Real and the Fake', in Jeffery Paul Chan et al. (eds), *The Big Aiiieeeee!: An Anthology of Chinese American and Japanese American Literature* (New York: Meridian, 1991), pp. 1–28.

32. Lawson Fusao Inada, *Legends from Camp* (Minneapolis: Coffee House Press, 1993).

33. Judith Kitchen, 'Auditory Imaginations: The Sense of Sound', *Georgia Review* 45.1 (Spring 1991), pp. 154–69. Quoted in Lawrence Trudeau (ed.), *Asian American Literature: Reviews and Criticism of Works by American Writers of Asian Descent* (Detroit: Gale Research, 1999), p. 263.

34. Li-Young Lee, *The City in Which I Love You* (Brockport, NY: BOA Editions, 1990).

35. See Marjorie Perloff, *Poetry On & Off the Page: Essays for Emergent Occasions* (Evanston, IL: Northwestern University Press, 1998) for a valuable survey of new directions in the field.

36. Helen Vendler, *Soul Says: On Recent Poetry* (Cambridge, MA: Belknap Press, 1995), pp. 6–7.

37. See Dani Cavallaro's summary of subjectivity in *Critical and Cultural Theory* (New Brunswick, NJ: Athlone Press, 2001), pp. 86–97.

38. Charles Bernstein, *My Way: Speeches and Poems* (Chicago: University of Chicago Press, 1999), pp. 8–9, 39–40, 96.

39. Richard Silberg, *Reading the Sphere: A Geography of Contemporary American Poetry* (Berkeley, CA: Berkeley Hills Books, 2002).

40. For an overview of these developments see Bernstein's essay 'Provisional Institutions', in *My Way*, pp. 145–54.

41. Alfred Arteaga, *Cantos* (San Jose, CA: Chusma House Publications, 1991).

42. Michael Palmer, *At Passages* (New York: New Directions, 1995); quotation from interview with Peter Gizzi in *Exact Change Yearbook* No. 1 (Boston: Exact Change, 1995), p. 167.

43. William Gass, 'The Art of Self: Autobiography in an Age of Narcissism', *Harper's Magazine*, May 1994, p. 43.

44. Paul John Eakin, *How Our Lives Become Stories: Making Selves* (Ithaca, NY: Cornell University Press, 1999), p. x.

45. Michiko Kakutani, 'Biography as Blood Sport', *New York Times*, 20 May 1994, Section B1.

46. Bret Easton Ellis, *American Psycho* (London: Picador, 1991).

47. Norman Mailer, 'Children of the Pied Piper', *Vanity Fair*, 54.3 (March 1991), pp. 154–9, 220–1.

48. David Foster Wallace, 'E Unibus Pluram', *Review of Contemporary Fiction* 13.2 (Summer 1993), p. 182.

49. Larry McCaffery, 'An Interview with David Foster Wallace', *Review of Contemporary Fiction* 13.2 (Summer 1993), pp. 127–50.

50. A. O. Scott , 'The Panic of Influence', *New York Review of Books*, 10 February 2000, p. 40.

51. Dennis Cooper, *Frisk* (London: Serpent's Tail, 1992), p. 38. For a similar argument see Julian Murphet, *Literature and Race in Los Angeles* (New York: Cambridge University Press, 2001), pp. 94–105.

52. Cooper, *Frisk*, pp. 113–14.

53. Ibid., p. 94.

54. Ibid., p. 87.

55. Kasia Boddy, 'Conversation with Dennis Cooper', *Critical Quarterly* 37.3 (Autumn 1995), p. 104.

56. Dennis Cooper, *Guide* (London: Serpent's Tail, 1998), p. 46.

57. Ibid., p. 102.

58. Cooper, *Frisk*, p. 128.
59. Murphet, *Literature and Race*, p. 105.
60. David Foster Wallace, *Infinite Jest* (Boston: Little, Brown, 1996), p. 839.
61. As the title's reference to *Hamlet* reminds us, the novel is a work of mourning not only for the dead patriarch but for the dead entertainer, the 'fellow of infinite jest' that Hamlet remembers in Yorick.
62. Paul Giles, 'Sentimental Posthumanism: David Foster Wallace', *Twentieth-Century Literature* 53.3 (Fall 2007), pp. 327–44.
63. Wallace, 'Federer as Religious Experience', *New York Times*, 20 August 2006, reprinted in the *Times*'s *Play* magazine, September 2006, p. 83.
64. James Wood, 'Human, All Too Inhuman', *The New Republic*, 24 July 2000, pp. 41–6. The piece is a review of British writer Zadie Smith's *White Teeth* which also accuses Salman Rushdie, Don DeLillo, Thomas Pynchon and David Foster Wallace.
65. Norman Mailer, *The Spooky Art: Some Thoughts on Writing* (New York: Random House, 2003), p. 294.
66. Philip Roth, *American Pastoral* (1997; London: Vintage, 1998), p. 35.
67. See Ross Posnock, *Philip Roth's Rude Truth: The Art of Immaturity* (Princeton, NJ: Princeton University Press, 2006), pp. 218–21.
68. Philip Roth, *I Married a Communist* (London: Vintage, [1998] 2005), p. 319.
69. Philip Roth, *The Human Stain* (London: Vintage, [2000] 2001), p. 335.
70. Roth, *American Pastoral*, p. 31.
71. Ibid., p. 20.
72. Ibid., pp. 281, 279.
73. For an insight into Roth's own views on 'the death of reading', see David Remnick's overview of Roth's career, 'Into the Clear', *New Yorker*, 8 May 2000, pp. 76–89.

2. Music and Radio

1. Steve Albini, 'The Problem with Music', *The Baffler* 5 (1993), reprinted in *Commodify Your Dissent: Salvos from* The Baffler (New York: Norton, 1997), pp. 164–76.
2. John Lovering, 'The Global Music Industry: Contradictions in the Commodification of the Sublime', in Andrew Leyshon, David Matless and George Revill (eds), *The Place of Music* (New York: Guilford Press, 1998), p. 49.
3. For a detailed history, see Louis Barfe, *Where Have All the Good Times Gone? The Rise and Fall of the Record Industry* (London: Atlantic Books, 2004).
4. Ibid., pp. 311–12, 326.
5. Dave Marsh, 'U2's Crash: Why Pop Flops', *The Nation*, 25 August–1 September 1997, pp. 18–21; Geoff Carter, 'U2 Live', *Las Vegas Sun*, 27 April 1997.
6. Mark Miller, 'Who Controls the Music?', *The Nation*, 25 August–1 September 1997, pp. 11–16.
7. Susan Douglas, *Listening In: Radio and the American Imagination* (New York: Times Books, 1999), pp. 314–18.
8. Peter J. Boyer, 'Bull Rush', *Vanity Fair*, May 1992, p. 106.
9. Douglas, *Listening In*, p. 297.

10. Keith Moerer, 'Who Killed Rock Radio?', *Spin*, February 1998, p. 74.
11. Jenny Toomey, 'Empire of the Air', *The Nation*, 13–20 January 2003, pp. 28–30.
12. Brent Staples, 'The Trouble With Corporate Radio: The Day the Protest Music Died', *New York Times*, 20 February 2003, Section A1, p. 30.
13. Paul Krugman, 'Channels of Influence', *New York Times*, 25 March 2003, Section A6, p. 17.
14. Mark Miller, 'Free the Media', *The Nation*, 3 June 1996, pp. 9–15; accompanying map of media ownership by Mark Miller and Janine Jacquet, pp. 23–27. Relevant dissenting websites are www.radiodiversity.com, www.projectcensored.org and www.freedomforum.org.
15. Douglas, *Listening In*, pp. 354–6.
16. Mark Andersen quoted in Jason Middleton, 'D.C. Punk and the Production of Authenticity', in Roger Beebe, Denise Fulbrook and Ben Saunders (eds), *Rock Over the Edge: Transformations in Popular Music Culture* (Durham, NC: Duke University Press, 2002), p. 352.
17. Michael Azerrad, 'Grunge City', *Rolling Stone*, 16 April 1992, p. 43.
18. Dave Grohl quoted in Michael Azerrad, *Come As You Are: The Story of Nirvana* (London: Virgin Books, 1993), p. 214.
19. Greil Marcus, 'Notes on the Life and Death and Incandescent Banality of Rock 'n' Roll', *Esquire*, August 1992, p. 69.
20. 'A Cry in the Dark': transcript of Courtney Love's taped message for Seattle Center memorial, *Rolling Stone*, 2 June 1994, p. 40.
21. Lawrence Grossberg, 'Is Anybody Listening? Does Anybody Care? On "The State of Rock"', in Andrew Ross and Tricia Rose (eds), *Microphone Fiends: Youth Music and Youth Culture* (New York: Routledge, 1994), p. 52.
22. Lawrence Grossberg, 'The War Against Kids, and the Rebecoming of US Modernity', *Postcolonial Studies* 6.3 (2003), pp. 327–49.
23. Grossberg, 'Is Anybody Listening?', in Ross and Rose (eds), *Microphone Fiends*, p. 56.
24. Joanne Gottlieb and Gayle Wald, 'Smells Like Teen Spirit: Riot Grrrls, Revolution and Women in Independent Rock', in Ross and Rose (eds), *Microphone Fiends*, p. 250.
25. 'riot grrrl' manifesto from fanzine *Bikini Kill* (July 1991), reprinted in David Brackett (ed.), *The Pop, Rock and Soul Reader* (New York: Oxford University Press, 2005), pp. 438–41.
26. See Gottlieb and Wald on the role women performers have traditionally played in deflecting a homoerotic gaze in rock: Ross and Rose (eds), *Microphone Fiends*, p. 259.
27. Fred Schruers, 'Sheryl', *Rolling Stone*, 14 November 1996, p. 70.
28. Chris Heath, 'The Caged Bird Sings Fiona', *Rolling Stone*, 22 January 1998, p. 68.
29. Christopher John Farley, 'Hip-Hop Nation', *Time* magazine, 8 February 1999, p. 56.
30. David Gates et al., 'Decoding Rap Music', *Newsweek*, 19 March 1990, pp. 60–3.
31. Jerry Adler et al., 'The Rap Attitude', *Newsweek*, 19 March 1990, p. 58.
32. Thomas Schumacher, 'This is a Sampling Sport: Digital Sampling, Rap Music

and the Law in Cultural Production', *Media, Culture and Society* 17.2 (1995), pp. 253–73.

33. Murray Forman, 'Represent: Race, Space and Place in Rap Music', *Popular Music* 19.1 (2000), p. 74.

34. Statistics from Thomas Dumm, 'The New Enclosures: Racism in the Normalised Community', in Robert Gooding-Williams (ed.), *Reading Rodney King: Reading Urban Uprising* (New York: Routledge, 1993), p. 190 and George Lipsitz, 'We Know What Time It Is', in Ross and Rose (eds), *Microphone Fiends*, p. 18.

35. Jeffrey Schmalz, 'Adrift in America; Disaffection With National Leaders Sharpens in the Glare of Los Angeles', *New York Times*, 10 May 1992, Section 4, p. 1; John Leland, 'Rap and Race', *Newsweek*, 29 June 1992, pp. 46–53. Examples of the strange slippage between rap and heavy rock – the unconscious association presumably being 'if it's offensive, it's black' – can be found in the erroneous title of the *New York Times* article 'The 1992 Campaign; Vice President Calls Corporation Wrong For Selling Rap Song', 20 June 1992, and the *Newsweek* article 'The Rap Attitude' (see note 31 above), which manages to name metal band Guns N' Roses as one of rap's worst offenders.

36. C. Delores Tucker quoted in Nelson George, *Hip Hop America* (New York: Penguin, 1998), p. 189.

37. George, *Hip Hop America*, pp. 189–90.

38. R. A. T. Judy, 'On the Question of Nigga Authenticity', *boundary 2*, 21.3 (Autumn 1994), p. 229.

39. Quoted in Brackett, *The Pop, Rock and Soul Reader*, p. 421.

40. 'Bare life' is Giorgio Agamben's term for the new political subjectivity that is increasingly displacing the classical concept of the citizen; it is the reality of the refugee, the concentration camp intern, the unhoused and the incarcerated. See Lindsay Waters for a preliminary application of Agamben to rap's discourse of 'nigga', 'Dreaming with Tears in My Eyes', *Transition* 74 (1997), pp. 78–102.

41. Kevin Powell, 'All Eyes on Him: Interview with Tupac Shakur', *Vibe*, February 1996.

42. Kai Fikentscher, *You Better Work! Underground Dance Music in New York City* (Hanover, NH: Wesleyan University Press, 2000), p. 78.

43. Quoted in Jon Savage, 'Machine Soul: a History of Techno', *Village Voice Rock and Roll Quarterly* (Summer 1993), p. 19.

44. Simon Reynolds, *Energy Flash: A Journey through Rave Music and Dance Culture* (London: Picador, 1998), pp. 210–11.

45. Banks from 'Mike Banks über Underground Resistance', interview, *De:Bug* 109, 10 Feb 2007, http://www.de-bug.de/texte/4639.html; Mills from Reynolds, *Energy Flash*, p. 221.

46. Neil Strauss, 'The Next Big Thing Or the Next Bust?', *New York Times*, 26 January 1997.

47. Simon Reynolds, 'Post-Rock', *Village Voice*, 29 August 1995, reprinted in Christoph Cox and Daniel Warner (eds), *Audio Culture: Readings in Modern Music* (New York: Continuum, 2004), p. 359.

48. Robert Fink, 'Elvis Everywhere: Musicology and Popular Music Studies at the Twilight of the Canon', in Beebe et al., *Rock Over the Edge*, p. 79.

49. Karl Taro, 'Meet the Napster', *Time* magazine, 2 October 2000, p. 62.

50. John Alderman, *Sonic Boom: Napster, MP3, and the New Pioneers of Music* (London: Fourth Estate, 2001), pp. 9–10.
51. John Perry Barlow, 'The Next Economy of Ideas: Will Copyright Survive the Napster Bomb? Nope, but Creativity Will', *Wired*, October 2000, pp. 240–2, 252; Jesse Freund, 'Listen Up', interview with Chuck D, *Wired*, March 1999, p. 139.
52. The current website, Napster 2.0, is a pay service that retains only the name from the original company, after it was bought by BMG during the trial and later sold to Roxio.
53. Robert Fink, *Repeating Ourselves: American Minimal Music as Cultural Practice* (Berkeley, CA: University of California Press, 2005), p. 21.
54. Anahid Kassabian, 'Ubiquitous Listening', in David Hesmondhalgh and Keith Negus (eds), *Popular Music Studies* (London: Arnold, 2002), pp. 131–42.

3. Film and Television

1. Bruce Cumings, *War and Television* (London: Verso, 1992), p. 2.
2. Peter Arnett, *Live From the Battlefield* (London: Bloomsbury Press, 1994), p. 342.
3. See accounts in Cumings, *War and Television*, Philip M. Taylor, *War and the Media: Propaganda and Persuasion in the Gulf War* (Manchester: Manchester University Press, 1992) and W. Lance Bennett and David Paletz (eds), *Taken By Storm: The Media, Public Opinion, and US Foreign Policy in the Gulf War* (Chicago: University of Chicago Press, 1994).
4. Elaine Scarry, 'Watching and Authorising the Gulf War', in Marjorie Garber et al. (eds), *Media Spectacles* (New York: Routledge, 1993), pp. 63–4.
5. Daniel Hallin and Todd Gitlin, 'The Gulf War as Popular Culture and Television Drama', in Bennett and Paletz, *Taken By Storm*, pp. 149–64.
6. See Peter Arnett's account of the interview in his memoir *Live From the Battlefield* (London: Bloomsbury, 1994), pp. 372–402.
7. Jean Baudrillard's three articles written for the French newspaper *Libération* in January, February and March 1991 are collected in *The Gulf War Did Not Take Place* trans./intro Paul Patton (Sydney: Power Publications, [1991] 1995).
8. See Paul Virilio, *War and Cinema* (London: Verso, [1984] 1998) and companion volume *The Vision Machine* (Bloomington, IN: Indiana University Press, 1994).
9. Orlando Patterson, 'Race, Gender and Liberal Fallacies', *New York Times*, 20 October 1991, Section 4, p. 15.
10. See Kimberlé Crenshaw, 'Whose Story is it Anyway? Feminist and Antiracist Appropriations of Anita Hill', in Toni Morrison (ed.), *Race-ing Justice, Engendering Power* (London: Chatto & Windus, 1993), pp. 402–40. Crenshaw assisted Hill's defence team during the hearings. For a background to the movement, see Crenshaw, *Critical Race Theory: The Key Writings* (New York: New Press, 1995).
11. Manning Marable, 'Clarence Thomas and the Crisis of Black Political Culture', *Race-ing Justice*, pp. 61–85.
12. Michael Stone quoted in Robert Gooding-Williams (ed.), *Reading Rodney King, Reading Urban Uprising* (New York: Routledge, 1993), p. 186.

13. Richard Lacayo, 'Anatomy of an Acquittal', *Time* magazine, 11 May 1992, p. 42.

14. Marita Sturken and Lisa Cartright, *Practices of Looking: An Introduction to Visual Culture* (New York: Oxford University Press, 2001), pp. 286–90.

15. David Ellis et al., 'L.A. Lawless', *Time* magazine, 11 May 1992, pp. 26–30.

16. William Staples, *Everyday Surveillance: Vigilance and Visibility in Postmodern Life* (Lanham, MD: Rowman & Littlefield, 2000), p. 51.

17. George Lipsitz, 'The Greatest Story Ever Sold', in Toni Morrison and Claudia Brodsky Lacour (eds), *Birth of a Nation'hood: Gaze, Script and Spectacle in the OJ Simpson Case* (London: Vintage, 1997), pp. 3–30.

18. See *Chandler* v. *Florida*, 1981.

19. Jeff Goodell, 'The Supreme Court', *Wired* 3.03 (March 1995), p. 121.

20. Judge Ito quoted in Douglas Kellner, *Media Spectacle* (New York: Routledge, 2003), p. 105.

21. Michael Eisner, Walt Disney Co. Annual Report 1993, quoted in William Kunz, *Culture Conglomerates: Consolidation in the Motion Picture and Television Industries* (Lanham, MD: Rowman & Littlefield, 2007), p. 41.

22. Geoff King, *American Independent Cinema* (New York: I. B. Tauris, 2005), pp. 21–6.

23. Peter Biskind, *Down and Dirty Pictures: Miramax, Sundance and the Rise of the Independent Film* (London: Bloomsbury 2004), pp. 65, 81, 144–8, 189.

24. Ibid., p. 127.

25. Susan Sontag, 'The Decay of Cinema', *New York Times*, 26 February 1996, Section 6, p. 60.

26. Jeffrey Sconce, 'Movies: A Century of Failure', in Jeffrey Sconce (ed.), *Sleaze Artists: Cinema at the Margins of Taste, Style and Politics* (Durham, NC: Duke University Press, 2007), pp. 273–309.

27. See Jeffrey Pence, 'Postcinema / Postmemory', in Paul Grainge (ed.), *Memory and Popular Film* (Manchester: Manchester University Press, 2003), pp. 237–56.

28. James Schamus, 'The Pursuit of *Happiness*: Making an Art of Marketing an Explosive Film', *The Nation*, 5–12 April 1999, p. 34.

29. Jean Baudrillard, *The Transparency of Evil: Essays on Extreme Phenomena* (London: Verso, 1993), pp. 121–2.

30. Sean Cubitt, *The Cinema Effect* (Cambridge, MA: Massachusetts Institute of Technology Press, 2004), p. 220.

31. Allan Sekula, 'Between the Net and the Deep Blue Sea (Rethinking the Traffic in Photographs)', *October* 102 (Fall 2002), p. 17.

32. Fowler quoted in William Baker, 'On the State of American Television', *Daedalus* 136.2 (Spring 2007), p. 142.

33. Figures from Ron Becker, *Gay TV and Straight America* (New Brunswick, NJ: Rutgers, 2006), n. 251–2.

34. Jeffrey Sconce, 'What If?: Charting Television's New Textual Boundaries', in Lynn Spigel and Jan Olsson (eds), *Television After TV: Essays on a Medium in Transition* (Durham, NC: Duke University Press, 2004), pp. 107–9.

35. Sara Gwenllian Jones, 'Web Wars: Resistance, Online Fandom and Studio Censorship', in Mark Jancovich and James Lyons (eds), *Quality Popular Television* (London: BFI, 2003), p. 166.

36. Emily Nussbaum, 'Must-See Metaphysics', *New York Times*, 22 September 2002, Section 6, p. 56.
37. Nancy San Martin, '"Must See TV": Programming Identity on NBC Thursdays', in Jancovich and Lyons, *Quality Popular Television*, pp. 32–47.
38. Becker, *Gay TV and Straight America*, p. 182.
39. See, for instance, Jon Kraszewski, 'Country Hicks and Urban Cliques: Mediating Race, Reality and Liberalism on MTV's *The Real World*', in Susan Murray and Laurie Ouellette (eds), *Reality TV: Remaking Television Culture* (New York: New York University Press, 2004), pp. 205–22.
40. Elizabeth Kolbert, 'At Work With Matt Groening; The Fun of Being Bart's Real Dad', *New York Times*, 25 February 1993, Section C1.
41. Peter Parisi, 'Black Bart Simpson: Appropriation and Revitalization in Commodity Culture', *Journal of Popular Culture* 27.1 (Summer 1993), pp. 125–42.
42. Nick Griffiths, 'America's First Family', *Times Magazine*, 15 April 2000, pp. 25, 27–8.
43. Ibid., p. 27.
44. See Eva Cherniavsky, '"Karmic Realignment": Transnationalism and Trauma in *The Simpsons*', *Cultural Critique* 41 (Winter 1999), pp. 139–57.
45. Paul Wells, *Animation and America* (Edinburgh: Edinburgh University Press, 2002), pp. 159–60.

4. Art and Architecture

1. David Wojnarowicz, 'Postcards from America: X-Rays from Hell', in Nan Goldin (ed.), *Witnesses: Against Our Vanishing* (New York: Artists Space, 1989).
2. See Steven Dubin, *Arresting Images: Impolitic Art and Uncivil Actions* (New York: Routledge, 1992).
3. Nancy Spector, *Felix Gonzalez-Torres* (New York: Guggenheim Museum Publications, 1995), pp. 14–15.
4. Quoted in Spector, *Felix Gonzalez-Torres*, pp. 147, 150.
5. Coco Fusco, 'The Other History of Intercultural Performance', in *English is Broken Here: Notes on Cultural Fusion in the Americas* (New York: New Press, 1995), pp. 37–63.
6. Hal Foster, *The Return of the Real* (Cambridge, MA: Massachusetts Institute of Technology Press, 1996), pp. 171–203.
7. Interview with Fred Wilson, *Inside the Studio: Two Decades of Talks with Artists in New York* (New York: Independent Curators International, 2004), pp. 198–200.
8. Coco Fusco, *The Bodies That Were Not Ours and Other Writings* (New York: Routledge, 2001), p. 16.
9. Arthur Danto, 'The 1993 Whitney Biennial', *The Nation*, 19 April 1993, reprinted in *The Wake of Art: Criticism, Philosophy and the Ends of Taste* (Amsterdam: G+B Arts International, 1998), p. 174; Peter Plagens, 'Fade From White', *Newsweek*, 15 March 1993, p. 72.
10. 'The Politics of the Signifier: A Conversation on the Whitney Biennial', *October* 66 (Fall 1993), p. 7.

11. Abject art's antecedents were explored in another Whitney exhibition also from 1993: *Abject Art: Repulsion and Desire in American Art.*

12. Antoni quoted in Martha Buskirk, *The Contingent Object of Contemporary Art* (Cambridge, MA: Massachusetts Institute of Technology Press, 2003), p. 252.

13. 'The recovered memories are often times wish fulfilment – it's not recovery at all. The past is actually a screen memory, a construction of present desires.' Mike Kelley, 'Repressed Architectural Memory Replaced with Psychic Reality', *Architecture New York* 15 (1996), p. 39.

14. Howardena Pindell, 'Diaspora/Realities/Strategies', paper given at 'Trade Routes, History, Geography, Culture: Towards a Definition of Culture in the late 20th Century', Johannesburg Biennale, October 1997, updated with a new postscript, January 2002, http://web.ukonline.co.uk/n.paradoxa/pindell.htm.

15. Mark Reinhardt, 'The Art of Racial Profiling': catalogue essay for exhibition *Kara Walker: Narratives of a Negress* (Cambridge, MA: Massachusetts Institute of Technology Press, 2003), p. 121.

16. Cornell West, 'The New Cultural Politics of Difference', *October* 53 (1990), pp. 93–109. Reprinted in Simon During (ed.), *The Cultural Studies Reader* (London and New York: Routledge, 1993), pp. 203–20.

17. 'Kara Walker: Ill-Will and Desire': interview with Jerry Saltz, *Flash Art* 191 (November/December 1996), pp. 82–6.

18. *Kara Walker: Narratives of a Negress*, p. 55.

19. Elizabeth Hayt, 'Monuments of Junk Artfully Compacted', *New York Times*, 2 May 1999, Section 2, p. 25.

20. Roxana Marcoci, 'The Anti-Historicist Approach: Brancusi, "Our Contemporary"', *Art Journal* 59.2 (Summer 2000), p. 34.

21. Ibid.

22. The title refers obliquely to Phineas T. Barnum's prank in which signs saying 'To the Egress' in his American Museum on Broadway were merely a device for shepherding gullible spectators towards the exit.

23. See Dave Hickey, *The Invisible Dragon: Four Essays on Beauty* (Los Angeles: Art Issues Press, 1995).

24. Gregory Crewdson, *Dream of Life* (Salamanca: Ediciones Universidad de Salamanca, 1999), p. 28.

25. *Philip Lorca diCorcia* (New York: Museum of Modern Art, 1995), p. 50.

26. Brandon Taylor, *Art Today* (London: Laurence King, 2005), p. 232.

27. Paul Pfeiffer, commentary from *Art: 21*, ed. Marybeth Sollins (New York: Harry N. Abrams, Inc., 2003), p. 196.

28. Fredric Jameson, *Postmodernism: Or, The Cultural Logic of Late Capitalism* (London & New York: Verso, 1991), pp. 70–7.

29. Exhibition notes, *Bill Viola*, cur. David Ross and Peter Sellars, November 1997–January 2000 (Paris & New York: Flammarion, with Whitney Museum of American Art).

30. Bill Viola, 'Video Black – The Mortality of the Image', in Doug Hall and Sally Jo Fifer (eds), *Illuminating Video: An Essential Guide to Video Art* (New York: Aperture, 1990), p. 477.

31. Interview with Ben Lewis in the television programme *Art Safari*, episode 'Matthew Barney: Church of Cremaster' (Ben Lewis, BBC 2003).

32. *Art Safari*. Benjamin Buchloh probably went too far when he called Barney

'a proto-totalitarian artist . . . a small-time Richard Wagner who mythifies the catastrophic conditions of existence under late capitalism'. Hal Foster, Rosalind Krauss, Benjamin Bucloch and Yves-Alain Bois, *Art Since 1900: Modernism, Antimodernism, Postmodernism* (New York: Thames & Hudson, 2004), p. 673.

33. Johanna Drucker, *Sweet Dreams: Contemporary Art and Complicity* (Chicago: University of Chicago Press, 2005), p. xii.
34. Round-table discussion, 'The Predicament of Contemporary Art', in Foster et al., *Art Since 1900*, p. 679.
35. Franco Moretti, 'MoMA2000: The Capitulation', *New Left Review* 4 (July 2000), pp. 98–102.
36. Julian Stallabrass, *Art Incorporated: The Story of Contemporary Art* (Oxford: Oxford University Press, 2004), p. 186.
37. Foster et al., *Art Since 1900*, p. 673.
38. Drucker, *Sweet Dreams*, p. 39.
39. Rem Koolhaas, 'Whatever Happened to Urbanism?', in Rem Koolhaas and Bruce Mau, *S, M, L, XL* (New York: Monacelli Press, 1998), pp. 958–71.
40. Mike Davis, *City of Quartz: Excavating the Future in Los Angeles* (New York: Vintage Books, 1992), pp. 238–40.
41. Jeremy Gilbert-Rolfe with Frank Gehry, *Frank Gehry: The City and Music* (Amsterdam: G+B Arts International, 2001), p. 112; Martin Filler, *Makers of Modern Architecture* (New York: New York Review of Books, 2007), pp. 178–9.
42. Greg Lynn, 'Architectural Curvilinearity: The Folded, the Pliant and the Supple' (1993), excerpted in Charles Jencks and Karl Kropf (eds), *Theories and Manifestoes of Contemporary Architecture*, 2nd edn (Chichester: Wiley Academy, 2006), p. 127. For a critical perspective on Gehry, see Allan Sekula, 'Between the Net and the Deep Blue Sea (Rethinking the Traffic in Photographs)', *October* 102 (Fall 2002), pp. 3–34.
43. Miwon Kwon, *One Place After Another: Site-Specific Art and Locational Identity* (Cambridge, MA: Massachusetts Institute of Technology Press, 2002).
44. Ilya and Emilia Kabakov, artist commentary for *The Palace of Projects* (1998), available at http://www.ilya-emilia-kabakov.com.
45. Sollins, *Art: 21*, p. 57.
46. Hsieh announced he had 'given up' making art in the new millennium, though his complaint about continuing interest in his activities indicates this was not an easy move to make: 'If I am painting a house, people say I am painting or I am doing a performance. But it is *not* . . .' Tehching Hsieh in conversation with Delia Bajo and Brainard Carey, *The Brooklyn Rail*, August–September 2003, http://www.thebrooklynrail.org/arts/sept03/tehchinghsieh.html.

5. Digital Culture

1. 'The U.S. Now Has One Computer for Every Three People', Computer Industry Almanac Press Release, 28 April 1995, http://www.c-i-a.com/pr0495.htm.
2. Steven Jones, 'The Bias of the Web', in Andrew Herman and Thomas Swiss (eds), *The World Wide Web and Contemporary Cultural Theory* (New York: Routledge, 2000), pp. 171–82.

3. See David Lyon, *Surveillance Society: Monitoring Everyday Life* (Buckingham & Philadelphia: Oxford University Press, 2001) for an overview of some of these issues.

4. Sean Cubitt, *The Cinema Effect* (Cambridge, MA: Massachusetts Institute of Technology Press, 2004), p. 97.

5. Andrew Ross, *Real Love: In Pursuit of Cultural Justice* (New York: Routledge, 1998), p. 29.

6. Chip Morningstar and F. Randall Farmer, 'The Lessons of Lucasfilm's *Habitat*' (1991), in Noah Wardrip-Fruin and Nick Montfort (eds), *The New Media Reader* (Cambridge, MA: Massachusetts Institute of Technology Press, 2003), pp. 663–77.

7. Julian Dibbell, 'A Rape in Cyberspace; or how an evil clown, a Haitian trickster spirit, two wizards, and a cast of dozens turned a database into a society' (1993), in David Bell (ed.), *Cybercultures: Critical Concepts in Media and Cultural Studies*, Vol. III (New York: Routledge 2006), pp. 289–307.

8. Howard Rheingold, *The Virtual Community: Homesteading on the Electronic Frontier* (Cambridge, MA: Massachusetts Institute of Technology Press, [1993] 2000), pp. 191–3.

9. A survey in 1992 judged that 50 per cent of all posts on the WELL were contributed by only 1 per cent of its users: see Marc Smith, 'Voices from the WELL: The Logic of the Virtual Commons', http://www.sscnet.ucla.edu/soc/csoc/papers/voices/Voices.htm.

10. Rheingold, *The Virtual Community*, p. 152.

11. Kevin Robins, 'Against Virtual Community: For a Politics of Distance', in *The Cybercultures Reader*, 2nd edn, p. 229.

12. Rheingold, *The Virtual Community*, p. 326.

13. Sherry Turkle, *Life on the Screen: Identity in the Age of the Internet* (New York: Simon & Schuster, 1995), p. 180.

14. David Bell, *An Introduction to Cybercultures* (New York: Routledge, 2001), pp. 127–8.

15. Post from Gareth Branwyn on WELL sex conference topic 265, 'Text Sex', 13 July 1992, quoted in Mark Dery, *Escape Velocity: Cyberculture at the End of the Century* (New York: Grove Press, 1996), p. 203.

16. See Lisa Nakamura, 'Race in / for Cyberspace: Identity Tourism and Racial passing on the Internet', in David Bell and Barbara Kennedy (eds), *The Cybercultures Reader*, 2nd edn (New York: Routledge, 2007) pp. 297–305.

17. Tom Spooner and Lee Rainie, 'African-Americans and the Internet', Pew Internet and American Life Report, 22 October 2000, http://www.pewinternet.org/PPF/r/25/report_display.asp.

18. John Perry Barlow, 'A Declaration of the Independence of Cyberspace', email message, 1996, reprinted in Peter Ludlow (ed.), *Crypto Anarchy, Cyberstates and Pirate Utopias* (Cambridge, MA: Massachusetts Institute of Technology Press, 2001), pp. 27–30.

19. Gary Rivlin, 'A Retail Revolution Turns 10', *New York Times*, 10 July 2005.

20. James Gleick, 'Accounting for Taste', *New York Times Magazine*, 25 October 1998, reprinted in *What Just Happened: A Chronicle from the Information Frontier* (New York: Abacus 2002), pp. 216–19.

21. See discussion on Plastic.com, 'EBay – What's Up With That?', http://www.

plastic.com/submit.html;op=userviewsub;subid=040604.07375279;sid=04/06/08/14100582.

22. Andrew Gumbel, 'Short Shrift for Unions in Amazon's Silicon Jungle', *The Independent*, 3 February 2001.

23. Rebecca Blood, 'Weblogs: a History and Perspective', 7 September 2000, http://www.rebeccablood.net/essays/weblog_history.html.

24. http://setiathome.ssl.berkeley.edu.

25. See the ruling *United States* v. *Thomas*, F.3d (6th Cir. 1996) requiring a California bulletin board to instal filters preventing offensive screens to be displayed in Tennessee; David Johnson and David Post, 'Law and Borders: The Rise of Law in Cyberspace' (1996), in Ludlow, *Crypto Anarchy, Cyberstates and Pirate Utopias*, n. 179.

26. This is a question asked by Richard Stallman, co-developer of the GNU-Linux operating system and a leading voice in the open source software movement. See 'The GNU Manifesto' (1985), reprinted in Noah Wardrip-Fruin and Nick Montfort (eds), *The New Media Reader* (Cambridge, MA: Massachusetts Institute of Technology Press, 2003), pp. 543–50.

27. Esther Dyson, 'Intellectual Value', *Wired* 3.07 (July 1995).

28. Nathan Newman, 'Prop 13 meets the Internet: How State and Local Govt Finances are becoming Road Kill on the Info Superhighway' (2001), in Ludlow, *Crypto Anarchy, Cyberstates and Pirate Utopias*, pp. 213–42.

29. Saskia Sassen, 'Digital Networks and the State: Some Governance Questions' (2000), in Bell and Kennedy, *The Cybercultures Reader* 2nd edn, pp. 582–93.

30. Philip Elmer Dewitt et al., 'On a Screen Near You', *Time* magazine, 3 July 1995, pp. 38–45.

31. *Reno* v. *ACLU*, 521 U.S. 844 (1997).

32. U.S. District Court for District of Columbia, 'Review of the Final Judgments by the United States and New York Group', 30 August 2007; http://www.usdoj.gov/atr/cases/f225600/225658.pdf.

33. Thomas Frank, 'The Rise of Market Populism', *The Nation*, 30 October 2000.

34. Max More, 'Principles of Extropy' Version 3.11, http://www.extropy.org/principles.htm.

35. Stelarc, 'Prosthetics, Robotics and Remote Existence: Postevolutionary Strategies', *Leonardo* 24.5 (1991), p. 591.

36. Dery, *Escape Velocity*, pp. 164–7.

37. Joel Garreau, *Radical Evolution: The Promise and Peril of Enhancing Our Minds, Our Bodies – and What It Means to Be Human* (New York: Doubleday, 2005), p. 11.

38. This point was made early on in the life of the HGP, in opposition to the 'a gene for . . .' discourse. See Ruth Hubbard, 'Genes as Causes', in Vananda Shiva and Ingunn Moser (eds), *Biopolitics: A Feminist and Ecological Reader on Biotechnology* (London: Zed Books, 1995), pp. 38–51.

39. Visible Human Project Home: http://www.nlm.nih.gov/research/visible/visible_human.html.

40. Catherine Waldby, *The Visible Human Project: Informatic Bodies and Posthuman Medicine* (New York: Routledge, 2000).

41. See Eugene Thacker, '. . . visible_human.html/digital anatomy and the hyper-texted body', www.ctheory.net, 2 June 1998.

42. Jean Baudrillard, *The Transparency of Evil: Essays on Extreme Phenomena*, trans. James Benedict (London: Verso, [1990] 1993), pp. 24–5.

43. Ibid., p. 25.

44. N. Katherine Hayles, *How We Became Posthuman: Virtual Bodies in Cybernetics, Literature and Informatics* (Chicago: University of Chicago Press, 1999), p. 288.

Conclusion

1. The term refers to Michael Hardt and Antonio Negri's ideas about the possibilities for resistance to a transnational corporate order that they call Empire. See *Empire* (Cambridge, MA: Harvard University Press, 2000) and *Multitude: War and Democracy in the Age of Empire* (New York: Penguin, 2004).

2. John Gray, *Heresies: Against Progress and Other Illusions* (London: Granta Books, 2004), pp. 52–3.

3. Thomas Frank, 'Why Johnny Can't Dissent', *Baffler* 6 (1995), reprinted in *Commodify Your Dissent: Salvos from* The Baffler (New York: Norton, 1997), pp. 31–45.

4. Winfried Fluck, 'Surface and Depth, Postmodernism and Neo-Realist Fiction'; Kristiaan Versluys (ed.), *Neo-Realism in Contemporary American Fiction* (Amsterdam: Rodopi, 1992), pp. 65–85.

5. Sean Cubitt, *The Cinema Effect* (Cambridge, MA: Massachusetts Institute of Technology Press, 2004), p. 235.

6. Arjun Appadurai, *Modernity at Large: Cultural Dimensions of Globalization* (Minneapolis: University of Minnesota Press, 1996), pp. 176–7.

7. Hayden quoted in Steven Pearlstein, 'Seattle Protests Open Up the Globalization Debate', *Washington Post*, 4 December 1999. For the politics of 'participatory discrepancy' see Eric Lott, *The Disappearing Liberal Intellectual* (New York: Basic Books, 2006), p. 161.

8. Vincent Bugliosi, 'None Dare Call It Treason', *The Nation*, 5 February 2001.

9. *Bush* v. *Gore*, 531 U.S. 98 (2000).

10. Derek Chollet and James Goldgeier, *America Between the Wars: From 11/9 to 9/11* (New York: Public Affairs, 2008), pp. 308–12.

11. Frank Rich, 'Journal: The Day Before Tuesday', *New York Times*, 15 September 2001, Section A, p. 23. Slavoj Žižek, 'Welcome to the Desert of the Real', email communication 15 September 2001, available at http://web.mit.edu/cms/reconstructions/interpretations/desertreal.html.

12. Philip Wegner, *Life Between Two Deaths, 1989–2001: U.S. Culture in the Long 1990s* (Durham, NC: Duke University Press, 2009), p. 9.

Bibliography

Introduction

Appadurai, Arjun, *Modernity at Large: Cultural Dimensions of Globalisation* (Minneapolis: University of Minnesota Press, 1996).

Barber, Benjamin, *Jihad vs McWorld* (London: Corgi, [1995] 2003).

Bauman, Zygmunt, *Globalization: The Human Consequences* (Cambridge: Polity Press, 1998).

Berger, Maurice, Brian Wallis and Simon Watson (eds), *Constructing Masculinity* (New York: Routledge, 1995).

Berlant, Lauren, *The Queen of America Goes to Washington City: Essays on Sex and Citizenship* (Durham, NC: Duke University Press, 1997).

Boym, Svetlana, *The Future of Nostalgia* (New York: Basic Books, 2001).

Bracewell, Michael, *The 1990s: When Surface Was Depth* (London: Flamingo, 2002).

Buell, Frederick, 'Nationalist Postnationalism: Globalist Discourse in Contemporary American Culture', *American Quarterly* 50.3 (September 1998), pp. 548–91.

Caplan, Richard and John Feffer (eds), *State of the Union 1994: The Clinton Administration and the Nation in Profile* (Boulder, San Francisco, Oxford: Westview Press, 1994).

Chollet, Derek and James Goldgeier, *America Between the Wars: From 11/9 to 9/11* (New York: Public Affairs, 2008).

Chow, Rey, *Ethics After Idealism: Theory – Culture – Ethnicity – Reading* (Bloomington, IN: Indiana University Press, 1998).

Chow, Rey, *The Protestant Ethnic and the Spirit of Capitalism* (New York: Columbia University Press, 2002).

Cockburn, Alexander, Jeffrey St. Clair and Allan Sekula, *Five Days That Shook the World: Seattle and Beyond* (New York: Verso, 2000).

Cole, Alyson M., *The Cult of True Victimhood: From the War on Welfare to the War on Terror* (Stanford, CA: Stanford University Press, 2007).

Crockatt, Richard and Allan Lloyd Smith, 'The United States after Reagan', in Malcolm Bradbury & Howard Temperley (eds), *Introduction to American Studies*, 3rd edn (London: Longman, 1998), pp. 321–44.

Davis, Mike, *Magical Urbanism: Latinos Reinvent the U.S. City* (New York: Verso, 2000).

Davis, Philip and Fred Waldstein (eds), *Political Issues in America Today: The 1990s Revisited* (Manchester: Manchester University Press, 1996).

Delgado, Richard and Jean Stefancic, *Critical Race Theory: An Introduction* (New York: New York University Press, 2001).

Faludi, Susan, *Backlash: The Undeclared War Against Women* (London: Chatto & Windus, [1991] 1992).

Faludi, Susan, *Stiffed: The Betrayal of Modern Man* (London: Chatto & Windus, 1999).

Felski, Rita, *Doing Time: Feminist Theory and Postmodern Culture* (New York: New York University Press, 2000).

Fraser, Steven (ed.), *The Bell Curve Wars: Race, Intelligence and the Future of America* (New York: Basic Books, 1995).

Fukuyama, Francis, *The End of History and the Last Man* (London: Hamish Hamilton, 1992).

Giles, Paul, *Virtual Americas: Transnational Fictions and the Transatlantic Imaginary* (Durham, NC: Duke University Press, 2002).

Giroux, Henry, *Stealing Innocence: Youth, Corporate Power, and the Politics of Culture* (New York: St. Martin's Press, 2000).

Grainge, Paul, *Monochrome Memories: Nostalgia and Style in Retro America* (Westport, CT: Praeger, 2002).

Guinier, Lani and Gerald Torres, *The Miner's Canary: Enlisting Race, Resisting Power, Transforming Democracy* (Cambridge, MA: Harvard University Press, 2002).

Hill, Mike, *After Whiteness: Unmaking an American Majority* (New York: New York University Press, 2004).

Hollinger, David, *Postethnic America: Beyond Multiculturalism* (New York: Basic Books, 1995).

Hutchings, Robert L. (ed.), *At the End of the American Century: America's Role in the Post Cold War World* (Washington, DC: Woodrow Wilson Center Press, 1998).

Huyssen, Andreas, *Twilight Memories: Marking Time in a Culture of Amnesia* (New York: Routledge, 1995).

Jameson, Fredric and Masao Miyoshi (eds), *The Cultures of Globalisation* (Durham, NC: Duke University Press, 1998).

Kelley, Robin, *Yo' Mama's Disfunktional!: Fighting the Culture Wars in Urban America* (Boston: Beacon Press, 1997).

Kimmel, Michael, *Manhood in America* (New York: Free Press, 1996).

Lauter, Paul, *From Walden Pond to Jurassic Park: Activism, Culture and American Studies* (Durham, NC: Duke University Press, 2001).

Lechner, Frank J. and John Boli, *The Globalization Reader*, 3rd edn (Oxford: Blackwell, 2008).

Lipsitz, George, *American Studies in a Moment of Danger* (Minneapolis: University of Minnesota Press, 2001).

Lott, Eric, *The Disappearing Liberal Intellectual* (New York: Basic Books, 2006).

Lubiano, Wahneema (ed.), *The House that Race Built* (New York: Vintage, 1998).

Marable, Manning, *Race Reform and Rebellion: The Second Reconstruction and Beyond in Black America 1945-2006*, 3rd edn (New York: Palgrave, 2007).

Omi, Michael and Howard Winant, *Racial Formation in the United States from the 1960s to the 1990s*, 2nd edn (New York: Routledge, 1994).

Pease, Donald (ed.), *The Futures of American Studies* (Durham, NC: Duke University Press, 2002).

Putnam, Robert, *Bowling Alone: The Collapse and Revival of American Community* (New York: Simon & Schuster, 2000).

Rasmussen, Birgit Brander et al. (eds), *The Making and Unmaking of Whiteness* (Durham, NC: Duke University Press, 2001).

Reed, Adolph, *Class Notes: Posing As Politics and Other Thoughts on the American Scene* (New York: New Press, 2001).

Remnick, David (ed.), *The New Gilded Age: The New Yorker Looks at the Culture of Affluence* (New York: Random House, 2000).

Ross, Andrew, *The Chicago Gangster Theory of Life: Nature's Debt to Society* (New York: Verso, 1994).

Schier, Steven (ed.), *The Postmodern Presidency: Bill Clinton's Legacy in U.S. Politics* (Pittsburgh: University of Pittsburgh Press, 2000).

Schlesinger, Arthur Jr, *Disuniting America: Reflections on a Multicultural Society* (New York: Norton, 1992).

Seltzer, Mark, 'Wound Culture: Trauma in the Pathological Public Sphere', *October* 80 (Spring 1997), pp. 3–26.

Sennett, Richard, *The Corrosion of Character: The Personal Consequences of Work in the New Capitalism* (New York: Norton, 1998).

Smith, Paul, *Millennial Dreams: Contemporary Culture and Capital in the North* (London: Verso, 1997).

Stiglitz, Joseph, *The Roaring 1990s: Why We're Paying the Price for the Greediest Decade in History* (London: Penguin, [2003] 2004).

Wallerstein, Immanuel, *The End of the World as We Know It: Social Science for the Twenty-First Century* (Minneapolis: University of Minnesota Press, 1999).

Wallerstein, Immanuel, *The Decline of American Power: The U.S. in a Chaotic World* (New York: New Press, 2003).

Wegner, Philip, *Life Between Two Deaths, 1989-2001: U.S. Culture in the Long 1990s* (Durham, NC: Duke University Press, 2009).

Wolf, Naomi, *Fire With Fire: The New Female Power and How it Will Change the 21st Century* (London: Vintage, 1994).

Yudice, George, *The Expediency of Culture: Uses of Culture in the Global Era* (Durham, NC: Duke University Press, 2003).

Fiction and Poetry

Annesley, James, *Blank Fictions: Consumerism, Culture and the Contemporary American Novel* (London: Pluto Press, 1998).

Annesley, James, *Fictions of Globalization: Consumption, the Market and the Contemporary American Novel* (London: Continuum, 2006).

Bernstein, Charles, *My Way: Speeches and Poems* (Chicago & London: University of Chicago Press, 1999).

Bigsby, Christopher, *Contemporary American Playwrights* (Cambridge: Cambridge University Press, 1999).

Birkerts, Sven, *The Gutenberg Elegies: The Fate of Reading in an Electronic Culture* (Winchester, MA: Faber and Faber, 1994).

Buell, Frederick, *National Culture and the New Global System* (Baltimore: Johns Hopkins University Press, 1994).

Chan, Jeffery Paul et al., *The Big Aiiieeeee!: An Anthology of Chinese American and Japanese American Literature* (New York: Meridian, 1991).

Dimock, Wai-chee, 'Deep Time: American Literature and World History', *American Literary History* 13.4 (Winter 2001), pp. 755–75.

Eakin, Paul John, *How Our Lives Become Stories: Making Selves* (Ithaca, NY: Cornell University Press, 1999).

Farr, Cecilia Konchar, *Reading Oprah: How Oprah's Book Club Changed the Way America Reads* (Albany, NY: State University of New York Press, 2005).

Franzen, Jonathan, 'Perchance to Dream: In the Age of Images, a Reason to Write Novels', *Harper's Magazine*, April 1996.

Grassian, Daniel, *Hybrid Fictions: American Literature and Generation X* (Jefferson, NC: McFarland, 2003).

Green, Jeremy, *Late Postmodernism: American Fiction at the Millennium* (New York: Palgrave, 2005).

Grice, Helena et al., *Beginning Ethnic American Literatures* (Manchester: Manchester University Press, 2001).

Gysin, Fritz, 'From Modernism to Postmodernism: Black Literature at the Crossroads', in Maryemma Graham (ed.), *The Cambridge Companion to the African American Novel* (Cambridge: Cambridge University Press, 2004), pp. 139–55.

Lee, A. Robert, *Multicultural American Literature: Comparative Black, Native, Latino/a and Asian American Fictions* (Edinburgh: Edinburgh University Press, 2003).

Levine, Lawrence, *The Opening of the American Mind: Canons, Culture, and History* (Boston: Beacon Press, 1996).

Lowe, Lisa, *Immigrant Acts: On Asian American Cultural Politics* (Durham, NC: Duke University Press, 1996).

Michaels, Walter Benn, 'Empires of the Senseless: (The Response to) Terror and (the End of) History', *Radical History Review* 85 (Winter 2003), pp. 105–13.

Millard, Kenneth, *Contemporary American Fiction: An Introduction to American Fiction Since 1970* (Oxford: Oxford University Press, 2000).

Morrison, Toni, *Playing in the Dark: Whiteness and the Literary Imagination* (Cambridge, MA: Harvard University Press, 1992).

Murphet, Julian, *Literature and Race in Los Angeles* (Cambridge: Cambridge University Press, 2001).

Myers, B. R., 'A Reader's Manifesto', *Atlantic Monthly*, July/August 2001, pp. 104–22.

Perloff, Marjorie, *Poetry On and Off the Page: Essays for Emergent Occasions* (Evanston, IL: Northwestern University Press, 1998).

Posnock, Ross, *Philip Roth's Rude Truth: The Art of Immaturity* (Princeton, NJ: Prinecton University Press, 2006).

Poulin, A. Jr. and Michael Waters (eds), *Contemporary American Poetry* (Boston: Houghton Mifflin, 2006).

Prosser, Jay (ed.), *American Fiction of the 1990s* (New York: Routledge, 2008).

Scholes, Robert, *The Rise and Fall of English* (New Haven, CT: Yale University Press, 1999).

Silberg, Richard, *Reading the Sphere: A Geography of Contemporary American Poetry* (Berkeley, CA: Berkeley Hills Books, 2002).

Vendler, Helen, *Soul Says: On Recent Poetry* (Cambridge, MA: Belknap Press, 1995).

Wallace, David Foster, 'E Unibus Pluram', *Review of Contemporary Fiction* 13.2 (Summer 1993), pp. 151–94.

Wallace, David Foster (ed.), *Review of Contemporary Fiction* (*Spring 1996*): *The Future of Fiction* (Normal, IL: Dalkey Archive Press, 1996).

Wallace, Mark and Steven Marks (eds), *Telling it Slant: Avant-Garde Poetics of the 1990s* (Tuscaloosa: University of Alabama Press, 2002).

Wong, Shawn, *Asian American Literature: A Brief Introduction and Anthology* (New York: HarperCollins, 1996).

Wood, James, 'Human, All Too Inhuman: The Smallness of the "Big" Novel', *New Republic*, 24 July 2000, pp. 41–5.

Music and Radio

Barfe, Louis, *Where Have All the Good Times Gone?: The Rise and Fall of the Record Industry* (London: Atlantic Books, 2005).

Beebe, Roger et al., *Rock over the Edge: Transformations in Popular Music Culture* (Durham, NC: Duke University Press, 2002).

Bennett, Andy et al., *The Popular Music Studies Reader* (New York: Routledge, 2006).

Brackett, David (ed.), *The Pop, Rock, and Soul Reader* (New York: Oxford University Press, 2005).

Chang, Jeff, *Can't Stop Won't Stop: A History of the Hip Hop Generation* (London: Ebury Press, 2005).

Crawford, Richard, *America's Musical Life: A History* (New York: Norton, 2001).

D, Chuck with Yusuf Jah, *Fight the Power: Rap, Race and Reality* (Edinburgh: Payback Press, 1997).

Douglas, Susan, *Listening In: Radio and the American Imagination* (New York: Times Books, 1999).

Dyson, Michael Eric, *Between God and Gangsta Rap: Bearing Witness to Black Culture* (New York: Oxford University Press, 1996).

Forman, Murray and Mark Anthony Neal (eds), *That's the Joint!: The Hip-Hop Studies Reader* (London: Routledge, 2004).

George, Nelson, *Hip Hop America* (New York: Viking Penguin, 1998).

Grossberg, Lawrence, *Dancing in Spite of Myself: Essays on Popular Culture* (Durham, NC: Duke University Press, 1997).

Hull, Geoffrey, *The Recording Industry* (New York: Routledge, 2004).

Kitwana, Bakari, *Why White Kids Love Hip Hop: Wankstas, Wiggers, Wannabes, and the New Reality of Race in America* (Cambridge, MA: Basic Civitas Books, 2006).

Kun, Josh, *Audiotopia: Music, Race, and America* (Berkeley, CA: University of California Press, 2005).

Kureishi, Hanif and Jon Savage, *The Faber Book of Pop* (London: Faber, 1995).

Leyshon, Andrew et al., *The Place of Music* (New York: Guilford Press, 1998).

Lipsitz, George, *Footsteps in the Dark: The Hidden Histories of Popular Music* (Minneapolis: University of Minnesota Press, 2007).

Neal, Mark Antony, *What the Music Said: Black Popular Music and Black Popular Culture* (New York: Routledge, 1999).

Reynolds, Simon, *Energy Flash: A Journey through Rave Music and Dance Culture* (London: Picador, 1998).

Ross, Andrew and Tricia Rose (eds), *Microphone Fiends: Youth Music and Youth Culture* (New York: Routledge, 1994).

Swiss, Thomas et al., *Mapping the Beat: Popular Music and Contemporary Theory* (Malden, MA: Blackwell, 1998).

Toop, David, *Ocean of Sound: Aether Talk, Ambient Sound and Imaginary Worlds* (London: Serpent's Tail, 1995).

Werner, Craig, *Music, Race and the Soul of America* (Edinburgh: Payback Press, 2000).

Film and Television

Barker, Martin, *From* Antz *to* Titanic*: Reinventing Film Analysis* (London: Pluto Press, 2000).

Becker, Ron, *Gay TV and Straight America* (New Brunswick, NJ: Rutgers University Press, 2006).

Biskind, Peter, *Down and Dirty Pictures: Miramax, Sundance and the Rise of the Independent Film* (London: Bloomsbury, 2004).

Black, Joel, *The Reality Effect: Film Culture and the Graphic Imperative* (New York: Routledge, 2002).

Brooker, Peter and Will Brooker (eds), *Postmodern After-Images: A Reader in Film, Television and Video* (London: Arnold, 1997).

Byrne, Eleanor and Martin McQuillan, *Deconstructing Disney* (London: Pluto, 1999).

Collins, Jim et al., *Film Theory Goes To The Movies* (New York: Routledge, 1993).

Cubitt, Sean, *The Cinema Effect* (Cambridge, MA: Massachusetts Institute of Technology Press, 2004).

Davies, Jude and Carol Smith, *Gender, Ethnicity and Sexuality in Contemporary American Film* (Edinburgh: Keele University Press, 1997).

Davies, Philip John and Paul Wells (eds), *American Film and Politics from Reagan to Bush Jr* (Manchester: Manchester University Press, 2002).

Manthia Diawara (ed.), *Black American Cinema* (New York: Routledge, 1993).

Dovey, John, *Freakshow: First Person Media and Factual TV* (London: Pluto Press, 2000).

Edgerton, Gary, *The Columbia History of American Television* (New York: Columbia University Press, 2007).

Edgerton, Gary and Brian Rose, *Thinking Outside the Box: A Contemporary Television Genre Reader* (Lexington, KY: University of Kentucky Press, 2005).

Edmundson, Mark, *Nightmare on Main Street: Angels, Sadomasochism, and the Culture of Gothic* (Cambridge, MA: Harvard University Press, 1999).

Garber, Marjorie et al., *Media Spectacles* (New York: Routledge, 2003).

Giroux, Henry, *Breaking into the Movies: Film and the Culture of Politics* (Oxford: Blackwell, 2002).

Grainge, Paul (ed.), *Memory and Popular Film* (Manchester: Manchester University Press, 2003).

Hammond, Michael and Lucy Mazdon, *The Contemporary Television Series* (Edinburgh: Edinburgh University Press, 2005).

Hart, Roderick, *Seducing America: How Television Charms the Modern Voter* (New York: Oxford University Press, 1994).

Hillier, Jim (ed.), *American Independent Cinema: A Sight and Sound Reader* (London: BFI Publishing, 2001).

Holmes, Su and Deborah Jermyn, *Understanding Reality Television* (New York: Routledge, 2004).

hooks, bell, *Reel to Real: Race, Sex and Class at the Movies* (New York: Routledge, 1996).

Jancovich, Mark and James Lyons (eds), *Quality Popular Television* (London: BFI Publishing, 2003).

Kellner, Douglas, *Media Spectacle* (New York: Routledge, 2003).

King, Geoff, *New Hollywood Cinema: An Introduction* (London: I. B. Tauris, 2002).

King, Geoff, *American Independent Cinema* (New York: I. B. Tauris, 2005).

Kunz, William, *Culture Conglomerates: Consolidation in the Motion Picture and Television Industries* (Lanham, MD: Rowman & Littlefield, 2007).

Leverette, Marc et al., *It's Not TV: Watching HBO in the Post-Television Era* (New York: Routledge, 2008).

Levy, Emanuel, *Cinema of Outsiders: The Rise of American Independent Film* (New York: New York University Press, 1999).

Lewis, Jon (ed.), *The End of Cinema as We Know It: American Film in the 1990s* (London: Pluto Press, 2002).

Lyon, David, *Surveillance Society: Monitoring Everyday Life* (New York: Oxford University Press, 2001).

Murray, Susan and Laurie Ouellette, *Reality TV: Remaking Television Culture* (New York: New York University Press, 2004).

Natoli, Joseph, *Hauntings: Popular Film and American Culture 1990–1992* (Albany, NY: State University of New York Press, 1994).

Neale, Steve and Murray Smith, *Contemporary Hollywood Cinema* (New York: Routledge, 1998).

Newcomb, Horace, *Television: The Critical View*, 6th edn (New York: Oxford University Press, 2000).

Newman, Kim (ed.), *Science Fiction / Horror: A Sight and Sound Reader* (London: BFI Publishing, 2002).

Pfeil, Fred, *White Guys: Studies in Postmodern Domination and Difference* (New York: Verso, 1997).

Sandler, Kevin S. and Gaylyn Studlar (eds), *Titanic: Anatomy of a Blockbuster* (New Brunswick, NJ: Rutgers University Press, 1999).

Sekula, Allan, 'Between the Net and the Deep Blue Sea (Rethinking the Traffic in Photographs)' *October* 102 (Fall 2002), pp. 3–34.

Spigel, Lynn and Jan Olsson (eds), *Television After TV: Essays on a Medium in Transition* (Durham, NC: Duke University Press, 2004).

Stabile, Carol A. and Mark Harrison (eds), *Prime Time Animation: Television Animation and American Culture* (London: Routledge, 2003).

Wells, Paul, *Animation and America* (Edinburgh: Edinburgh University Press, 2002).

Williams, Linda and Michael Hammond (eds), *Contemporary American Cinema* (New York: Oxford University Press, 2006).

Willis, Susan, *High Contrast: Race and Gender in contemporary Hollywood Film* (Durham, NC: Duke University Press, 1997).

Art and Architecture

Bal, Mieke, *Looking In: The Art of Viewing* (Amsterdam: Gordon & Breach, 2001).

Buskirk, Martha, *The Contingent Object of Contemporary Art* (Cambridge, MA: Massachusetts Institute of Technology Press, 2003).

Curtis, William, *Modern Architecture Since 1900*, 3rd edn (Upper Saddle River, NJ: Prentice Hall, 1996).

Danto, Arthur *The Wake of Art* (Amsterdam: Gordon & Breach, 1998).

Doss, Erika, *Twentieth-Century American Art* (Oxford: Oxford University Press, 2002).

Drucker, Johanna, *Sweet Dreams: Contemporary Art and Complicity* (Chicago: University of Chicago Press, 2005).

Filler, Martin, *Makers of Modern Architecture: From Frank Lloyd Wright to Frank Gehry* (New York: New York Review of Books, 2007).

Elwes, Catherine, *Video Art: A Guided Tour* (London: I. B. Tauris, 2005).

Foster, Hal, *The Return of the Real: the Avant-Garde at the End of the Century* (Cambridge, MA: Massachusetts Institute of Technology Press, 1996).

Foster, Hal et al., *Art Since 1900: Modernism, Antimodernism, Postmodernism* (New York: Thames & Hudson, 2004).

Frampton, Kenneth, *Modern Architecture: A Critical History*, 4th edn (London: Thames & Hudson, 2007).

Fraser, Andrea, *Museum Highlights* (Cambridge, MA: Massachusetts Institute of Technology Press, 2005).

Fusco, Coco, *The Bodies That Were Not Ours and Other Writings* (New York: Routledge, 2001).

Gossel, Peter and Gabriele Leuthauser, *Architecture in the 20th Century*, Vol. 2 (London: Taschen, 2005).

Harrison, Charles and Paul Wood, *Art in Theory, 1900-2000: An Anthology of Changing Ideas*, 2nd edn (Malden, MA: Blackwell, 2002).

Hickey, Dave, *The Invisible Dragon: Four Essays on Beauty* (Los Angeles: Art Issues Press, 1993).

Hopkins, David, *After Modern Art 1945–2000* (New York: Oxford University Press, 2000).

Hughes, Robert, *Culture of Complaint: The Fraying of America* (London: Harvill Press, 1993).

Jencks, Charles and Karl Kropf, *Theories and Manifestoes of Contemporary Architecture*, 2nd edn (Chichester: Wiley Academy, 2006).

Jones, Amelia (ed.), *A Companion to Contemporary Art Since 1945* (Oxford: Blackwell, 2006)

Joselit, David, *American Art Since 1945* (London: Thames & Hudson, 2003).

Kelley, Mike, *Foul Perfection: Essays and Criticism* (Cambridge, MA: Massachusetts Institute of Technology Press, 2003).

Kester, Grant, *Conversation Pieces: Community and Communication in Modern Art* (Berkeley, CA: University of California Press, 2004).

Kwon, Miwon, *One Place After Another: Site-Specific Art and Locational Identity* (Cambridge, MA: Massachusetts Institute of Technology Press, 2002).

October roundtable: 'The Politics of the Signifier: A Conversation on the Whitney Biennial', *October* 66 (Fall 1993), pp. 3–27.

Orvell, Miles, *American Photography* (New York: Oxford University Press, 2003).

Perl, Jed, *Eye Witness: Reports from an Art World in Crisis* (New York: Basic Books, 2000).

Ross, Andrew, 'The Great Un-American Numbers Game', in John Hartley and Roberta Pearson (eds), *American Cultural Studies: A Reader* (New York: Oxford University Press, 2000), pp. 287–301.

Sandler, Irving, *Art of the Postmodern Era: from the Late 1960s to the Early 1990s* (New York: HarperCollins, 1996).

Schavemaker, Margriet and Mischa Rakier (eds), *Right About Now: Art & Theory Since the 1990s* (Amsterdam: Valiz, 2007).

Schor, Mira, *Wet: On Painting, Feminism, and Art Culture* (Durham, NC: Duke University Press, 1997).

Sollins, Marybeth (ed.), *Art: 21* (New York: Harry N. Abrams, Inc., 2003).

Stallabrass, Julian, *Art Incorporated: The Story of Contemporary Art* (New York: Oxford University Press, 2004).

Taylor, Brandon, *Art Today* (London: Laurence King, 2005).

Tribe, Mark and Reena Jana, *New Media Art* (Los Angeles: Taschen, 2006).

Wallis, Brian et al., *Art Matters: How the Culture Wars Changed America* (New York: New York University Press, 1999).

Welchman, John, *Art After Appropriation: Essays on Art in the 1990s* (London: Gordon & Breach, 2001).

Digital Culture

Bell, David, *An Introduction to Cybercultures* (New York: Routledge, 2001).

Bell, David (ed.), *Cybercultures: Critical Concepts in Media and Cultural Studies* (New York: Routledge, 2006).

Bell, David and Barbara Kennedy (eds), *The Cybercultures Reader*, 2nd edn (New York: Routledge, 2007).

Darley, Andrew, *Visual Digital Culture: Surface Play and Spectacle in New Media Genres* (New York: Routledge, 2000).

Dery, Mark, *Escape Velocity: Cyberculture at the End of the Century* (New York: Grove Press, 1996).

Featherstone, Mike and Roger Burrows, *Cyberspace, Cyberbodies, Cyberpunk: Cultures of Technological Embodiment* (London: Sage, 1995).

Galloway, Alexander, *Protocol: How Control Exists After Decentralization* (Cambridge, MA: Massachusetts Institute of Technology Press, 2004).

Gleick, James, *What Just Happened: A Chronicle from the Information Frontier* (New York: Abacus, 2002).

Haraway, Donna, *Modest Witness@Second Millennium: FemaleMan Meets Oncomouse* (New York: Routledge, 1996).

Hayles, N. Katherine, *How We Became Posthuman: Virtual Bodies in Cybernetics, Literature and Informatics* (Chicago: University of Chicago Press, 1999).

Ludlow, Peter (ed.), *Crypto Anarchy, Cyberstates and Pirate Utopias* (Cambridge, MA: Massachusetts Institute of Technology Press, 2001).

Lyon, David, *Surveillance Society: Monitoring Everyday Life* (New York: Oxford University Press, 2001).

Manovich, Lev, *The Language of New Media* (Cambridge, MA: Massachusetts Institute of Technology Press, 2000).

Margolis, Michael and David Resnick (eds), *Politics as Usual: The Cyberspace 'Revolution'* (Thousand Oaks, CA: Sage, 2000).

Mitchell, William J., *City of Bits: Space, Place, and the Infobahn* (Cambridge, MA: Massachusetts Institute of Technology Press, 1996).

Mitchell, William J., *Me++: The Cyborg Self and the Networked City* (Cambridge, MA: Massachusetts Institute of Technology Press, 2003)

Mosco, Vincent, *The Digital Sublime: Myth, Power and Cyberspace* (Cambridge, MA: Massachusetts Institute of Technology Press, 2004).

Nayar, Pramod, *Virtual Worlds: Culture and Politics in an Age of Cybertechnology* (New Delhi: Sage, 2004).

Rheingold, Howard, *The Virtual Community: Homesteading on the Electronic Frontier* (Cambridge MA: Massachusetts Institute of Technology Press, [1993] 2000).

Shiva, Vananda and Ingunn Moser, *Biopolitics: A Feminist and Ecological Reader on Biotechnology* (London: Zed Books, 1995).

Tofts, Darren et al., *Prefiguring Cyberculture: An Intellectual History* (Cambridge, MA: Massachusetts Institute of Technology Press, 2002).

Trend, David (ed.), *Reading Digital Culture* (Oxford: Blackwell, 2001).

Wardrip-Fruin, Noah and Nick Montfort (eds), *The New Media Reader* (Cambridge, MA: Massachusetts Institute of Technology Press, 2003).

Wertheim, Margaret, *The Pearly Gates of Cyberspace: a History of Space from Dante to the Internet* (New York: Norton, 1999).

Index

abject art, 139–43
Abuse Excuse, The (Dershowitz), 19
Akerman, Chantal, 165
Aladdin (Clements and Musker), 111, 130, 131
Albini, Steve, 65–6
Alexie, Sherman, 45
Al-Qaeda, 206
Amazon.com, 171, 183, 184
American Beauty (Mendes), 16
American Pastoral (Roth), 62, 63–4
American Psycho (Ellis), 55–6
Amos, Tori, 80
animation, 127–32
Antoni, Janine, 141
Anzaldúa, Gloria, 45
Appadurai, Arjun, 202
Apple, Fiona, 80, 81
Arnett, Peter, 99, 101
Arteaga, Alfred, 53
Auster, Paul, 43, 55

Babes in Toyland, 79
Backlash (Faludi), 16–18
Banks, Mike, 91–2
Barlow, John Perry, 95, 182, 183
Barney, Matthew, 154, 156–8
Basic Instinct (Verhoeven), 16
Baudrillard, Jean, 101–2, 118, 196–7
Beastie Boys, 83, 94
Beavis and Butt-Head, 77–8, 123, 127

Benjamin, Walter, 39–40
Berlant, Lauren, 5–6, 14–15, 26
Berlin Wall, 11, 207, 208
Bernstein, Charles, 51
Bikini Kill, 78, 79
blank fiction, 55–6
blogging, 184–5
Bly, Robert, 18
Bowling Alone (Putnam), 31–3
Boym, Svetlana, 3–4
Brooks, Meredith, 80, 81
Buchloch, Benjamin, 159
Buell, Frederick, 30, 36
Buffy the Vampire Slayer, 123, 124, 125
Bush, Barbara, 14
Bush, George H. W., 11, 98, 128
Bush, George W., 10, 204–6, 207

Cable News Network (CNN), 97, 98, 99, 101, 103
Cameron, James, 119–20
cell phone, 170
'Changes' (Tupac), 88
CHERRY Makita – Honest Engine Work (Rhoades), 146–7
Chuck D, 87–8, 95
Clear Channel, 70, 71
Clinton, Bill, 4–5, 11–12, 85, 127, 173, 185, 194, 206
Clinton, Hillary, 14

Cobain, Kurt, 66, 73–5, 76, 78, 87, 89, 200
Colapinto, John, 43
colour-blindness, 13, 20, 22–4, 130, 181
Communications Decency Act, 182, 186, 189–90
computer games, 170, 171, 172
conglomeration in media industries, 65–6, 67–8, 70–2, 110–12
Contract With America, 5
Cooper, Dennis, 57–9
Cops, 124, 126
Cosby Show, The, 107, 128, 130
Coupland, Douglas, 55
Court TV, 97, 108–9, 126
Cremaster (Barney), 154, 156–8
Crewdson, Gregory, 150–1
Critical Race Theory, 104
Crow, Sheryl, 80, 81
Cubitt, Sean, 119, 174, 202
Culture of Complaint, The (Hughes), 19
Currin, John, 150

Dances With Wolves (Costner), 16
Davis, Mike, 25, 162
DeLillo, Don, 43, 61
Dershowitz, Alan, 19
de Tocqueville, Alexis, 10, 32
Dibbell, Julian, 177–8
diCorcia, Philip-Lorca, 150, 151–2
Dion, Mark, 164
Disney Corporation, 70, 110, 111–12, 127, 131
Disuniting of America, The (Schlesinger), 18
downsizing, 7
Dr Dre, 83, 95
Dreamworks SKG, 111, 131
Drexciya, 91
Drucker, Johanna, 52, 158, 159–60
Drudge Report, The (Drudge), 185
D'Souza, Dinesh, 19

Eakin, Paul John, 53–4
eBay.com, 171, 172, 183–4
Educational Complex (Kelley), 143
Electronic Frontier Foundation, 182, 189
Ellen, 125
Ellis, Bret Easton, 55–6
End of History and the Last Man, The (Fukuyama), 9–10
Enola Gay, 3
Enron, 6
ER, 125
Erdrich, Louise, 45
Everett, Percival, 43
Etzioni, Amitai, 31

Falling Down (Schumacher), 16, 25
Faludi, Susan, 16–18
Fight Club (Fincher), 16
Fink, Robert, 93, 96
Fire With Fire (Wolf), 17
Forrest Gump (Zemeckis), 174
Foster, Hal, 138, 140, 158
Fragment of a Crucifixion (After Francis Bacon) (Pfeiffer), 154
Frank, Thomas, 200–1
Frankenberg, Ruth, 25
Franzen, Jonathan, 43, 61
Friends, 123, 125
Frisk (Cooper), 57–9
Fukuyama, Francis, 9–10
Fusco, Coco, 138, 139

Garreau, Joel, 192–3
Gass, William, 53
Gates, Bill, 7, 8–9, 175, 190
Gehry, Frank, 160, 161–3
Giles, Paul, 28, 60
Gilligan, Carol, 14
Gingrich, Newt, 5
Gioia, Dana, 35–6
globalisation, 26–31, 163–6, 202
Gober, Robert, 141–2
Godzilla (Emmerich), 112

Goldin, Nan, 81, 136
González, Elián, 202
Gonzalez-Torres, Felix, 136–8, 146
Google.com, 172, 183
Gordon, Douglas, 153
Gore, Al, 169, 175, 187, 205
Gray, John, 16
Greenspan, Alan, 6
Greeting, The (Viola), 155
Groening, Matt, 127, 128–30
Grossberg, Lawrence, 76–7, 90
grunge music, 72–3
Guggenheim Bilbao, 161–3
Guinier, Lani, 4
Gulf War, 98–102, 202

hacktivism, 186
Hand that Rocks the Cradle, The
   (Hanson), 16
Hanna, Kathleen, 78
Happiness (Solondz), 116–18
Hayles, N. Katherine, 197
Heads series (diCorcia), 152–3
*Heath Anthology of American
   Literature, The* (Lauter), 44, 51
Hill, Anita, 14–15, 17, 42, 102–4
hip-hop, 66, 81–9, 93–4
Holliday, George, 105, 106, 140
Hollinger, David, 26
Hollywood series (diCorcia), 151–2
house music, 90
Hover series (Crewdson), 151
How the Irish Became White
   (Ignatiev), 25
Hsieh, Tehching, 165, 166–7
Huan, Zhang, 165, 166, 167
Hughes, Robert, 19
Human Genome Project, 7, 194–5
Human Stain, The (Roth), 62, 63
Hussen, Andreas, 2–3
Hypothetical? (Simpson), 139

Ice Cube, 82, 83–4
Ice-T, 82, 85, 105

Ignatiev, Noel, 25
Illiberal Education (D'Souza), 19
I Married a Communist (Roth), 62,
   63
Inada, Lawson Fusao, 48–9
Independent Media Centre
   (Indymedia), 185–6
Infinite Jest (Wallace), 59–60
Iron John (Bly), 18
'It was a Good Day' (Ice Cube),
   83–4

Jameson, Fredric, 2, 155
Jen, Gish, 46
Johnson, Lyndon, 12, 20
Jurassic Park (Spielberg), 112

Kabakov, Ilya and Emilia, 165–6
Kelley, Mike, 142–3, 146
Kilimnik, Karen, 160
King, Rodney, 22, 84, 104, 106–7,
   139, 140
Knight, Suge, 86, 88
Koresh, David, 98
Kyoto Protocol, 205

Last Seduction, The (Dahl), 16
Lee, Ang, 29
Lee, Li-Young, 49–51
Lewinsky, Monica, 5, 12, 173, 185
Ligon, Glen, 139
Lilith Fair, 80
Limbaugh, Rush, 16, 69–70
Lion King, The (Allers and
   Minkoff), 112, 130, 131
Los Angeles riots, 46, 84, 85, 105–6
Love, Courtney, 75
Lyotard, Jean-François, 2

Mailer, Norman, 56, 61
Man Coming Out of Woman
   (Gober), 141–2
Mapplethorpe, Robert, 19, 136, 139,
   152

Marable, Manning, 21–2, 104
Markson, David, 43
Martinez, Daniel, 139–40
Matrix, The (Wachowski brothers), 102, 199–201, 206
May, Derrick, 91
McCarthy, Paul, 142, 146
Meccatuna (Rhoades), 147–8
Memento (Nolan), 3, 199
Men are from Mars, Women are from Venus (Gray), 16
Microsoft, 8–9, 172, 173, 190–1
Million Man March, 18
Mills, Jeff, 91–2
Mining the Museum (Wilson), 138
Minority Report (Spielberg), 120, 194
Miramax Films, 111, 114
modernism, 135, 158–9
Morning After, The (Roiphe), 17
Morissette, Alanis, 80, 81
Morrison, Toni, 25, 37–42, 43
Mortar and Pestle (Antoni), 141
Mosely, Walter, 45
mp3 audio format, 94, 96, 170, 172
MTV, 28, 77–8, 126
Mudhoney, 73
Mukherjee, Bharati, 45, 61
museum architecture, 160
Museum of Modern Art, 158–9
My Brother / Brancuzi (Rhoades), 147
My America (Hard to Acclimatize) (Huan), 166
My New York (Huan), 166

Nader, Ralph, 205
Napster, 94–6, 172, 186, 187, 189
National Organisation of Women, 13
neobaroque cinema, 119–20, 202
neoliberalism, 6–7, 33, 188, 202
neorealism, 201–2

Nevermind (Nirvana), 72, 74
new independent cinema, 112–18
Ng, Fae Myenne, 47
Nirvana, 72, 73–5
North American Free Trade Association (NAFTA), 27
Notes on the Margin of the Black Book (Ligon), 139
nostalgia, 3, 16, 33, 55, 70, 74, 89

Oklahoma City bombing, 5
Oprah's Book Club, 36–7
Orlan, 191–2
Oursler, Tony, 154

Palace of Projects (Kabakovs), 165
Palmer, Michael, 53
Paradise (Morrison), 37, 38, 40–2
Perfect Moment, The (Mapplethorpe), 136
Pfeiffer, Paul, 154
Pilgrimage – Wind and Water (Huan), 166
Piss Christ (Serrano), 135–6
Pixar Studios, 131
Player, The (Altman), 170
Playing in the Dark (Morrison), 25, 42
post-cinema, 116–17, 119–21, 201
post-ethnicity, 26, 201
post-feminism, 13, 17–18, 201
posthumanism, 131–2, 191–7, 201
postmodernism, 2, 54–61, 158, 201
Postmodernism, Or, The Cultural Logic of Late Capitalism (Jameson), 2
post-rock, 92–3, 201
Powers, Richard, 43
Prince of Egypt, The (Chapman and Hickner), 131
Project for a New American Century, 10
Proposition 209, 21
Public Enemy, 82, 83, 85, 88, 95

Pulp Fiction (Tarantino), 114, 115–16
Putnam, Robert, 31–3

quality TV, 121–6

reality TV, 126–7
Real World, The, 126–7
Reich, Robert, 27
Remnick, David, 7
Reno v. *ACLU*, 189–90
Reynolds, Simon, 91, 93
Rheingold, Howard, 175, 178–80, 181
Rhoades, Jason, 146–8
Riot Grrrl, 78–80, 81
Road Ahead, The (Gates), 9
rock music, 66, 72–8
Roediger, David, 25
Roh-Spaulding, Carol, 47
Roiphe, Katie, 17
Rosler, Martha, 155, 165
Roth, Philip, 62–4
Rubins, Nancy, 146
Rules, The (Fein and Schneider), 16

Saddam Hussein, 98, 101
Schlesinger, Arthur, Jr, 18
Scream (Craven), 170
Seattle protests, 7, 28, 203–4, 207
Second Means of Egress (Sze), 148–9
Seinfeld, 123
Sekula, Allan, 121, 165
Sennett, Richard, 8
September 11th 2001, 205–7, 208
Serra, Richard, 135, 137, 146
Serrano, 135
Shakur, Tupac, 22, 66, 87–9
Simmons, Russell, 82
Simpson, Lorna, 138–9
Simpson, O. J., 22–4, 53, 63, 69, 104, 108, 109
Simpsons, The (Groening), 122, 123, 128–30

situation comedy (sitcom), 122, 123, 125, 128–9
Slavery! Slavery! . . . (Walker), 144
Smalls, Biggie, 22, 87, 88
'Smells Like Teen Spirit' (Nirvana), 74–5, 78
Snoop Dogg, 83, 87
Solondz, Todd, 116–18
Sommers, Christina Hoff, 17
Souza, Al, 146
Spears, Britney, 80
Spielberg, Steven, 119–20
Starr, Kenneth, 173
Stelarc, 191–2
Stephanopolous, George, 12
Stern, Howard, 16, 69–70
Stiglitz, Joseph, 6, 7
Suh, Do-Ho, 165, 166
surveillance, 97–8, 187–8
synergy, 110, 111
Sze, Sarah, 146, 148–9

talk radio, 68–70
Tarantino, Quentin, 115
techno, 90–2
Telecommunications Act, 6, 70–1, 182
Terminator 2 (Cameron), 112
Thomas, Clarence, 14, 20, 42, 102–4
Three Kings (Russell), 102
Tilted Arc (Serra), 135
Titanic (Cameron), 119–21
Total Recall (Verhoeven), 3
Toy Story (Lasseter), 127, 131–2
Toy Story 2 (Lasseter), 131–2
transnationalism, 26, 28–30, 61, 202
Tucker, Dolores, 85–6
Turkle, Sherry, 180
turntablism, 93–4
Two Undiscovered Amerindians Visit the West (Fusco and Gómez-Peña), 138
Typical American (Jen), 46

United States v. *Microsoft*, 190–1
Universal Studios, 110, 111, 112, 116–17
Untitled (Lover Boys) (Gonzalez-Torres), 137–8

Venice Biennale, 148, 155, 164
video art, 134, 152–8
Viola, Bill, 154, 155–6
Viramontes, Helena, 45
Virtual Community, The (Rheingold), 178–80
virtual reality, 175–81
Visible Human Project (VHP), 171, 195–6
Vizenor, Gerald, 45

Wages of Whiteness, The (Roediger), 25
Walker, Kara, 144–5
Wallace, David Foster, 56–7, 59–61, 202

West, Cornell, 145
Whedon, Joss, 124–5
whiteness, 25–6
White Women, Race Matters (Frankenberg), 25
Whitney Biennial, 134, 139, 147, 163, 166
Wideman, John Edgar, 45
Wilson, Fred, 138, 139
Winant, Howard, 12
Winfrey, Oprah, 36–8
Wojnarowicz, David, 136
Wolf, Naomi, 17
World Trade Center, 11, 206, 208
World Trade Organization, 203
World Wide Web, 8, 94, 169, 172, 182, 203
Wurtzel, Elizabeth, 53

X-Files, The, 124, 125

Yuskavage, Lisa, 150